The Critical Reception of Henry James

Studies in American Literature and Culture:
Literary Criticism in Perspective

Scott Peeples, Series Editor
(*Charleston, South Carolina*)

About *Literary Criticism in Perspective*

Books in the series *Literary Criticism in Perspective* trace literary scholarship and criticism on major and neglected writers alike, or on a single major work, a group of writers, a literary school or movement. In so doing the authors — authorities on the topic in question who are also well-versed in the principles and history of literary criticism — address a readership consisting of scholars, students of literature at the graduate and undergraduate level, and the general reader. One of the primary purposes of the series is to illuminate the nature of literary criticism itself, to gauge the influence of social and historic currents on aesthetic judgments once thought objective and normative.

The Critical Reception of
Henry James
Creating a Master

Linda Simon

CAMDEN HOUSE
Rochester, New York

Copyright © 2007 Linda Simon

All Rights Reserved. Except as permitted under current legislation,
no part of this work may be photocopied, stored in a retrieval system,
published, performed in public, adapted, broadcast, transmitted,
recorded, or reproduced in any form or by any means,
without the prior permission of the copyright owner.

First published 2007 by Camden House
Reprinted in paperback and transferred to digital printing 2010

Camden House is an imprint of Boydell & Brewer Inc.
668 Mt. Hope Avenue, Rochester, NY 14620, USA
www.camden-house.com
and of Boydell & Brewer Limited
PO Box 9, Woodbridge, Suffolk IP12 3DF, UK
www.boydellandbrewer.com

Paperback ISBN-13: 978-1-57113-441-7
Paperback ISBN-10: 1-57113-441-7
Hardback ISBN-13: 978-1-57113-319-9
Hardback ISBN-10: 1-57113-319-4

Library of Congress Cataloging-in-Publication Data

Simon, Linda, 1946–
    The critical reception of Henry James: creating a master / Linda Simon.
      p. cm. — (Studies in American literature and culture: literary criticism in perspective)
    Includes bibliographical references (p.) and index.
    ISBN-13: 978-1-57113-319-9 (hardcover: alk. paper)
    ISBN-10: 1-57113-319-4 (hardcover: alk. paper)
    1. James, Henry, 1843–1916—Criticism and interpretation—History.
I. Title. II. Series.

PS2124.S56 2007
813'.4—dc21

2007018053

A catalogue record for this title is available from the British Library.

This publication is printed on acid-free paper.
Printed in the United States of America.

Cover photo: Henry James in Rome, 1899. Photo by Giuseppi Primoli.
By permission of the the Houghton Library, Harvard University.

Contents

Acknowledgments	vi
Introduction	1
1: A Mirror for Americans: Contemporary Criticism, 1866–1916	10
2: Instructions to the Reader: James's Prefaces to the New York Edition	27
3: The Cult of Henry James, 1918–1960	42
4: A Life of the Master: Leon Edel's *Henry James* and Its Influence on Criticism	61
5: Critical Revisions: James in the Academy	75
6: Jamesian Consciousness: Mind, Morality, and the Problem of Truth	95
7: Gender, Sexuality, Intimacy	114
Selected Henry James Bibliography	137
Works Consulted	141
Index	157

Acknowledgments

JAMES WALKER AND SCOTT PEEPLES have been extraordinarily helpful, insightful, and generous throughout the process of my writing this book; I could not wish for better editors. Working with them and all the staff at Camden House has been a singularly wonderful experience. Professors Kristin Boudreau and Pierre Walker read the manuscript at different stages and offered thoughtful and useful suggestions. I thank them for their enthusiasm for this project and for their careful consideration of my work. I am continually grateful to my colleagues at Skidmore College for the fine intellectual community of which I am privileged to be a part.

L. S.
April 2007

Introduction

> *Nothing, of course, will ever take the place of the good old fashion of "liking" a work of art or not liking it: the most improved criticism will not abolish that primitive, that ultimate test.*
> — Henry James, "The Art of Fiction"

ALTHOUGH SOME OF JAMES'S contemporary critics deemed him just short of a great writer, history has elevated Henry James to indisputable preeminence in the American canon. Even before Leon Edel underscored the epithet "The Master" in his multi-volume biography (the first volume appeared in 1953), James was the novelist with whom every major American critic grappled. Van Wyck Brooks, Richard Blackmur, F. O. Matthiessen, F. W. Dupee, Lionel Trilling, Edmund Wilson: these writers and hundreds more had their say about the works of Henry James. In the second half of the twentieth century and into our own time, this attention has multiplied; in the kaleidoscopic world of literary scholarship, James has been considered from myriad critical vantage points. This volume in the *Literary Criticism in Perspective* series examines the trajectory of writings about James, beginning with responses to James's works in the newspapers and magazines of his time and ending with an examination of the current critical focus on sexuality and gender, morality, and the nature of consciousness.

"To criticise," James wrote in his preface to *What Maisie Knew*, "is to appreciate, to appropriate, to take intellectual possession, to establish in fine a relation with the criticised thing and make it one's own" (Blackmur 155). James's definition offers a gloss on the changing temper of criticism in the past 135 years. The "criticised thing," at various times during this period, has been not merely a particular novel or short story, but the idea of genre itself, the author and his life, the role and authority of the reader, the process of creation, and a wide range of cultural contexts. In addition, we can see a similar change in the meaning of James's phrase "to take intellectual possession." More than a century of criticism reveals a shift in the critic's identity from a reviewer whose audience consisted mainly of newspaper and magazine readers, to a public intellectual conscious of his or her role in shaping cultural values, to a literary scholar with a readership largely in the academy.

James's early critics, in his own time and for generations after his death, wrote for a nonspecialist, educated public; their articles and reviews appeared in general interest magazines, such as the *Atlantic* and the *Nation*, where

James's fiction also appeared. From the 1920s through the 1940s, such critics felt pressure to defend art in the context of social and political problems; in the case of James's art, that defense proved, for some, a strenuous challenge. The burgeoning of academia, especially after the Second World War, brought with it a new role and a new readership for those writing seriously about literature; increasingly, critics were scholars addressing others in the academy, fellow scholars and their graduate students. Literary criticism has become associated with various theoretical schools of thought — feminism, for example, or Marxism, structuralism, New Historicism, cultural studies, and queer studies. Because James has provided fertile territory for exploration through the lens of many theoretical perspectives, because contemporary scholarship feeds a thriving "James industry," James's place in the literary canon is increasingly assured.

One way of tracing evolving critical trends is by looking at some of the casebooks published primarily for classroom use. Successive Norton Critical Editions of any of James's works, for example, reveal a shift in attention to one "criticised thing" or another, and also a change in the critic's training, sense of audience, and intellectual aims. The first edition of *Tales of Henry James*, edited by Christof Wegelin and published in 1984, contains essays, several from the 1940s, concerned with aesthetics, language, form, and such themes as Daisy Miller's limitations of experience and the effects of haunting in "The Beast in the Jungle." Only briefly does one critic touch, gingerly, the hint of homosexuality in "The Pupil" (Wegelin). By 2003, the second edition, edited by Wegelin and Henry B. Wonham, offered several essays on sexuality and homoeroticism, which by then were major themes among scholars writing on "The Pupil." The collection includes Philip Horne's "The Master and the 'Queer Affair' of the Pupil," John Carlos Rowe's "Gender, Sexuality, and Work in *In the Cage*," and Eve Kosofsky Sedgwick's "The Beast in the Closet" (Wegelin and Wonham).

In the first Norton Critical edition of James's popular *The Turn of the Screw*, edited by Robert Kimbrough (1966), a few articles ventured beyond the traditional readings of the tale, as summarized by Eric Solomon in "The Return of the Screw": "either the governess is a villain (conscious or unconscious) and there are no ghosts; or there are ghosts, and the children may be villains or innocents, but the governess is an innocent struggling against supernatural evil" (Kimbrough 237). Freudian interpretations — especially that of Edmund Wilson, whose 1934 essay "The Ambiguity of Henry James" seemed to many critics to misread the tale entirely — argued that the tale was an exploration of the existence and consequences of the governess's sexual repression. According to Mark Spilka, however, in "Turning the Freudian Screw: How Not to Do It," this psychoanalytic reading characterized the governess as "neurotic or insane [who] sees no apparitions: she merely records her own hallucinations and their damaging effect on two innocent children" (245). Spilka, though, believes that such an interpretation imposes "modern attitudes" on the story and gets in the way of our apprehending James's intention to offer social criticism. Although Spilka acknowledges "the tale's erotic ambiguities," James, he argues, "has poignantly revealed the moral and psychic cost of hothouse life," in which the well-intentioned young governess "proceeds to fight the invading evil [of sexuality] in the name of hothouse purity and domestic sainthood" (252). She is not inflicting her own sexual repressions on the children; she is as much a victim of Victorian prudery as they are.

The second Norton edition, published thirty-three years later and edited by Deborah Esch and Jonathan Warren, paid overt attention to how James's work has been understood in different historical contexts. This edition included many responses to the themes of ghosts, spiritualism, and psychical phenomena, some from contemporary reviews, which urged readers to consider responses to the tale at a time when ghosts were seen not exclusively as imaginative constructions but, quite possibly, evidence of the soul's existence beyond the body. Tzvetan Todorov, writing on "The Fantastic," distinguishes between the uncanny, in which "the laws of nature remain intact and permit an explanation of the phenomena described," and the marvelous, where "new laws of nature must be entertained to account for the phenomena." The fantastic, Todorov argues, urges readers to navigate between the two genres in order to interpret the tale. In "The Turn of the Screw," the reader's perception of the supernatural "constitutes a screen" that concentrates the reader's attention "on the act of perception [so] that we never know the nature of what is perceived (what are the vices of the discharged tutor and governess?). Anxiety predominates here . . ." (Esch and Warren 194, 196). Shoshana Felman begins her article "Henry James: Madness and the Risks of Practice (Turning the Screw of Interpretation)" with several questions: "What does the act of turning a screw have to do with literature? What does the act of turning a screw have to do with psychoanalysis? Are these two questions related? If so, might their relationship help to define the status of literature?" (Esch and Warren 196). These questions relate to her arguments about the theme of sexuality and madness in James's tale, but more importantly reflect a new critical, or meta-critical, perspective: on the process of literary interpretation itself, on how readers make meaning. Paul Armstrong extends this inquiry in "History and Epistemology," which considers debates "between conflicting communities of readers" (Esch and Warren 245).

Such articles represent late twentieth-century critical perspectives, which are identified and explained in the second edition of Bedford/St. Martin's volume on *The Turn of the Screw*, edited by Peter G. Beidler, part of its Case Studies in Contemporary Criticism (2004). The Bedford edition contains essays from the perspective of reader-response, psychoanalytic, gender, and Marxist criticism, each of which is introduced as orientation for each critical article. Organizing criticism as representative of various theoretical perspectives teaches students, for whom the volume is aimed, about "the current critical and theoretical ferment in literary studies" (v), a ferment far different from the responses of James's contemporary reviewers, who argued about how successfully James evoked horror and how artistically he conveyed his tale. As the Bedford Case Study and the two Norton editions of James's tales and "The Turn of the Screw" demonstrate, James's works have invited new questions for each generation of readers, and they have provoked new possibilities for interpretation.

This volume, as it traces the focus of critical attention, illuminates each generation's desires, standards, anxieties, and expectations. What is a novel or short story? What use does it have in a community's cultural life? What is the relationship between the author and his characters? Between an author and his readers? What makes a work of fiction worthy of the time invested in reading it? These questions are implicit in criticism of any writer, and especially of James. Furthermore, the volume illuminates the history of critical writing from the late nineteenth century, when assessment of literature lay in the hands of reviewers whose interest in fiction was aesthetic or humanistic; through the early to mid-twentieth century when critics questioned the power of literature to inspire social change; to our own time, when outlets for belletristic criticism are diminishing and scholarship has created specialized readerships and, often, rarefied critical language.

In the 1870s, James's contemporaries — many early critics were part of his social circle — privileged European novelists over American. They read George Eliot and Gustave Flaubert, Charles Dickens and Emile Zola, writers who reflected the rich artistic culture of Great Britain and France. Seeking a comparable American writer, these critics focused on James's works as mirrors of American identity and sought to establish James's place in the nation's newly evolving indigenous literary culture. While some critics praised him as heir to such European writers as Honoré de Balzac and Dickens, others regretted that James did not develop a more distinctly American voice; and still others insisted on his literary indebtedness to the country's only other renowned novelist, Nathaniel Hawthorne. James's early reviewers had mixed responses to his works, evaluating them according to expectations honed by European writers. These reviewers looked for a strong plot, clearly defined characters, and a satisfying ending. Their expectations were not always met; while many admired James's talent for minute observation and his interest in the ambiguities of his characters' minds, others were dismissive of works that seemed devoid of plot and a happy and conclusive ending. As James noted in "The Art of Fiction," a "good" novel might have one or another attribute, according to critics:

> One would say that being good means representing virtuous and aspiring characters, placed in prominent positions; another would say that it

depends on a "happy ending," on a distribution at the last of prizes, pensions, husbands, wives, babies, millions, appended paragraphs, and cheerful remarks. Another still would say that it means being full of incident and movement, so that we shall wish to jump ahead, to see who was the mysterious stranger, and if the stolen will was ever found, and shall not be distracted from this pleasure by any tiresome analysis or "description." But they would all agree that the "artistic" idea would spoil some of their fun. (*Literary Criticism* 48)

While James's early works — *The American* (1879), for example, and *Washington Square* (1881) — seemed conventional enough to please readers, as James's career progressed, many reviewers became frustrated by what they deemed his "fussy" language and defiantly "artistic" ideas. Many critics, also, were impatient with the slow pace of his novels, his insistence on focusing on thought rather than action, and his attenuated descriptions. Although he won the accolade "the Master" — James's story "The Lesson of the Master," published in the *Universal Review* in 1888, inspired the epithet — that praise, unhappily for James, did not translate into sales. Chapter 1 focuses on how James was understood by his contemporaries throughout his career.

Despite James's appreciation by some early critics, as his style became increasingly difficult, and his critics grew increasingly impatient with convoluted sentences and repetitions of theme, James took on the role as advocate for his own works. His twenty-four volume *New York Edition*, published from 1907 to 1909, represents his attempt to speak to a new generation of readers as well as to revive his reputation among those of his own generation. This edition offered instructions to the reader in the form of prefaces to each volume. In these prefaces, James not only reconstructs what he says were the germs of inspiration for his works, but directs the reader to his themes, explains his connection to his characters, and suggests his characters' connection to his readers. Chapter 2 examines critical responses to these prefaces at the time that they were written and after, and considers their impact in shaping both the reading public and James's literary reputation.

After James's death in 1916, criticism waned. Even the publication of Percy Lubbock's two-volume edition of James's letters in 1920 did not help to inspire new interest, and articles about his works numbered barely two dozen a year. In the 1920s and 1930s, his reputation became contested as such modernists as Ezra Pound, T. S. Eliot, and Virginia Woolf embraced him, while other critics, notably Van Wyck Brooks and Vernon Parrington, questioned his significance for a new age beset with social and political problems that, they argued, made James's work irrelevant.

Yet James's works never were eclipsed; as a reviewer of *The Europeans* had noted in 1879, James was a writer for "a highly respectable and well-read class, which may be termed the 'upper middle cultured'" (Hayes 60).

This rarefied audience remained interested in James for many decades. That interest burgeoned in 1943, the centennial of James's birth. In fifty-nine critical essays, articles, and memoirs, James's reputation was reassessed, and his accomplishments lauded. Included among the celebrants were Edmund Wilson, Lionel Trilling, Philip Rahv, and many other well-respected critics. James's works, many long out of print, were republished in paperback, accessible now to another generation of readers. With essays about James in many popular magazines such as the *New Republic*, the *Saturday Review of Literature*, and even *Vogue*, critics helped to move James into a prominent position in the newly sanctified American canon. Critics mined biographical studies and selections of correspondence to explicate James's work, examine his goals and achievements as an artist, and argue for his relevance in a new age. Chapter 3 explores these responses.

The publication of Leon Edel's Freudian reading of James's life (1953–72), along with Edel's editing of James's letters and notebooks, deepened possibilities both for contextualizing his works and for critical debate. Although there had been some biographical information available before Edel's massive study, notably F. O. Matthiessen's *The James Family* (1947) and memoirs by such writers as Simon Nowell-Smith, Hugh Walpole, and Theodora Bosanquet, these works seemed cursory in the light of Edel's detailed biography. Because Edel has had such a pervasive and extensive influence on James studies, Chapter 4 is devoted to examining his work: his background and motivation for writing about James, the reception and impact of his biography, and his effect on James scholarship.

In 1973, when the last volume of Edel's massive James biography was published, Philip Rahv noted that James's reputation, which had waxed and waned during his lifetime and for decades after, once again had waned. That assessment, though, was not accurate: James no longer was the topic of articles in popular magazines, but instead his work was taken up vigorously by the academy. Criticism intended for a general readership gave way to scholarship intended for other scholars. Chapter 5 examines these scholarly perspectives, some of which complicated and extended formal and theoretical questions that had begun in the 1930s, and some of which connected James's work more intrinsically to his life. From the 1960s through the 1980s, scholars explored such issues as the philosophical grounding of James's fiction, his portrayal of women, and his social criticism. Rather than waning, James's reputation was bolstered by attention from the academy.

From the 1980s to the present, we can see a flourishing James industry as scholars have brought new critical perspectives to bear on James's works by examining them in the light of New Historicism, feminist and queer theory, cultural studies, and both psychological and philosophical studies of consciousness. "As a novelist," John Carlos Rowe writes, "he has been held up as the master of realism, modernism, and postmodernism in quick succession. As a theorist, he has been claimed by New Critics, phenomenological and reader-response critics, structuralists, and deconstructive critics. Cultural critics have identified his limitations, but often in ways that have testified to his generally progressive ideals and the subtlety of his understanding of how social power works." James's desires and goals, and his own anxieties "concerning sexuality, conventional gender roles, authorship, and nationalism at the turn of the last century" — anxieties that no current critic seems to doubt — seem congruent, Rowe adds, with our own (*Other* ix).

Rowe himself is a case study of the changing interest in James since the 1980s: in his *The Theoretical Dimensions of Henry James* (1984), one of the most influential books of this period, Rowe characterized James as "the prototypical modern and American expatriate" and "an especially appropriate figure for the study of the impact of contemporary theory on our ideas of the author, American literature, and international modernism" (*Theoretical* xi). That contemporary theory included "the psychology of influence, feminism, psychoanalysis, Marxism, phenomenology, and reader-response or *Rezeptionstheorie*" (xi). Fourteen years later, Rowe's *The Other Henry James* (1998) considered a different set of contemporary theories, focusing now on James's sexuality, on his challenge to ideas "of literary authority and mastery," and on his representation of "vast intricacies" of social systems (*Other* x). An interest in international modernism now has shifted: "This 'other' Henry James," Rowe writes, "helps us understand the difficult and interconnected qualities of our modern and now postmodern societies, so dependent on their means of communication . . ." (xi). For readers in 1998, Rowe argues, the complexities and ambiguities of James's style, which his contemporaries found so convoluted, now seems to represent a new reality.

In a perceptive introduction to her own book, *Portraying the Lady: Technologies of Gender in the Short Stories of Henry James* (2001), Donatella Izzo cautions us to recognize that new critical perspectives need to be conscious of their own historical and ideological contexts. "The recurring rhetoric of *transformation*" she writes, "runs the risk of substituting for the elitist Master of Form another image, opposed to but as critically reified as the preceding one and perhaps as unwilling to question its own premises" (5). Rowe's work, for example, which Izzo admires and extends in her study, has "strategic rather than heuristic value. The James revival dismisses James as formalist and aesthete, canonizes him anew on ideological and ethical premises, and ends up acclaiming him again as the Master: the King is dead, long live the King" (5). But, Izzo asks, is James the Master because of the intrinsic quality of his work, or do scholars, out of professional self-interest, aid in perpetuating the James industry, assuming James to be the Master who requires ever new readings of his work? While recognizing the intellectual investment that many scholars have made in James's work, Izzo responds that for her, at least, "James as a critic of ideology is neither theoretically nor critically incompatible with James as sophisticated artist of narrative techniques." Using the textual and formal approach that canonized James for past generations, Izzo contextualizes him "within feminist theory, gender studies, and critique of ideology" (6).

Criticism has abounded to such an extent that I devote two chapters, 6 and 7, mostly to works published in the last two decades. Chapter 6 focuses on Jamesian consciousness: mind, morality, and the problem of truth. Chapter 7 focuses on questions of intimacy, gender, and sexuality. If criticism has changed dramatically since James's contemporaries wrote about his work, still the same questions recur: what are we to make of James's apparent detachment from his characters? Why is love so fraught? How do his characters come to know one another and to apprehend their world? What is James's relationship to his readers? Where does James stand on the continuum from the nineteenth-century realist to the twentieth-century modernist to the twenty-first-century postmodernist?

In July, 2002, the Henry James Society held an international conference in Paris that reflected the state of current James studies. Among the participants presenting papers were scholars from France, Italy, Spain, England, Scotland, India, Canada, Russia, Bulgaria, Estonia, China, Japan, Korea, Australia, the Netherlands, South Africa, and the United States. Their interests were wide-ranging, theoretically diverse, and included focus not only on James's literary works, but renderings of those works into other media. In "Henry James, (Post)Modernist?" (2004), a perceptive essay about the past, present, and future of James studies, David McWhirter predicted that the transformation of James's novels into films, along with the increasing globalization of James's works, no doubt will open up new critical perspectives. What Henry James means to "us," will necessarily change as "us" becomes enlarged and culturally diverse. McWhirter sees these new readerships as offering an opportunity for fresh insights into James's ideas. James, he suggests, might be discovered again "in and through diverse cultural and critical traditions" that will create a postmodern James (185).

The future of James studies will be grounded in many of the works I consider here. Any study of literary criticism, of course, necessarily privileges some writers over others. I have tried to include in each chapter important voices in shaping James's critical reputation: writers who had influence on other critics, scholars whose work has been cited for their arguments and provocations. From the thousands of articles about James, however, this book selects relatively few for discussion. I trust that this selection will help readers understand how James became elevated to preeminence in our literary history; who his champions and detractors were; what he has meant to past generations of readers and critics; and, not least, what he means to us, now.

Works Cited

Armstrong, Paul B. "History and Epistemology: The Example of *The Turn of the Screw*." In Esch and Warren, 245–54.

Beidler, Peter G., ed. *The Turn of the Screw by Henry James*. 2nd ed. Boston: Bedford/St. Martin's, 2004.

Blackmur, Richard, ed. *The Art of the Novel: Critical Prefaces by Henry James*. New York: Scribner's, 1934.

Esch, Deborah, and Jonathan Warren, eds. *The Turn of the Screw by Henry James: A Norton Critical Edition*. 2nd ed. New York: Norton, 1999.

Felman, Shoshana. "Henry James: Madness and the Risks of Practice (Turning the Screw of Interpretation)." In Esch and Warren, 196–228.

Hayes, Kevin J., ed. *Henry James: The Contemporary Reviews*. Cambridge: Cambridge UP, 1996.

Izzo, Donatella. *Portraying the Lady: Technologies of Gender in the Short Stories of Henry James*. Lincoln: U of Nebraska P, 2001.

James, Henry. *Literary Criticism: Essays on Literature, American Writers, English Writers*. New York: The Library of America, 1984.

Kimbrough, Robert, ed. *The Turn of the Screw by Henry James*. New York: Norton, 1966.

McWhirter, David. "Henry James, (Post)Modernist?" *Henry James Review* 25, no. 2 (2004): 168–94.

Rahv, Philip. "Henry James and His Cult." In *Essays on Literature and Politics, 1932–1972*, edited by Arabel J. Porter and Andrew J. Dvosin, 93–104. Boston: Houghton Mifflin, 1978.

Rowe, John Carlos. *The Other Henry James*. Durham, NC: Duke UP, 1998.

———. *The Theoretical Dimensions of Henry James*. Madison: U of Wisconsin P, 1984.

Solomon, Eric. "The Return of the Screw." In Kimbrough, 237–45.

Spilka, Mark. "Turning the Freudian Screw: How Not to Do It." In Kimbrough, 245–53.

Todorov, Tzvetan. "The Fantastic." In Esch and Warren, 193–96.

Wegelin, Christof, ed. *Tales of Henry James*. New York: Norton, 1984.

Wegelin, Christof, and Henry B. Wonham, eds. *Tales of Henry James*. 2nd ed. New York: Norton, 2003.

1: A Mirror for Americans: Contemporary Criticism, 1866–1916

> *There are bad novels and good novels, as there are bad pictures and good pictures; but that is the only distinction in which I see any meaning. . . . The only classification of the novel that I can understand is into that which has life and that which has it not.*
>
> — Henry James, "The Art of Fiction"

JAMES DID NOT BURST, a fledgling, onto the literary scene with his first volume of stories, *A Passionate Pilgrim and Other Tales* (1875). Those stories, and other writings, already had been published in the *Atlantic Monthly* and the *Galaxy*; his first story, "A Tragedy of Error," appeared in the *Continental Monthly* in February, 1864 and his first reviewed story, "A Landscape Painter," appeared in the *Nation* in 1866 (Gard 3–4). By the time James's novels began to appear in book form in the 1870s, readers were familiar with them because they had been serialized, usually for more than a year. Reviewers, then, often confirmed, rather than shaped, the strong, but mixed, response that James elicited from readers. Some reviewers praised him as a "charming" and graceful fiction writer (Gard 4). But as William Dean Howells noted in his review of *A Passionate Pilgrim*, others felt an instant and abiding dislike. James, Howells said, "has not had to struggle with indifference, that subtlest enemy of literary reputations" (Vann 10). Yet he did have to struggle, throughout his career, to overcome persistent negative appraisal of his style and themes. As some reviewers saw it, James asked readers to reconceive their ideas about what a novel is, to distinguish between romance and realism, and to focus on the internal drama of a character's mind rather than on external events. Reviewers sometimes bristled at confronting these challenges, which became more demanding as James departed from traditional narrative and developed an idiosyncratic and, for many readers, difficult style.

Scholars divide James's works into three phases: early (1875 to mid-1880s), which includes *The American* (1877), *Daisy Miller* (1879), *Washington Square* (1880), *The Portrait of a Lady* (1881) and culminates with several collections of stories and travel essays; middle (mid-1880s to 1897), which includes *The Bostonians* (1886), *The Princess Casamassima* (1886), and *The Tragic Muse* (1890) and also James's writing for the stage, notably his play *Guy Domville*; and late (1897–1916), which includes some of his most stylistically and psychologically complex works, such as *The Sacred Fount* (1901), *The Wings of the Dove* (1902), *The Ambassadors*

(1903), and *The Golden Bowl* (1904). James's early period is characterized by mostly traditional narrative and the recurrence of an "international theme" that opposes American and European character and culture.

Although some reviewers criticized James's portrayal of Americans, many of his early works proved popular — especially *Daisy Miller*, whose strong-willed young heroine captivated readers — and were received with respect and admiration. As each work appeared, James waited anxiously for reviews, especially those published in what he deemed important publications. He worried about whether reviewers would understand him, and, of course, whether his books would sell. Increasingly, though, as he persisted with his literary experiments, he felt he could not predict critical responses nor the criteria by which he was judged. He felt tension between the dramatic, plot-driven fiction reviewers pressed him to write, and what he described as "the high state of development of my artistic conscience, which is so greatly attached to *form* that it shrinks from believing that it can supply it properly for *big* subjects, & yet is constantly studying the way to do so . . . I am determined," he wrote to his brother William in 1879, "that the novel I write this next year shall be 'big'" (Skrupskelis and Berkeley, vol. 1: 321). But his artistic conscience led to stylistic and thematic choices that precluded bigness, and he came to disparage reviewers. "The review," he wrote in "The Future of the Novel," is "in nine cases out of ten an effort of intelligence as undeveloped as the ineptitude over which it fumbles, and the critical spirit, which knows where it is concerned and where not, is not touched, is still less compromised, by the incident" (*Literary* 104). Eventually, rather than press his publishers and agent to send him reviews, he tried to avoid reading them. James's advice to his twenty-three year old nephew Edward Holton James, who had sent him a few of his stories for comments, reflects his hard-earned independence as a writer: "Take the most important subjects you can," James wrote to Edward in 1896, "and write about the most human and manly things. We live in a frightfully vulgar age; and twaddle and chatter are most imposed upon us. Suspect them — detest them — despise them" (Edel, *Letters*, 298).

Even before the mid-1880s, the arbitrary delineation of James's middle period, he had begun to experiment with narration and theme, sometimes to the distress of his reviewers. Experimentation, he remarked wryly in "The Future of the Novel," is essential if fiction is to live and thrive within a culture.

> A community addicted to reflection and fond of ideas will try experiments with the "story" that will be left untried in a community mainly devoted to traveling and shooting, to pushing trade and playing football. There are many judges, doubtless, who hold that experiments — queer and uncanny things at best — are not necessary to it, that its face has been, once for all, turned in one way, and that it has only to go straight before it. If that is what is actually doing in England and America the main thing

to say about its future would appear to be that this future will in very truth more and more define itself as negligible. (*Literary* 106)

As James's experiments met with resistance on the part of reviewers, he focused increasingly on tensions between art and life as in *The Aspern Papers* and "The Lesson of the Master"; on the pressures felt by any artist to represent reality, for example, in "The Real Thing"; and also on the social and moral issues that roiled his own society, women's suffrage and spiritualism in *The Bostonians*, political unrest and anarchy in *The Princess Casamassima*.

Despite his protests of commitment to his art, James also yearned for acclaim. Always aspiring to win a large audience, he turned to playwriting both as a way of making money and of enhancing his reputation. But both his experiments in fiction and his attempt at writing for the theater were not the successes for which he had hoped. The complexity that characterizes James's late period has been explained partly as a rejection of the demands of readers who refused him the accolades he coveted, partly as a resistance to nineteenth century fictional conventions, and partly as a manifestation of his own increasing interest in psychology and morality.

Criticism similarly can be seen as falling into three corresponding periods: early praise, even with some irritation at James's lack of interest in a vigorous plot; some confusion during James's middle period about the demands that he made on his readers; and distress from many reviewers during James's late period about the sheer difficulty of reading his works. Even sympathetic critics echoed William James's advice to his brother after he read *The Golden Bowl* in 1905: writing "in a very puzzled state of mind," William told Henry that he did not understand "the method of narration by interminable elaboration of suggestive reference" which, he said, "goes agin the grain of all my own impulses in writing. . . ." Acknowledging that the novel was brilliant, still, William wrote, "why won't you, just to please Brother, sit down and write a new book, with no twilight or mustiness in the plot, with great vigor and decisiveness in the action, no fencing in the dialogue, no psychological commentaries, and absolute straightness in the style?" (Skrupskelis and Berkeley, vol. 3: 301). When Henry's style became even more musty and convoluted, William despaired. "In this crowded and hurried reading age," he told Henry in 1907, "pages that require such close attention remain unread & neglected. You can't skip a word if you are to get the effect, and 19 out of 20 worthy readers grow intolerant . . . Give us *one* thing in your older directer manner, just to show that, in spite of your paradoxical success in this unheard of method, you *can* still write according to accepted canons" (Skrupskelis and Berkeley, vol. 3: 338). But William's advice, reiterated by many reviewers, did not influence the "unheard of method" to which Henry was so deeply committed.

What Is a Great Novel?

From the first, reviewers deemed James a literary, rather than popular, writer, expecting no less, it seemed, from the son of Henry James, Senior, whose writings were "well known," as a reviewer of *Roderick Hudson* put it in 1875, "for their rare union of subtlety of thought with vigor of style . . ." (Hayes 3). In the *New York Tribune*, to which Henry James, Senior occasionally contributed, a reviewer of *The American* noted that the younger James "inherits from his father a diction so rich and pure, so fluent and copious, so finely shaded yet capable of such varied service, that it is, in itself, a form of genius" (Hayes 21). Despite such generous praise, however, reviewers tended to agree on what they saw as James's shortcomings: his apparent lack of interest in plot, his frequent lack of success in creating interesting and believable characters, and his too frequent thematic focus on the contrast between Americans and Europeans, a contrast that did not show Americans to advantage.

Certainly reviewers agreed that James failed to meet his contemporaries' expectations for a novel driven by a vigorous plot and containing a climactic, conclusive, and preferably happy ending. A writer in the *North American Review*, for example, echoed others in noting that *Roderick Hudson* was "entirely peculiar," being a "study in character. There is no plot, strictly speaking . . ." (Gard 39). Although the reviewer praised James for creating "a marvellous mosaic, whose countless minute pieces are fitted with so much skill and ingenuity that a real picture is presented . . . ," still the mosaic of details yielded nothing more than a surface impression, "an absence of richness and relief, of all that is vivid and salient; there is a pervading lowness of tone, and flatness of tint" (Gard 41). Writing about *The Europeans* (1878) in the *Chicago Tribune*, a reviewer noted that James presented the tale as " 'a sketch.' It lacks the element of a great and sufficient motive, and the robust tone which we are accustomed to associate with full-grown books" (Hayes 52). This criticism recurred in many contemporary reviews, inspiring one reviewer of *The American* to ask "the dangerously broad question what a great novel really is" (Gargano, *Early Novels*, 38).

Acknowledging James's predilection for creating a sketch rather than a plot, reviewers focused on his characters. Here, while some reviewers praised James's talent at evoking richly dimensional characters, many were unsatisfied by characters with whom they could not fully sympathize — and with whom they believed James himself did not sympathize — or whose behavior they could not easily predict. Howells, in his largely appreciative review of *The Passionate Pilgrim*, thought the book "marvelous," and yet even he cautioned James about his attitude toward his characters, criticizing James's "tendency to expatiate upon his characters too much, and not to trust his reader's perception enough." While James was successful in telling his stories from a narrator's point of view, the fiction would be better, Howells wrote, "if the assumed narrator were able to keep himself from seeming to patronize the simpler-hearted heroes, and from openly rising above them in a worldly way" (Vann 16). Writing about *Roderick Hudson* in *Appleton's Journal*, one reviewer complained that "with all his knowledge of human nature and insight into character, Mr. James cannot conceive a *person*." He can trace cause and effect, he can show how outside influences shape a person's decision, but he cannot, this reviewer asserted, "seem able to construct in thought the process by which a person reveals his personality, and becomes individual in the apprehension of others.... The action of the story is curiously suggestive of a puppet-show" (Hayes 8). "He sits beside his characters," remarked a reviewer in the *New York Tribune*, writing about *The American* (1877), "observing and delineating their qualities and actions with marvelous skill, yet apparently untouched by any sympathy with them" (Hayes 21). While that reviewer praised James's mastery of dialogue, he also noted the protagonist's curious "lack of vitality" (Hayes 27). James, the reviewer decided, "writes like a man who has never known an enthusiasm" and feels himself superior to his characters and, most likely, his readers as well (Hayes 22).

This regret about a lack of emotional resonance recurred in reviews of many other novels. Writing about *The American* in the *North American Review*, Edward L. Burlingame noted that James considered it unnecessary for the reader to empathize with fictional characters. "It is not necessary that you should feel when the persons in this story feel — only that you should see that *they* are feeling. It is not needful that you should be in *rapport* with them, — that when a bundle of nerves is laid bare you should feel each one tingle..." (Gargano, *Early Novels*, 39). In responding to *Confidence* (1880), for example, while many reviewers praised "the artistic perfection of [James's] style, the keenness of his observation and the strength and brilliancy of his thought" (Hayes 95), most noted a number of shortcomings: an overly self-conscious cleverness of language; and the repetition of one theme — the contrast between the cultivated European sensibility and the rough, often barbaric, American. Christopher Newman, protagonist of *The American*, seemed to some reviewers to offer a negative portrait of all American men. Newman, one reviewer noted, "is so entirely lacking in attractive personal qualities, and ... so raw in his manner" that, while he may represent a certain type of businessman, he denigrates other Americans (Hayes 36). James's satirical portrait of the young American girl on the loose in Europe (*Daisy Miller*, 1879) and of New England reformers (*The Bostonians*, 1886) further justified reviewers' complaints about James's characterization of his countrymen and women.

By far the most prevalent objections to James, though, were focused on his style: too verbose, too detailed: in short, too literary. Some reviewers, like a *Chicago Tribune* writer considering *Washington Square* (1881), found James "too supercilious, too dilettante, [he] talks too much and says too little" (Hayes 101). Particularly irritating was the character of Catherine Sloper. "Mr. James appears to have set himself the task of portraying the mental features of a dull woman capable of a species of dumb devotion to a man who easily assumes the place of an ideal being in the somewhat arid waste of her life," wrote a reviewer in the *Atlantic* (Gard 92). A British reviewer writing in the *Pall Mall Gazette* expressed a common strain of irritation with *Washington Square*: "Like most, and perhaps all of his novels, 'Washington Square' seems to have been worked up with extraordinary case and skill — and come to nothing. We do not care two straws for the fate of the actors; we are merely concerned with the evident cleverness of the author" (Hayes 111). Yet the reviewer did care for James's portrayal of his country: "America is so near and remote, familiar and strange enough to awaken sympathy and curiosity in England — a combination of feeling most auspicious for a novelist. And what more could the heart of a writer desire than to have a new world at his feet waiting only to be written about and an audience waiting only to read?" (111).

In praising James's realism, a reviewer in the *Californian* stopped short of affirming James's ability to handle one theme: love. "A dignified quietude, a masterly dispassionateness, and a matter-of-fact realism, are qualities without which he would find it as impossible to appear in print as he would find it to appear in the street without his coat and shoes . . . ," the reviewer wrote. "But he ought not to try, under their bonds, to treat of such things as love at its utmost depth, crushed hearts, spoiled lives." James examines his characters with the perspective of a scientist, the reviewer asserted, analyzing feelings without evoking passion or sympathy. *Washington Square*, for all its elegance, was "painful reading" (Hayes 116).

The Portrait of a Lady (1881), which was published in three volumes, seemed unduly long and, to many, tedious: "Mr. James pays himself a graceful compliment in assuming the forbearance of his readers and reviewers when writing a novel of extraordinary length on a singularly unsensational subject," complained a reviewer in the *London Times* (Hayes 131). As a writer for the *Athenaeum* put it, "It is impossible not to feel that Mr. James has at last contrived to write a dull book" with too much description "in which the author goes on refining and distinguishing, as if unable to hit on the exact terms necessary to produce the desired effect" (Hayes 121). Concurring, a *New York Times* reviewer deemed *Portrait* "unsatisfactory in its beginning and in its end. It is spun out too much, and suffers the reader at times to exclaim at its dullness." Yet the reviewer conceded that James offered "a deeply interesting study of men and women, of motives and moods. In spite of a certain irritation which it will be likely to excite; in spite of not a little thinness and unnaturalness which belong to the characters; notwithstanding the care with which they have been finished and the skill with which they are presented, one is never quite content to lay aside the volume without knowing what has become of them so far as Mr. James is willing to let his reader know" (Hayes 125).

Isabel Archer was a more appealing female character than, say, Catherine Sloper, but a reviewer for the *Saturday Review* (England) found her "in truth, a rather selfish and heartless young lady, who acts as if the world were arranged in order to satisfy claims of her imagination" (Gard 98). James's refusal to provide a decisive and conclusive ending frustrated this reviewer, as it did others. "Mr. James devises a plot skillfully, and leads us up to a crisis where all our expectation is awake; but when the moment for action comes, he evades the catastrophe altogether, either — which is his most common method — by making his actors do nothing at all, or by making them do something which seems to be prompted by no reasonable motive" (Gard 98).

For some reviewers, James's interest in his characters' minds seemed almost scientific. W. C. Brownell, writing about *The Portrait*, remarked on the "microscopy" with which James revealed the personality of his characters and laid out for the reader's inspection the inner workings of their minds (Hayes 22, 147). Similarly, J. H. Morse, writing about *Portrait of a Lady*, felt that James's technique "satisfies the intellect and the observing faculties . . . but it does not satisfy the heart" (Gargano, *Early Novels*, 53).

Although most magazine and newspaper reviews were unsigned during this period of James's career, occasionally well-known writers published a defense of James's work. One of the most influential was William Dean Howells's 1882 article in the *Century*, the same magazine in which James often published. In fact, in the same issue as Howells's "Henry James, Jr.," James published a travel essay on Venice. Although James would drop the "Jr." from his name just a month later, when his father died, Howells made a point of James's inheritance of a "felicity of diction," which, while not so "racy" or "graphic" as the elder James's, still was striking. In tracing James's career over nearly twenty years, Howells admitted that his work was more popular among magazine editors than readers: "The flavor was so strange, that, with rare exceptions, they had to 'learn to like' it" (Gard 128). As Howells rehearsed common objections to James's work, he focused on readers' frustration over lack of plot. "Evidently it is the character, not the fate, of his people which occupies him," Howells explained; "when he has fully developed their character he leaves them to what destiny the reader pleases" (Gard 129). Fiction was changed, Howells explained patiently, from the days of Richardson and Fielding, and James was practitioner and harbinger of the new. The new novel, it seemed, required a cooperative and active reader: one who could read attentively, respond to nuance, and participate in the creation of the fiction by imagining a world beyond the pages of the work. "Will the reader be content to accept a novel which is an analytic study rather than a story, which is apt to leave him arbiter of the destiny of the author's creations?" Howells asked. "Will he find his account in the unflagging interest of their development?" (Gard 133). Howells saw in James's "growing popularity" evidence that a new readership awaited him. After all, he concluded, "stories were all told long ago; and now we want merely to know what the novelist thinks about persons and situations." We read James because he is "philosophic," an "annalist, or analyst," not because we want to be gratified by the contrivances of a plot (Gard 134).

As Donald Murray shows, Howells's essay generated anger among British readers because he elevated James above Dickens and Thackeray. Moreover, in the same month that Howells's "Henry James" appeared in America, Robert Louis Stevenson published "Gossip on Romance" in the British *Saturday Review*. That essay defended the plot-driven tale over the novel in which characters were examined and dissected. For the next two years, Murray tells us, critics on both sides of the debate contributed articles to magazines on both sides of the Atlantic, culminating in James's "The Art of Fiction," which James delivered at the Royal Institution in April, 1884 and published in *Longman's Magazine* the next fall.

In "The Art of Fiction," James responded both to the ongoing debate among critics and to more than a decade of criticism of his own works. He acknowledged that distinctions between the romance and the novel, the novel of incident and the novel of character, were made for the convenience of readers and critics, but had nothing to do with art. Each novel takes its own form depending on the reality that the writer wants to convey, he asserted, and that form "is to be appreciated after the fact: then the author's choice has been made, his standard has been indicated; then we can follow lines and directions and compare tones and resemblances" (*Literary* 55). The genre of a novel has no fixed template, James argued, and no "recipe." "Humanity is immense," he wrote, "and reality has a myriad [of] forms; the most one can affirm is that some of the flowers of fiction have the odor of it, and others have not; as for telling you in advance how your nosegay should be composed, that is another affair" (52). Still, despite James's caution, many critics throughout his career continued to try to categorize his fictions as certain types, either fulfilling their expectations or falling short. Not until late in his career did some critics understand that James was inventing a new kind of fiction and, in effect, a new reader.

James was painfully aware of the difference between Howells's appreciation of his talents and reviewers' assessments of his work, and as much as he wanted to be esteemed by writers he admired, still he courted reviewers and the readership that he felt they influenced and represented. In his next novels, *The Bostonians* (1885) and *The Princess Casamassima* (1886), he aimed for drama, broader strokes, and more compelling characterizations.

Passions and Dramas

After *The Bostonians* was serialized in the *Atlantic*, James confessed to William that he feared "a fiasco, as not a word, echo or comment on the serial . . . have come to me from any quarter whatever. This deathly silence seems to indicate that it has fallen flat. I hoped so much of it, & shall be disappointed — having got no money for it I hoped for a little glory" (Skrupskelis and Berkeley, vol. 2: 30). Nevertheless, when the novel appeared in book form, many reviewers found the melodramatic *Bostonians* more passionate, forceful, and, therefore, more successful than some of James's previous works: "the novel is full of novelty," asserted a writer in the *London Daily News*, ". . . novelty of character, and even of situation . . . and one leaves his story with a desire to hear more about certain of his characters . . ." (Hayes 153), certainly an unusual request from a reviewer. In the *Detroit Free Press*, an appreciative reviewer wrote, "Those who have become accustomed to hear Mr. James ridiculed and his novels decried will probably be mildly surprised to know that 'The Bostonians' really is a readable and interesting story which might almost have been written by a novelist without any peculiar or advanced views as to art in fiction" (Hayes 161).

Even more gratifying for James, *The Princess Casamassima*, which was published the following year, met with enthusiastic praise. Some considered it the most virile, sensational, and vital novel that James had yet written. "There is more flesh and blood in it than one finds in any of his foregoing novels . . . and the field is broader, the characters are more diversified, the central theme is more clearly defined, than one is wont to look for in Mr. James's essays in fiction," a reviewer in the *Literary World* observed (Hayes 189). Still, reviewers were impatient with the wordiness, the overwhelming delicacy of James's style. It was hard work reading James, although for some reviewers the effort was rewarded. "There is a mass of what, from a hasty reading, may be stigmatized as super-subtle analyses, ultra-refined phrases, fine-spun nothings," wrote Annie Logan in the *Nation*. "But a careful reading . . . will pretty surely acquit the author of such sins, and compel the recognition that, putting aside his skill as a novelist, he has written a book remarkable for the precision, elegance, and distinction of its style" (Hayes 193).

The Tragic Muse (1890), however, for some reviewers signaled a return to a novel that had "a curiously brilliant surface" that failed to dazzle. "There is something paradoxical in a success which leaves our real sympathies untouched," remarked a writer in the *Literary World* (Gard 208). George Saintsbury, who admitted to being an admirer of James, suggested that *The Idiot Asylum* might be an apt title for the novel because the characters' motivations were so maddeningly mysterious. The characters "come, like the language that they talk, of constant imitation and re-imitation, not of real life or of anything like real life, but of thrice and thirty times redistilled literary decoctions of life" (Gargano, *Early Novels*, 65). Horace Scudder, writing in the *Atlantic*, was one dissenter to this view: James's technique "proves to be the facile instrument of a master workman who is thinking of the soul of his art . . ." (Vann 22). In the light of mixed reviews of *The Tragic Muse* and Scudder's rejection of "The Pupil" for the *Atlantic*, James was delighted when a production of *The American* met with success upon its opening in Lancashire. The theater, he hoped, would afford him the popularity that eluded him elsewhere.

Another possibility for a larger audience also presented itself: newspaper syndication. As Charles Johanningsmeier details in an article about "The Real Thing" (2006), syndicated publication meant that James reached far more readers, in this case about 800,000, than he would reach in the magazines in which he usually appeared, and certainly more than he would reach when his works were sold as books. The newspaper editors who purchased the story from aggressive syndicator S. S. McClure took pains to present James as an accessible and important writer: advertisements for the impending publication called him "noted" and "celebrated"; but editors focused on selling the plot, too: "This is a peculiarly attractive tale and should not be missed by those who like a well-turned story," one editor wrote. Like other papers, the *Illustrated Buffalo Express* decided to publish the story in two parts, hoping that readers would buy a second issue to find out the ending. The paper characterized James as a writer "whose keen deft character analysis, polished humor, and artistic style have placed him among the first of short story writers and critics. He is an American by birth, European by education, and cosmopolitan by preference" (Johanningmeier 87). Certainly James's interest in newspaper syndication is consistent with his desire for a large readership, just as his efforts to break into the theater reflect his desire to enhance his reputation as more than a literary writer for a small elite.

James's hopes for *Guy Domville* reveal themselves in a letter to his brother William, written just a month before the play was to open in January 1895. "The play is small & simple," Henry wrote, "— only 3 acts — but pretty, I think interesting & distinctly 'emotional'; a little romantic story in an old-time (last century) setting. I have endeavoured to make it both very artful & very human — and it will not, at any rate, be a disgraceful work. It will be quite exquisitely mounted, dressed, &c & as well acted as London can act" (Skrupskelis and Berkeley, vol. 2: 329–30). The night before the play opened, Henry wrote with a shaking hand that he was "lonely & terrified" and asked for his brother's prayers (335). A few days later, he conveyed devastating news.

He had been too nervous to see the play, he said, but instead went to another theater to see Oscar Wilde's *The Ideal Husband*. Then, when he returned to his theater when the performance ended, he was persuaded to go on stage. The audience seated in the boxes and stalls were quick to applaud the author, but noisy derision from the gallery forced James to flee into the wings. James described the scene to William as horrifying: "an abominable ¼ of an hour during wh. all the forces of civilization in the house waged a battle of the most gallant, prolonged & sustained applause with the hoots & jeers & catcalls of the roughs, whose *roars* (like those of a cage of beasts at some infernal 'Zoo') were only exacerbated (as it were!) by the conflict.... Meanwhile," he added, "all *private* opinion is apparently one of extreme admiration — I have been flooded with letters of the warmest protest & assurance." Although James had attempted, he said, to make his play as "as broad, as gross, as simple, as clear" as he could, nevertheless the audience was so vulgar that even these strenuous efforts were not rewarded. He was certain that the play itself was "altogether the best thing I've done" and blamed the audience's reaction on their own stupidity (Skrupskelis and Berkeley, vol. 2: 337–38). As "tormenting & tragic" as the experience had been, he was comforted by the solace of his friends, and their friends. He knew better, he told William, than to take seriously the "rude" newspaper reviews. "It hasn't mattered to me," he said, "— for I have too long & too carefully watched their pronouncements, their standards, & know too much what they are.... The play has failed," he explained, "because it has been *unfamiliar*. It is an exceedingly skilful, considered & expert piece of construction — with a neatness of art, in this particular, that their measurement, their utterly unitiated sense, is too coarse & too stupid for." He had no doubt, he insisted, on his own " 'technical skill' " (Skrupskelis and Berkeley, vol. 2: 343–45). In this event, we can see the division that also marked two strains among reviewers of James's fiction: those who had no patience with the literary difficulties that James presented, and those who praised James's style and themes for precisely those complexities or, at least, for their social or intellectual affinity with the author.

Extraordinary Mannerisms

After his experience as a playwright, James told William that he was able to "get quickly detached & away from it" and to move on "to the better or fresher life of the next thing to come" (Skrupskelis and Berkeley, vol. 2: 343). Although he insisted that he had not lost confidence in his abilities as a writer, still he struggled with the threat of commercial failure, worried that negative reviews would have an impact on magazine publications, concerned that his readership was shrinking. *What Maisie Knew* and *The Spoils of Poynton* (1897), "The Turn of the Screw" (1898), *The Awkward Age* (1899), *The Sacred Fount* (1901), *The Wings of the Dove* (1902), *The Ambassadors* (1903), and *The Golden Bowl* (1904) are the major works of this period of James's career, and their reception can be characterized as a mixture of awed respect and persistent irritation. Reviewers may have been frustrated and sometimes bewildered by James's stylistic or thematic choices, but they did not doubt his stature as a major American novelist. As impatient as they were with the "clumsy and even wearisome" effect of James's overwhelming details and minute observations (review of *The Awkward Age*, Gard, 293), there was consensus that his work was both brilliant and, in its own way, fascinating. If one reviewer criticized the "intellectual remoteness" of *The Awkward Age* (Gard 298), another praised the "unflagging literary skill" of *Wings of the Dove* (Gard 319). If one reviewer of *Wings* expressed impatience with James's "inveterate habit of minute analysis" (Gard 332), another, writing about *The Ambassadors*, found the characters refreshingly appealing (Gard 359). Yet even those who praised James believed that he intended his works for only an elite readership.

The exception to this belief appeared in reviews of "The Turn of the Screw" (1898), where James, at last, seemed to have produced a tale that could be popular. A reviewer in the *New York Tribune* went so far as to assert that if James had written "The Turn of the Screw" earlier in his career, "his critics would have prophesied for him . . . a bright immortality . . . Why Mr. James should have hidden his light under a bushel for so long, no man, we suppose, will ever know." The tale was perfection itself: "it crystallizes an original and fascinating idea in an absolutely appropriate form. There is not a word which could be spared . . ." (Esch and Warren 150). Although some reviewers considered the theme of evil "distinctly repulsive" (Esch and Warren 151), the *Tribune* writer spoke for the majority: "We realize now that Mr. James, if he had known and had cared, could have been great" (Esch and Warren 150).

Some reviewers of James's late novels understood that his focus of interest was not plot, but the consciousness of his characters, and by late in the nineteenth century, when psychical research, spiritualism, early psychoanalysis, and tales of multiple personality were prominent in cultural life, this interest seemed defensible and even admirable. Reviewing *The Golden Bowl* in the *Academy*, a reviewer concluded that James "knows that modern domesticity is a thing of half-tints, even in its suffering; it bleeds but it does not bleed red. . . . Mr. James's extraordinary gift in detecting and expressing the most evanescent complexities of psychological feeling, subconscious or unconscious thought, has seemingly become a passion that he cannot for an instant disembarrass himself of it. It overpowers his instinct of proportion: he must analyze everything, important or trivial, with like minuteness and like prolixity" (Gard 376–77). Although some reviewers believed that such a focus on psychology was not worth writing a novel about, and others found James's circumlocutions too demanding, still, they lauded James's motivation and goals. Generous reviewers predicted that with an increase in attention to consciousness among readers, books such as *What Maisie Knew*, *The Sacred Fount*, and *The Golden Bowl* would become increasingly appreciated (Gard 447).

Publication of *The Golden Bowl* coincided with James's visit to America in 1904, a visit that generated accolades and attention to one of the country's most prominent men of letters. Some reviews, such as an unsigned piece in the *Athenaeum*, supported this reputation: the book "is a veritable triumph," the reviewer concluded, despite James's often "super-subtle" style (Gargano, *Late*, 57). Mary Moss, writing in the *North American Review*, called James "a marvelous hermit on a lonely isle; you must row out of the current to visit him.. . . . He has deserted the earth and hovers in a wonderful, labyrinthine dimension of his own" (Gargano, *Late*, 57). Many reviewers of *The Golden Bowl* used the occasion as a chance to offer an overview of James's career. James's "extraordinary mannerisms," it seemed to one reviewer, had become intensified in both *The Ambassadors* and *The Golden Bowl*, ensuring that he would appeal only to a "small and select audience," but an audience, nevertheless, who could "exalt his reputation far above the fame of his more popular fellows" (Hayes 418). "His demands on his readers are increasingly rigorous," asserted Claude Bragdon in *The Critic* (Hayes 420).

Those demands were so rigorous, in fact, that a reviewer in the *London Daily Chronicle* considered the reader to be James's "joint author" because of the effort that must be exerted to read between the lines and draw inferences from "the infinite complications of the mechanism" of the characters' minds (Hayes 361). James, in fact, saw this collaboration as a mark of a novelist's success. "In every novel," he wrote in an essay about George Eliot, "the work is divided between the writer and the reader; but the writer makes the reader very much as he makes his characters. When he makes him ill, that is, makes him indifferent, the writer does all. When he makes him well, that is, makes him interested, then the reader does quite half the labor" (*Literary* 922). This notion of artistic collaboration recurred in writings about James's late works and became evidence for critics' assertion that James was a precursor of modernism. Yet for many reviewers, James asked too much even of well-educated readers. Although some found *The Ambassadors* more successful than *The Wings of the Dove*, most agreed that James's late style was too convoluted. Rather than feel that James wanted his readers' cooperation, these reviewers felt that James did not care about his readers at all; he had simply turned away from their needs. Henry B. Fuller, writing in the *Chicago Evening Post*, felt that by the time James wrote *The Wings of the Dove*, he had "gone along refining on his own refinements until the delicate has become the impalpable, and the elusive the intangible, and the exquisite the all but imperceptible" (Hayes 365).

After the turn of the century, some well-known writers leapt to James's defense. Joseph Conrad, in an "appreciation" that reads like a eulogy, cited

James's claim that the novelist must have the cultural standing of an historian. "I think that the claim cannot be contested," Conrad wrote, "and that the position is unassailable. Fiction is history, human history, or it is nothing.... As is meet for a man of his descent and tradition, Mr. Henry James is 'the historian of fine conscience'" (Edel, *Collection*, 15). In 1913, Ford Madox Ford concurred with Conrad: "I consider Mr. James to be the greatest man now living. He, more than anybody, has observed human society as it now is, and more than anybody has faithfully rendered his observations for us" (Edel, *Collection*, 48–49); "... he is the only unbiassed, voluminous and truthful historian of our day. And, in our day, the greatest need of society is the historian who can cast a ray of light into the profound gloom, into the whirl of shadows, of our social agnosticism" (Edel, *Collection*, 66). Conrad's and Ford's hailing of James as a social critic underscored his success as a realist, whose characters represent palpable individuals grappling with their social, political, cultural, and even sexual passions.

Perhaps the most outspoken dissenter to this view was H. G. Wells, for whom James seemed isolated and cut off from the realities that others experienced. James's refusal to deal with passion, lust, belligerence, and violence seemed profound shortcomings. Similar assessments recurred in reviews of James's *The American Scene* (1907), the nonfiction response to his long trip through his native land. Many reviewers, respectful as they were of James's talents as a writer, believed that he was too cut off from his native land to see it clearly, too mired in the past to fully appreciate the present and imagine the future. He appeared, noted a reviewer in the *Nation*, "as a curiously alien observer. . . . Mr. James's chief interest lies in the hallowed associations of what he terms the 'whole precious past'; he has little but misgiving and suspicion for the new and untried" (Hayes 458). Fascinating and acutely observed as the book was, the reviewer saw James as "fundamentally incapable of getting inside the skin of the average American or of realizing that the outlook to such a citizen is by no means so dreary and 'common' as to himself" (Hayes 460). Like other reviewers, Frederic Taber Cooper, writing in the *North American Review*, saw *The American Scene* as continuous with James's fiction, the same vision, the same sensibility as *The Ambassadors* or *What Maisie Knew*. "In 'The American Scene' the method is the same, excepting that the temperament through which we behold places and people is that of the author himself. Moreover, it is a keenly self-conscious temperament, tremendously interested with its own sensations, and with finger constantly on pulse, to detect and record every momentary quickening" (Hayes 466). The perspective and mannerisms that irritated some reviewers of James's fiction became sources of praise in a work more overtly autobiographical.

An unusually perceptive commentator about James's works and predictor of his legacy was H. G. Dwight, himself a writer, who served as curator of the New York Author's Club from 1903 to 1906. In an essay that appeared in *Putnam's Monthly* in 1907, following the publication *The American Scene*, but before the publication of the New York Edition of his works, Dwight reflected James's reception among readers "neither willing to aclaim [*sic*] him nor able to ignore him" (Gard 440). Part of the reason for their disdain surely was James's difficult style; but partly, Dwight believed, was James's renunciation of his native land. "They can forgive almost any of his shortcomings before they can forgive his exile," Dwight concluded (447).

James demanded more from his readers than other novelists did, "more attention than many readers think a mere book deserves" (444). Unlike some readers who believed that James's perspective was coldly scientific, Dwight believed he was "concerned with the things of what we call, for lack of a better word, the soul. Indeed this interest has gradually superseded others in him, making all his later work a series of studies in the dark drama of the inner life" (444). James came closest of any writer, Dwight said, in reproducing thought and speech, with all of its hesitations and digressions, as if thought were "the breaking crests of a sea subject to cross currents and inconstant winds. The clauses, the parentheses, the intonations of daily life are of course familiar enough to our ears; but they still have a strangeness for eyes accustomed to the telegraphic brevity of the newspaper" (444). This goal of depicting the reality of the inner drama, what his brother William called the stream of human consciousness, posed the most difficulty for readers, especially American readers who, according to Dwight, were "the least sensitive to the movements of the inner life" (445). James, then, was not victim of his own style, but of a readership not sufficiently sophisticated to respond to that style.

James was ahead of his time, and Dwight looked forward to a later generation, more familiar with fiction that attended to the inner life of characters, more willing to validate a novelist whose interest was not plot but "in relating the scene of every day to the background of mystery against which it moves" (449). "If there is anything at all in what we vaguely called the *Zeitgeist*," Dwight argued, "it would seem that as consciousness increases, as we become more trained to the consequence of much that we have regarded as inconsequent, books like *What Maisie Knew* and *The Sacred Fount* and *The Golden Bowl* will take on for us a new significance" (447). Certainly Dwight proved correct, but it would not be until the mid-1940s that James's reputation took an upward turn. By then, critics had acclaimed the work of such writers as James Joyce and Virginia Woolf; the *Zeitgeist*, as Dwight had predicted, was completely transformed, and James was seen as the writer, "the first, in his generation, to open a door between English letters and the wider world" (449).

Works Cited

Conrad, Joseph. "An Appreciation." In Edel, *Collection*, 11–17.

Dwight, H. G. "H. G. Dwight on American Hostility to James, and Its Probable Causes." In Gard, 432–49.

Edel, Leon, ed. *Henry James: A Collection of Critical Essays*. Englewood Cliffs, NJ: Prentice Hall, 1963.

———, *Henry James: Selected Letters*. Cambridge, MA: Belknap Press of Harvard UP, 1987.

Esch, Deborah, and Jonathan Warren, eds. *The Turn of the Screw by Henry James: A Norton Critical Edition*. 2nd ed. New York: Norton, 1999. Review in *Outlook*, 29 October 1898: 151; *New York Tribune*, 23 October 1898: 150–51.

Ford, Ford Madox. *Henry James: A Critical Study*. New York: Octagon Books, 1964 [1913].

Gard, Roger, ed. *Henry James: The Critical Heritage*. London: Routledge, 1968.

Gargano, James W., ed. *Critical Essays on Henry James: The Early Novels*. Boston: G. K. Hall, 1987.

———. *Critical Essays on Henry James: The Late Novels*. Boston: G. K. Hall, 1987.

Garland, Hamlin. "'I Have Lost Touch with My Own People.'" In *Henry James, Interviews and Recollections*, edited by Norman Page, 91–95. London: Macmillan, 1984.

Hayes, Kevin J., ed. *Henry James: The Contemporary Reviews*. Cambridge: Cambridge UP, 1996.

Howells, William Dean. "Henry James, Jr." *Century* 25, no. 1 (1882): 25–29.

———. Review of *The Passionate Pilgrim*. In Vann, 10–16.

James, Henry. *Literary Criticism: Essays on Literature, American Writers, English Writers*. New York: The Library of America, 1984.

Johanningsmeier, Charles. "How Real American Readers Originally Experienced James's 'The Real Thing.'" *Henry James Review* 27, no. 1 (2006): 75–99.

Murray, Donald M. "Henry James and The English Reviewers, 1882–1890." *American Literature* 24, no. 1 (March 1952): 1–20.

Scudder, H. E. Review of *The Tragic Muse*. In Vann, 19–22.

Skrupskelis, Ignas, and Elizabeth Berkeley, eds. *The Correspondence of William James*. Vol. 1, *William and Henry, 1861–1884*. Charlottesville: U of Virginia P, 1992.

———. *The Correspondence of William James*. Vol. 2, *William and Henry, 1885–1896*. Charlottesville: U of Virginia P, 1993.

———. *The Correspondence of William James*. Vol. 3, *William and Henry, 1897–1910*. Charlottesville, U of Virginia P, 1994.

Tuttleton, James, ed. *The American by Henry James: A Norton Critical Edition.* New York: Norton, 1978. Review of *The American, Nation,* 11 January 1877: 389–90; *Independent,* 17 May 1877: 391.

Vann, J. Don, ed. *Critics on Henry James.* Coral Gables, FL: U of Miami P, 1972.

Wells, H. G. "Of Art, Of Literature, Of Mr. Henry James." In *Henry James and H. G. Wells: A Record of their Friendship, Their Debate on the Art of Fiction, and Their Quarrel,* edited by Leon Edel and Gordon N. Ray, 234–60. Urbana: U of Illinois P, 1958.

2: Instructions to the Reader: James's Prefaces to the New York Edition

> *The critic's first duty in the presence of an author's collective works is to seek out some key to his method, some utterance of his literary convictions, some indication of his ruling theory. The amount of labor involved in an inquiry of this kind will depend very much upon the author. In some cases the critic will find express declarations; in other cases he will have to content himself with conscientious inductions.*
> — Henry James, "The Novels of George Eliot"

IN LATE JULY 1905, HENRY JAMES was sixty-two; he just had returned to England from a long and emotional trip to America, a country he had not seen in decades. The cultural changes he noted urged him to look back not only at his youth, but at the whole of his life and career. He returned, then, in a reflective, biographical mood that emerged in his essays published as *The American Scene* (1907) and, most significantly, in his new project: a specially printed and bound multi-volume edition of his works. He would call it the New York Edition, in honor, he said, of his birthplace and, perhaps, in recognition of the preeminence of that city — more than London or Paris — as the vibrant cultural capital of the future.

In a long memorandum to his publisher, Charles Scribner's Sons, James laid out his plans for the edition, a compendium of his "principal novels — that is with the exception possibly of one" — and of selected stories, which, he hoped, "will gain in significance and importance, very considerably, by a fresh grouping or classification, a placing together . . . of those that will help each other . . ." He would revise, "re-touch," as he put it, especially the early works. Most important, he would write for each volume "a freely colloquial and even, perhaps, as I may say, confidential preface or introduction . . . a frank critical talk about its subject, its origin, its place in the whole artistic chain, and embodying, in short, whatever of interest there may be to be said about it." This project was different from anything he had ever done, he said, even though he had written much criticism, and he felt "a certain freshness of appetite" at the prospect of this kind of intimate disclosure to the reader. The memorandum reads as if James is recounting a beautiful image seen in a dream, a glowing image of "dignity and beauty," something solid, elegant, gleaming: a commemoration to his lifework, to his native city, and to the spirit of creativity that shaped his fictions (Edel 366–67).

One measure of his personal investment in the project can be seen in his decision to illustrate each volume with a photograph as frontispiece, and his choice of Alvin Langdon Coburn as photographer. James had met the twenty-three year old photographer in New York and was impressed. This "young American expert," he wrote to Scribner's, would provide the images, "consummately photographed," of "some scene, object or locality" appropriate to his fiction. For this project, James explained to Scribner's, he wanted something artistically different from the line drawings that sometimes accompanied his magazine pieces (Edel 407–8). There is no doubt that although James considered Coburn an expert, he also expected to collaborate fully in the choice of scene, object, or locality. In London, he accompanied Coburn through city streets pointing out specific sites that would be appropriate for his books. A particular doorway in St. John's Wood for *The Tragic Muse*, an evocatively foggy moment in Portland Place for *The Golden Bowl*, reflect James's aesthetic desires. When Coburn traveled to Paris and Venice, James sent him minute instructions about where to walk, what to look for, even how to direct his cabman: "once you get the Type into your head, you will easily recognise specimens by walking about in the *old* residential and 'noble' parts of the city," he assured Coburn in a memorandum. Not only the particular site was important, but also "some ingeniously-hit-upon angle of presentment" and most certainly the evocation of mood (Edel 417).

James's uncharacteristic move to include illustrations in the New York Edition serves as additional evidence for both his desire for a popular readership and a desire, as Ira Nadel argued in "Visual Culture: The Photo Frontispieces to the New York Edition," "to reassert the link between [his] fiction and the physical world. The carapace of reality they create helps defend his work from charges of abstraction . . ." (McWhirter 107). By associating his work with the exciting new technology of photography, James suggested that his fiction was equally exciting and modern. Although throughout his career, James had professed his disdain of illustrations because they threatened to compete with — or even usurp — the power of the word, he exerted such meticulous control of Coburn that the resulting images did not so much represent scenes of the texts as echo them. Moody and painterly, the photographs evoked a feeling of nostalgia for the worlds that James evoked in prose. "Each photograph illustrates, makes visible, not this or that detail in the text," J. Hillis Miller concluded in "The 'Grafted' Image," "but a general type or idea that the text magically evokes. . . . Each photograph would thereby be kept subsidiary to the text, posing no danger of overwhelming it" (McWhirter 141). Separated from the text by a page of tissue, the photographs, in fact, seemed an auxiliary to the prefaces, serving as James's attempt to control the reader's response to the newly revised work.

With volumes appearing over the course of three years, James hoped that the New York Edition would insure his reputation as a major novelist.

Surely he believed that that reputation must be reflected in the physical appearance of the books. In May, 1906, when Scribner's sent him sample pages, he exulted: "It seems to me handsome and charming, and abates nothing of the *dignity* of aspect which was, for this presentment of my books, my dream and desire" (Edel 403). By the time James began to work on his edition there had already been such multi-volume commemorative sets, finely bound, gilded, and specially watermarked, of the works of such writers as Rudyard Kipling, Robert Louis Stevenson, George Meredith, and Honoré de Balzac. As Eric Leuschner points out in an article giving historical context for James's project, the deluxe edition was a nineteenth-century convention that "enshrined" writers (26), although Leuschner notes that by the early twentieth century, the market for such editions had diminished considerably. Nevertheless, James believed that market did exist, and his decision to publish a deluxe edition speaks to his coveting of a readership and, certainly, his hopes for royalties. Not marketed through bookstores, the deluxe edition was sold as a complete set by subscription. It was, therefore, a collector's item; and James had great hopes that he would attract many collectors.

Besides alluding to a potential financial benefit, James's letters to friends as he worked on the edition underscore his desire to revise and reinvigorate his reputation. "Its *raison d'être*," he wrote to Robert Herrick in August 1905, "is in its being selective as well as collective, and by the mere fact of leaving out certain things (I have tried to read over *Washington Square* and *can't*, and I fear it must go!) I exercise a control, a discrimination, I treat certain portions of my work as unhappy accidents . . ." (Edel 371). In effect, he edited his image for posterity. James told Scribner's that the works most revised were *Roderick Hudson*, *The American*, and *Portrait of a Lady*; especially with *Portrait*, James hoped that revisions would give it "a new lease of such life as it may still generally aspire to" (Edel 408–9). Along with *Washington Square*, James omitted his first novel, *Watch and Ward*, because he considered it no more than a youthful effort and *The Europeans* because it would require extensive rewriting; he also decided not to republish *Confidence*, *The Other House*, and *The Sacred Fount*. As Michael Anesko explained in *"Friction with the Market": Henry James and the Profession of Authorship* (1986), a study that changed the way scholars understood James's relationship to the business of writing, some of James's selections were made for financial, rather than aesthetic, reasons, connected to the permissions fees he had to pay for reprinting his works (Anesko 148). When Scribner's suggested omitting *The Bostonians* for economic reasons, for example, James quickly agreed (Anesko 153). That novel, especially, seemed to James to require extensive revision to meet his new standards of excellence. If James saw the edition as supporting his identity as the Master, then, as Martha Banta has noted, he was content to define his mastery only in certain of his works.

Keys to the House of Fiction

When the first volumes began to appear in 1907, the publication of Henry James's New York Edition seemed to some readers indeed a cause for celebration. An article in the *Literary Digest* (1908) explained why: many of James's works, long out of print, were hard to find except in secondhand bookstores; the new edition made them available to a new generation of readers. Moreover, these readers could enjoy "the fine, ample, and dignified volumes" with their clear type, generous margins, and fine paper featuring "the author's own initials as a water-mark." While it dismayed some that James had revised several of his early works for the new project, others deemed the revisions "an advantage" because of "the greater sense of unity the entire body of work will present." Most important, the New York Edition contained James's prefaces, "the feature of the highest value" that allowed readers a glimpse of the writer's craft: "the germ of the story, the process of its growth and the environment that offered favoring aids to its furtherance." James, the article continued, was unusually candid about his own assessment of his works, about their success or failure, strengths or shortcomings. The prefaces "furnish the key to the whole admirable work he has accomplished; and show it as a goodly structure, reared upon a coherent plan, tho years have been expended in the fashioning of it" (Review, *Literary Digest*, 418).

This response has been debated ever since. Criticism has ranged from praise to exasperation, from critics taking the prefaces as invitations into James's creative world to those seeing the prefaces as distancing and exclusionary, characterized by unintended irony, overt duplicity, and lack of self-knowledge. As novelist Graham Greene ruefully remarked in *The Lost Childhood and other Essays* (1952), "We must always remain on our guard while reading these prefaces, for at a certain level no writer has really disclosed less" (40). James's contemporary Edmund Gosse concurred: "I have to confess that these prefaces constantly baffle my eagerness," he recalled in a memoir. "Not for a moment would I deny that they throw interesting light on the technical craft of a self-respecting novelist, but they are dry, remote, and impersonal to a strange degree. It is as though the author felt a burning desire to confide in the reader, whom he positively button-holes in the endeavor, but that the experience itself evades him, fails to find expression, and falls stillborn, while other matters, less personal and less important, press in and take their place against the author's wish" (18). The changing arc of criticism can be explained, in part, by changes in critics' assumptions about sources of creativity; questions about the extent to which any writer understands the full and nuanced context and implications of his or her own literary choices; and awareness of the intersections between a writer and a reader that create a text.

We see early critics, such as Percy Lubbock and Richard Blackmur, trusting James's self-knowledge and candor, and assuming that an author's identity is monolithic, stable, and consistent; this perspective invokes and helps to create an image of an author in control of his art, able to recover his original intentions for a work, to revise in order to achieve those intentions more precisely, and to articulate his aesthetic motivation and achievements. These critics also concur with James's portrayal of the novelist as an individual who, as Dorothy Hale put it in "Henry James and the Invention of Novel Theory" (1998), "most transparently expresses his unique 'impression' of life" and at the same time "does not allow his own views to prevent life from making its 'impression' on him" (Freedman 84–85). The artist, then, possesses a special vision, allowing him to see more and more deeply through any of the million windows into what he called "the house of fiction." And yet, Hale asserts, "As James takes pains to emphasize, all that distinguishes one viewer from another in the house of fiction is the 'need' and the 'pressure' of the 'individual will.' No viewing position is privileged; no window offers a more accurate or more preferable understanding of life than another . . ." (83–84). This image of the artist as acutely sensitive to impressions available to others, compelled to self-expression by some inner need or pressure, sharing his vision with his fortunate readers, appealed to many of James's early critics. They created for their own readers an iconic and canonical Henry James. We can infer that James meant to convey this image because of his reaction to Lubbock's praise for the New York Edition in the *Times Literary Supplement* in July 1909; Lubbock's piece, James wrote to a friend, was an "admirable and exquisite article" (Edel 525, 526 n. 1)

The New Critics, writing generations later, did not contradict such portrayals; as Hershel Parker argued in *Flawed Texts and Verbal Icons: Literary Authority in American Fiction* (1984), they focused exclusively on James's formal and aesthetic choices in revisions for the New York Edition and did not question James's claims in the prefaces. As Dorothy Hale also noted, James underscored an "aesthetic theory that values artistic form to the exclusion of other sorts of meaning," and he claims "that what he calls 'life' has, by comparison, no value at all until it becomes 'formed' through art" (80). Formalist critics, Parker saw, produced "a string of more or less mechanical studies in which James is found to be a good reviser or, very seldom, is found to have revised incautiously . . ." (*Flawed* 105). René Wellek, in his essay "Henry James's Literary Theory and Criticism" (1958), although deeming the prefaces "disappointing" and finding the "exaltation" about them "extravagant," did not question their usefulness for insights into James's life and career. "They tell us where and when a book was written, what was the 'germ' of the story — a remembered figure, an anecdote told at dinner, a mood recaptured — or they explain, expand, and develop the theme of the novel or indulge in general reflections on manners and life" (293–94).

In general, formalist critics who wrote about the prefaces did not correlate textual variants of James's novels to come to their own conclusions about James's achievements, nor did they relate the different stages of revision — and often there had been several, including the New York Edition — to James's life and goals at the time; they did not consult James's notebooks, which were published in 1947, nor his letters, a selection of which also appeared in print. Instead, they took at face value James's disclosures about his motivations, the various inspirations for his stories, his aesthetic goals, and his hopes for his readers' responses. "The enduring appeal of the old notion of achieving the archetype," Parker notes, "is obvious from the number of critics who espoused it, but it turns out under examination to be very curious indeed." No writer, Parker argues, "can intend to mean something before he is able to state that meaning in words" (*Flawed* 106).

An exception to the spate of New Critical approaches to the prefaces, in articles that continued for decades after the 1930s and 40s, is Sister Stephanie Vincec's 1976 article, "'Poor Flopping *Wings*': The Making of Henry James's *The Wings of the Dove*." Not satisfied with James's preface to untangle her confusion about the novel, Vincec researched his creative process by reading his notebooks, letters, and previous revisions of the book. How, she asked, did his original goals become transformed when he revised? How do those goals coincide with what he remembered as he wrote the preface? Her conclusion contradicts the New Critical affirmation of James's aesthetic achievement. "The historical record," Vincec tells us, ". . . makes it doubtful that James re-read the entire novel before he composed his Preface to *The Wings of the Dove*. Comparison of the Preface with the 1894 *Notebook* plans for the novel shows that he also failed to refer to them in 1908, for, while he was able to recall the initial idea for the story, he had obviously forgotten how radically he had altered it during the course of that early examination of the potential it embodied" (91). In writing some of the prefaces, James apparently did consult his notebooks. But for other prefaces, evidence is lacking as to whether he wrote the preface before or after or during the revision process; James may have created a fiction about his own goals to match the new achievements he believed he had attained.

Vincec's contextual approach, an exception in the 1970s, has become a model for recent criticism. In the past few decades, the prefaces have come under scrutiny by critics and scholars, such as the contributors to David McWhirter's *Henry James's New York Edition* (1995), who examine James's project in the context of cultural and professional pressures, the exigencies of his life, the marketplace, his family legacy, and even his sexuality. For these critics, the concept of the author is protean and contingent; and James himself, far from exerting his authority over his texts, appears in his prefaces to be vulnerable, questing, fluctuating, complex, and contradictory.

The Ideal Reader

James's contemporary reviewers examined the prefaces one by one, as they appeared in successive volumes of the New York Edition. That response, though, changed after 1934, when Richard Blackmur collected the prefaces into a volume that he titled *The Art of the Novel*. Critics came to see this collection as a whole — another of James's literary productions — guided by Blackmur, who saw James's reflections about writing as a manual for readers as well as for prospective writers (viii). In his introduction, Blackmur provided a gloss on the prefaces that focused on no less than thirty-three concerns, some developed in every preface, and others localized in one or two. James always dealt with five connected subjects: "The Relation of Art and the Artist. The Relation of Art and Life. Art, Life, and the Ideal. Art and Morals. Art as Salvation for its Characters" (xiv). In addition, James always pointed out difficulties in composition and exhorted his readers to show care and appreciation: "One burden of the Prefaces," Blackmur noted, "was to prove how much the reader would see if only he paid attention and how much he missed by following the usual stupid routine of skipping and halting and letting slide" (xvii).

To help focus his reader's attention, James pointed out five recurring themes: the international encounter; literary or artistic life; eminent, great, or historical characters; the relationship of the living to the dead; and ghosts and the supernatural. Besides these themes, to which James devoted much of his prefaces, he touched on some other matters that concerned him: the difference between romance and realism, the rendering of geographical places, and, most notably, the creation of a central intelligence or consciousness that acts, according to Blackmur, as the "commanding centre" of the tales (xxiii). Depending on the fiction, James also might discuss the effects of time, the creation of wonder or bewilderment, the necessity of fools, and such writerly concerns as the development of anecdote, first-person narrative, improvisation, foreshortening, or irony.

Many essays in McWhirter's collection consider Blackmur's influence in shaping readers' perceptions of the prefaces. According to Ross Posnock, in "Breaking the Aura of Henry James," Blackmur's introduction, first published in a 1934 essay in a special issue of *Hound and Horn*, marked James's "official canonization" (25). In Blackmur's view, James believed that "an ideal vision" could be achieved "in the informed imagination"; that "art was the viable representation of moral value"; and that "in the degree that the report was intelligent and intense the morals were sound" (xv). James's emphases, Blackmur concluded, "were on intelligence — James was avowedly the novelist of the free spirit, the liberated intelligence — on feeling, and on form" (xxxviii). As Posnock sees it, however, Blackmur's James was essentially contradictory: "a definitive, fixed image of an author always skeptical of the static, whose restless mind's most characteristic movement is an immanent one that conceives the way out as the way through." Blackmur produced an homage rather than explication, and because of his canonizing introduction, Posnock argues, a "cramped aura of sanctity has grown around what might be called James's cultural presence" (26).

Herschel Parker agreed, asserting that publishing the prefaces as an edition in itself separated them from the novels to which they were attached and therefore distorted James's intention in writing them. In lifting the prefaces from their contexts, Blackmur insists that they represent a unified theory of literature that James did not elaborate on his own. What James did consider, Parker argues, was the act of creativity and his relationship to his reader. "Throughout the prefaces," Parker notes, "James describes his role as author in various ways, including bricklayer, builder, conjurer, craftsman, creator, critic of life, dramatist, fabulist, magician, painter, and parent" (*Flawed* 36). James often accuses the reader of not reading correctly and of having expectations of the author that James will not meet. He resists the idea that the public can "own" a writer. In fact, Parker says, "James sees himself above most of his readers — sees himself as an artist, a poet — far different from the mass consumers of the commercial public" (*Flawed* 35).

As Paul Armstrong argued as well in "Reading James's Prefaces and Reading James," the prefaces — even if read along with their respective fictions — do not really fulfill the goals that James articulated: to help the reader anticipate and explicate the text to which they refer. They do not orient the reader, but rather deflect the reader's attention to consider the rarefied process of creation. Frequently, they portray the setting in which James first had the idea for his fiction, delineating the process from the "germ" of a story to its flowering.

That process, John Carlos Rowe noted in *The Theoretical Dimensions of Henry James* (1984), sometimes eluded James, motivating him to create a likely fiction describing the moment of creation. "Given the failure of the author-turned-reader to discover the germinal origin for the literary work — the point at which it would mark its difference from life and thus justify the author's identity — James must swerve from such a threat of ontological dislocation and offer instead certain 'dramatizations' of what must be termed his imaginary 'scenes of writing,' extemporized versions of that origin now lost" (237). These scenes convey to readers more than inspiration; they also create a fictional portrait of the artist as a young man.

Similarly, as William Stafford had pointed out in 1963, the prefaces also contain literary allusions "to those writers whose works represent precedents James specifically wishes to avoid and . . . those whose works embody precedents, techniques, and accomplishments he hopes to emulate or forward" (65). The prefaces, then, serve as a kind of intellectual autobiography of the artist. But in leading readers to the source of creation, in setting the works in the context of great works of literature, James suggests that only those who can emulate his own sensibility will fully apprehend the ways his experiences became transformed into art. Since readers necessarily respond idiosyncratically, they are bound to be frustrated: "By inviting readers to come with him back to those origins," Armstrong adds, "James asserts his own authority over works whose history he alone is privileged to know, even as the inconclusivenss of his private associations tells the reader that, for us as for the author, the responsibility for discovering and creating meaning is one's own" (135–36). James, however, was suspicious about his readers' ability to create meaning.

Besides elaborating on his authority as an artist, the prefaces reflect James's assumptions about his contemporary readers, especially about their shortcomings, and suggest his vision of the ideal reader. James instructs the reader in how to develop what Armstrong calls a sense of "doubleness" that is James's perspective in his fiction. The reader, according to James, should both attend to the fiction and observe himself attending to the fiction. "The dilemma for James's readers," Armstrong argues, "is that one cannot simultaneously observe something and observe oneself observing it. You can go back and forth between these attitudes, but you can't do both at the same time" (128). Trying to do both — or at least successfully observing oneself in the act of reading — would generate a self-consciousness that James seems to believe would benefit his readers, would make them more acutely appreciative of his particular talents as a writer. Yet Armstrong and other scholars believe that James's prefaces work instead to disorient and disempower readers.

Sharon Cameron, in *Thinking in Henry James* (1989), analyzed a reader's possible disorientation as it relates to James's overriding theme of consciousness, a term that Cameron takes great pains to interrogate. James held that his characters' consciousness was central to every novel, but Cameron suggests "that there is no single conception of consciousness in the novels and also, as the relation between Prefaces and novels suggests, that there is no *developing* sense of a Jamesian consciousness" (42). She maintains that in each preface, James attempted "to revise, in the sense of redetermine, the reader's understanding of the central consciousness in the novel that follows" (37). James, therefore, was prescriptive, positing definitions of consciousness that necessarily would alter a reader's interpretation of a novel or tale by directing readers to notice, for example, "that it takes a central consciousness to register shifts of power" (40). Along with the novels, then, Cameron argues that James's prefaces "do not simply represent characters thinking; they also raise the question of what thinking is, of how it can be made to register, and albeit disconcertingly, of *where* it might do so" (42). As we will see in chapter 6, Cameron argues, furthermore, that James conceived consciousness not as harbored within individuals, but as a pervasive force that transcends each individual mind.

James's prescriptive tone led scholars such as Vivienne Rundle, in "Defining Frames: The Prefaces of Henry James and Joseph Conrad" (1995), to extend arguments such as those proposed by Armstrong and Cameron and to conclude that the prefaces created "protective barriers between novel and reader" through James's "insistence upon his own assessment and analysis of the novels, his repeated disparagement of the reading public's critical faculties, his emphasis on the distinction between the inferior real reader and the supersubtle 'ideal' reader, and his delight in specifying the particular historical scene of the writing of the novel. All these maneuvers combine to denigrate James's readers, to exclude them from the narrative system of his oeuvre and to deny them critical authority over his works" (71). One of James's letters to his publishers supports this conclusion: when Scribner's limited him to 120,000 words per volume of short stories, he apprised them that he would edit his prefaces at a "cost" "of some critical animadversion on certain things missed by the reader, things that might rather confidently have been looked for: or perhaps I had better say that I *should* apprehend something of that sort were there more serious or attentive criticism nowadays to reckon with" (Edel 407).

Rundle feels that the prefaces show James distinguishing between the critics whose judgment so irritated and hurt him, and the ideal reader who could be only himself. The ideal reader would be "passive, receptive, appreciative, often even grateful" whose sensibilities somehow would merge with that of the author (74, she is quoting James). "Clearly, the ideal reader of James's work is not expected to challenge the author with an active contribution to the creation of the text; rather s/he must passively acquiesce to the author's vision . . ." (74). This assessment contradicts some of James's contemporary reviewers, who complained about the burden that James placed on readers, requiring them to be active collaborators in order to understand his fictions.

Prefaces as Autobiography

Unlike Stafford, who saw the prefaces as an intellectual and literary autobiography, many scholars in McWhirter's collection explore a wide range of issues in self-representation. As Philip Cohen noted in his review of the collection, many contributors ask, "What sorts of conflicts and problems might arise from framing the Edition's contents — some greatly revised, some little revised, and some unrevised — with prefaces in which an older James with concerns new and different from those he held years ago attempts to recall and comment on the origins and aims of his work?" (4). Certainly James himself admitted that writing the prefaces was partly an autobiographical project, and McWhirter agrees that the aim of the project was less to question " 'what it was' than 'who I am.' And this latter question depends for James not on *a* sense of the past, on a totalizing narrative of what was, but on a capacity for establishing multiple, often contradictory lines of connection, relation, and responsiveness to the past" ("Senses of the Past" 152). James's tone in the prefaces is sometimes nostalgic, looking back on a younger writer and wondering if it is possible to revive the feelings he had when working on past fictions. Sometimes that nostalgia blurs into bewilderment; sometimes, as McWhirter notes, remembering seems to generate "terrified reactions to the multiple past selves his astonishing 'reach of reminiscence' discovers" ("Senses of the Past" 153).

The process of writing the prefaces, James tells us, did seem to evoke memories that he thought were lost — an achievement that he describes in the preface to *The American*: "It is a pleasure to perceive how again and again the shrunken depths of old work yet permit themselves to be sounded or — even if rather terrible the image — 'dragged': the long pole of memory stirs and rummages the bottom, and we fish up such fragments and relics of the submerged life and the extinct consciousness as tempt us to piece them together" (Blackmur 26). Although James characterizes this process of digging up the past as pleasurable, his images — of shrunken depths, submerged relics, and dead memories — are, as he admits, "rather terrible" and menacing. As he pieces together the fragments of his past, he is tempted not only to give them coherence, but also refinement: to clean them up, so to speak, when he serves them to readers as his aesthetic legacy. Certainly he engaged in this process of selecting and cleansing in his several autobiographical volumes, *A Small Boy and Others* (1913), *Notes of a Son and Brother* (1914), and *The Middle Years* (1917), a project that James began after his brother William's death in 1910. But whether this process of selection reflected James's sense of who he had become, or rather the image he wanted readers to accept, remains an open question for scholars.

In his 2005 study of Henry James and William Dean Howells, Rob Davidson argues that in his prefaces, James discloses only those biographical details that create a portrait of the artist, and he deflects the reader's attention away from himself in any other role and toward the text. The prefaces, then, reveal "a strategy for foregrounding aesthetic questions before questions of biography, history, and so forth. . . . This Jamesian paradox — wanting the artistic text read on its own terms, while simultaneously allowing for the possibility that the figured artist might be 'glimpsed' vis-a-vis the text — is found through the Prefaces in James's celebration of the creative process of artistic submersion" (200, 201–2). The man with whom the reader becomes intimate, then, is a character as invented as any of the characters in James's fictions. "It is James the Artist we hear in the Prefaces. He is our guide and mentor," Davidson writes. "James the Man is kept out of sight" (204).

Yet as discreet as James intended to be in his prefaces, they have seemed to some recent scholars even more revealing than the works James offered as autobiography. McWhirter notes the "disturbing implications" of evidence of racism and xenophobia in the prefaces ("Senses of the Past" 152). Sara Blair and Eve Sedgwick focus on autobiographical allusions to gender and sexuality. As Blair examines what she calls "the imprint of sentimental ideology" of the prefaces (65), she argues that James engaged in "a strategic form of self-representation" (58) in which his "gestures of self-erasure and self-exposure" (73) undermine the idea of an "authorial will to power" (70) that seems stereotypically male; instead, she suggests, James's autobiographical "gestures" show his identification with female consciousness. By representing authorship "as a kind of domestic activity," by "revisiting domestic architecture to account for the origins of his own texts," James distances himself from the commercial, and male, marketplace (60–61). The prefaces, Blair concludes, form "a text of self-representation inscribed, in its forms and its formalism, its artistic flourishes and its artful dodges, with the motive of engendering a literary mastery that puts the social consequences of mastery at issue" (73).

Sedgwick also explores the question of gender: examining the connection between James's voice as the Master and his portrait of himself as a younger writer, Sedgwick argues that James's relationship to this younger writer is homoerotic. "The speaking self of the prefaces," Sedgwick writes, "does not attempt to merge with the potentially shaming or shamed figurations of its younger self, younger fictions, younger heroes; its attempt is to love them. That love is shown to occur both in spite of shame and, more remarkably, through it" (216). Sedgwick sees in portraying himself as a young writer, James, in effect, has created a fictional character, as distant as the characters in his novels. Like Blair, Sedgwick characterizes James's self in the prefaces as female: inhabiting domestic space, nurturing his characters, and in fact parenting them in anecdotes of male parturition. "In a number of places . . . James more or less explicitly invokes *Frankenstein* and all the potential uncanniness of the violently disavowed male birth. But he invokes that uncanniness in order to undo it, or at least do something further with it, by offering the spectacle of — not his refusal — but his eroticized eagerness to recognize his progeny even in its oddness" (216).

Although Sedgwick argues for James's homoerotic relationship to his younger self, she distinguishes between conflating homosexuality with the idea of shame that she thinks is more critical in understanding James, especially in his prefaces. Queerness, she says, relates less to homosexuality — not all homosexuals can be described as "queer" — than to "those whose sense of identity is for some reason tuned most durably to the note of shame" (238). Whereas Sedgwick does not consider the reasons for James's feeling of shame in her article on the prefaces, other scholars and biographers, especially those questioning James's homosexuality, take up the problem as they examine James's fictions, autobiographies, and letters.

Because James wrote his prefaces over time, scholars have become interested in specific prefaces as representative of particular biographical moments: Melanie Ross, for example (2005), looked at the preface to *The Golden Bowl*, the last that James wrote for his New York Edition, as evidence of his own process of thinking and recollecting in the final stages of the publication of his commemorative project. According to Ross, James experienced the process of remembering as a kind of transcription of emerging visual images; for James, it is this feeling of searching that most vividly characterizes consciousness. Walking the streets of London seeking sites for photographs for the edition's frontispieces, James enacted the search for past images that he was conducting in his mind. James's depiction of this search reproduces the "tracks" of his consciousness as he recollected the sources of the novel, sometimes frustrated at his inability to make connections transparent. As Philip Horne noted in "The Question of Our Texts," James's writing about his own work — in his notebooks and especially his prefaces, is characterized by "inspiring candor as well as . . . provoking concealments and silences" (Freedman 76).

In "The Logic of Delegation in *The Ambassadors*" (1986), Julie Rivkin sees the preface to that novel as exemplary of James's project of reviving his "cherished intentions" (820), but instead creating a paradoxical situation for the reader: suggesting his own disappointment at what is missing from the fiction. Rivkin draws upon Jacques Derrida's "logic of supplementarity," which holds that a "supplement, like the ambassador, is a stand-in supposed to alter nothing of that which it stands in for; it is defined as an addition having no effect on the original to which it is being joined" (819). In James's prefaces, writing that "ostensibly completes the project, telling the story that has not been told" in fact "reminds us of that which is absent. . . . By supplementing the novel with the story of its composition, the preface also inevitably hints at the intended novel that never got written" (820).

James had hoped for both renewed attention and commensurate royalties from the publication of the New York Edition, but those hopes were not fulfilled. In 1908, he was shocked at receiving from his literary agent a check for a mere $211. Yet his desire to shape his reputation for posterity still was alive: he turned to autobiography, which gave him a new opportunity to select, revise, and invent the past; and, in 1910, he set a huge bonfire and burned most of his private letters. He did not, he explained to his friend Annie Fields, want to leave those documents "at the mercy of any accidents, or even of my executors!" (Edel 541). As far as possible, he would control the future identity of Henry James.

Works Cited

Anesko, Michael. "The Eclectic Architecture of Henry James's New York Edition." *"Friction with the Market": Henry James and the Profession of Authorship*, 141–62. New York: Oxford UP, 1986.

Armstrong, Paul B. "Reading James's Prefaces and Reading James." In McWhirter, 125–37.

Banta, Martha. "The Excluded Seven: Practice of Omission, Aesthetics of Refusal." In McWhirter, 240–60.

Blackmur, Richard, ed. *The Art of the Novel: Critical Prefaces by Henry James*. New York: Scribner's, 1934.

Blair, Sara. "In the House of Fiction: Henry James and the Engendering of Literary Mastery." In McWhirter, 58–73.

Buelens, Gert, ed. *Enacting History in Henry James: Narrative, Power, and Ethics*. Cambridge: Cambridge UP, 1997.

Cameron, Sharon. "The Prefaces, Revision, and Ideas of Consciousness." *Thinking in Henry James*, 32–82. Chicago: U of Chicago P, 1989.

Cohen, Philip. "The Lesson of the Master: The New York Edition, James Studies, and Contemporary Textual Scholarship." Review of McWhirter. *Studies in the Novel* 31, no. 1 (Spring 1999): 98–116.

Davidson, Rob. *The Master and the Dean: The Literary Criticism of Henry James and William Dean Howells*. Columbia: U of Missouri P, 2005.

Edel, Leon, ed. *Henry James Letters*. Vol. 4. Cambridge, MA: Belknap Press of Harvard UP, 1984.

Freedman, Jonathan, ed. *The Cambridge Companion to Henry James*. Cambridge: Cambridge UP, 1998.

Gosse, Edmund. *Aspects and Impressions*. New York: Scribner's, 1922.

Greene, Graham. *The Lost Childhood and other Essays*. New York: Viking, 1952.

Hale, Dorothy J. "Henry James and the Invention of Novel Theory." In Freedman, 79–101.

Horne, Philip. "The Question of Our Texts." In Freedman, 63–78.

James, Henry. *Literary Criticism: Essays on Literature, American Writers, English Writers*. New York: The Library of America, 1984.

Leuschner, Eric. " 'Utterly, Insurmountably, Unsaleable': Collected Editions, Prefaces, and the 'Failure' of Henry James's New York Edition." *Henry James Review* 22, no. 1 (2001): 24–40.

Lubbock, Percy. *The Craft of Fiction*. New York: Scribner's, 1921.

McWhirter, David, ed. *Henry James's New York Edition: The Construction of Authorship*. Stanford, CA: Stanford UP, 1995.

———. " 'A Provision Full of Responsibilities': Senses of the Past in Henry James's Fourth Phase." In Buelens, 148–65.

Miller, J. Hillis. "The 'Grafted' Image: James on Illustration." In McWhirter, 138–41.

Nadel, Ira. "Visual Culture: The Photo Frontispieces to the New York Edition." In McWhirter, 90–108.

Parker, Herschel. "The Authority of the Revised Text and the Disappearance of the Author: What Critics of Henry James Did with Textual Evidence in the Heyday of the New Criticism." *Flawed Texts and Verbal Icons: Literary Authority in American Fiction*, 85–114. Evanston, IL: Northwestern UP, 1984.

Posnock, Ross. "Breaking the Aura of Henry James." In McWhirter, 23–28.

Review of *The Novels and Tales of Henry James*. *Literary Digest*, 21 March 1908: 418.

Rivkin, Julie. "The Logic of Delegation in *The Ambassadors*." *PMLA* 101, no. 5 (October 1986): 819–31.

Ross, Melanie H. "'The Mirror with a Memory': Tracking Consciousness in the Preface to *The Golden Bowl*." *Henry James Review* 26, no. 3 (Fall 2005): 246–55.

Rowe, John Carlos. *The Theoretical Dimensions of Henry James*. Madison: U of Wisconsin P, 1984.

Rundle, Vivienne. "Defining Frames: The Prefaces of Henry James and Joseph Conrad." *Henry James Review* 16, no. 1 (1995): 66–92.

Salmon, Richard. *Henry James and the Culture of Publicity*. Cambridge: Cambridge UP, 1997.

Sedgwick, Eve. "Shame and Performativity: Henry James's New York Edition Prefaces." In McWhirter, 206–39.

Stafford, William T. "Literary Allusions in James's Prefaces." *American Literature* 35, no. 1 (March 1963): 60–70.

Vincec, Sister Stephanie. "'Poor Flopping *Wings*': The Making of Henry James's *The Wings of the Dove*." *Harvard Library Bulletin* 24 (January 1976): 60–93.

Wellek, René. "Henry James's Literary Theory and Criticism." *American Literature* 30, no. 3 (November 1958): 293–321.

3: The Cult of Henry James, 1918–1960

> *The air of reality . . . seems to me to be the supreme virtue of a novel — the merit on which all its other merits . . . helplessly and submissively depend.*
>
> — Henry James, "The Art of Fiction"

FOR NEARLY THIRTY YEARS after James died, critical articles about him usually numbered fewer than two dozen each year. This response would not have surprised T. S. Eliot, who, in 1918, predicted that James always would be "regarded as the extraordinarily clever but negligible curiosity" understood by only "a few intelligent people" (854). After Percy Lubbock's two-volume edition of James's letters was published in 1920, the number of articles rose to thirty-two; even the publication of Lubbock's *The Craft of Fiction* (1921), which closely considered James's *The Ambassadors, The Wings of the Dove,* and *The Awkward Age,* failed to generate renewed interest. Only sixteen articles appeared in 1922, and the number continued at nearly that level, with few exceptions, until 1943, the centenary of James's birth. "When I went to college in the thirties," writer Hortense Calisher recalled, "we were scarcely taught James, in favor of his genteel shadow, Howells" (58). André Gide, writing in the *Yale Review* in 1930, suggests why: "Undoubtedly these novels of James are marvels of composition . . . We can marvel at the delicacy, at the subtlety of the gear wheels, but all his characters are like the figures of a clock, and the story is finished when they have struck the curfew; of themselves they return to the clockcase and to the night of our forgetting" (643). For all of James's obvious intelligence, Gide argued, his characters were soulless and his tales "without color, without flavor" (641). This sense of James as passionless, his fictions contrived, his characters simply puppets in his masterful hands — these assessments recur throughout the 1920s and 1930s. Besides dismissing James's fiction for being soulless, a few critics asserted that his work was irrelevant, too refined and romantic for an age that demanded gritty realism.

In April, 1934, however, a special edition of the journal *Hound and Horn* was devoted to essays about James by writers such as Francis Ferguson, Marianne Moore, Stephen Spender, and Edmund Wilson. The stature of the contributors underscored James's significance to serious readers. Shortly after this publication, Richard Blackmur, already a noted critic, published James's prefaces as a collection that allowed readers to consider James's own assessment of his craft and to trace the autobiographical seeds of his fiction. The prefaces — accessible and seemingly forthright — responded to compelling critical interests in James's artistry and in his life. To some scholars, these two publications mark the beginning of James's ascension in American letters.

The canonization of James became assured in the 1940s, when James was revitalized and, in a sense, reinvented by critics who championed him as a master of his craft, a moralist, and a proto-modernist. James's centenary in 1943 caused a healthy spike in articles: fifty-nine, by writers who included some of the most prominent American critics and scholars,: among them, Jacques Barzun, Blackmur, Witter Bynner, Alfred Kazin, F. O. Matthiessen, Katherine Anne Porter, Philip Rahv, William Troy, H. G. Wells, and Morton Zabel. Although the number of articles returned to its usual level in 1944, Matthiessen's *Henry James: The Major Phase* was published in that year to considerable attention from reviewers in newspapers, magazines, and literary journals. Matthiessen took his place as a leading James advocate, but he was not alone: writers such as F. R. Leavis, Philip Rahv, Edmund Wilson, Yvor Winters, and Lionel Trilling ensconced James firmly in the literary canon.

From 1918 to 1960, with a few exceptions, the most visible writers considering James may well be considered critics rather than scholars: they published widely on arts and letters; their articles appeared in general interest magazines, such as the *Saturday Review of Literature* and the *New Republic*; and their books, published by trade presses, were addressed to educated, nonspecialized readers. Of course, articles about James also appeared in scholarly journals, such as *Nineteenth-Century Fiction* and *American Literature*; and especially toward the end of this period, books increasingly appeared from academic presses. The matter of Henry James, though, was not relegated to the academy, and the questions these critics asked were focused on a few recurring themes: who was James as a man and an artist? How were his works relevant to a society vastly changed from the one he depicted in his fiction? If he was great, where does that greatness lie?

Portraits of the Artist

In the 1920s and '30s and even '40s, articles about James often were written by men and women who had known him, and they combine an assessment of his work with personal anecdotes. Some of these biographical details served to embellish an image that already had been established during James's lifetime: a man with an abundant social life who somehow kept himself apart from others, whose life was dominated by his writing, whose mannerisms of speech — hesitancy and rumination — were similar to his literary style. In her memoir *A Backward Glance* (1934) Edith Wharton, for example, described the "elaborate hesitancies" of his conversation (Vann 50). "His latest novels," she wrote, "for all their profound moral beauty, seemed to me more and more lacking in atmosphere, more and more severed from that thick nourishing human air in which we all live and move" (Gard 343). When she asked him why he stripped his characters in *The Golden Bowl* "of all the *human fringes* we necessarily trail after us through life?" he was surprised and hurt by her question: "This sensitiveness to criticism or comment of any sort had nothing to do with vanity; it was caused by the great artist's deep consciousness of his powers, combined with a bitter, a life-long disappointment at his lack of popular recognition" (Gard 343).

In his 1922 memoir, *Aspects and Impressions*, Edmund Gosse, recalling his first meeting with James, described him as "grave, extremely courteous, but a little formal and frightened, which seemed strange in a man living in constant communication with the world" (27). Gosse confirmed how James took other people's stories as germs of his fiction, a practice that led Gosse to conclude that James used others, without respecting their privacy, in the service of his art. "I speak of *The Author of Beltraffio*," Gosse wrote, "and after thirty-five years I may confess that this extraordinarily vivid story was woven around a dark incident in the private life of an eminent author known to us both, which I, having told Henry James in a moment of levity, was presently horrified and even sensibly alarmed to see thus pinnacled in the broad light of day" (30). Preying on his friends revealed a certain ungentlemanly arrogance, and H. G. Wells, in his *Experiment in Autobiography*, perpetuated an image of James that underscored both his arrogance and aloofness: novelists, as James saw them, were "artists of a very special and exalted type. He was concerned about their greatness and repute. . . . One could not be in a room with him for ten minutes," Wells recalled, "without realizing the importance he attached to the dignity of this art of his" (Edel and Ray 216–17). Still, if James seemed overbearing to Wells, he charmed others.

As late as 1943, Witter Bynner, Cyril Clemens, Shane Leslie, Compton MacKenzie, and Logan Pearsall Smith each published a reminiscence of James, several recalling childhood memories of meeting the famous author. G. K. Chesterton remembered James as his courtly neighbor in Rye when Wells came to visit. Cyril Clemens recounted anecdotes of meetings between James and Marie Belloc Lowndes. Elizabeth Jordan remembered meeting James at a dinner party in London. In 1949, Simon Fleet portrayed "The Nice American Gentleman" who was remembered at Rye; and John LaFarge described James's relationship with his parents, the artist John LaFarge and his wife Margaret. All of these memories cohered into the portrait of a genteel writer who might have stepped from the pages of his books. It was a portrait that increasingly seemed out of place in a changing world.

The Expatriate

In the 1920s, the debate over James's reputation was roiled by two influential critics: Van Wyck Brooks and Vernon Parrington. For the next decade and more, no critic writing could ignore their attack on James as effete and irrelevant to American life. Brooks already had established his reputation with such works as *The Wine of the Puritans* (1909), *America's Coming of Age* (1915), and *The Ordeal of Mark Twain* (1920), when he took on Henry James. In *America's Coming of Age*, Brooks maintained that American culture was characterized by a gap between elite highbrows and vulgar lowbrows. What America needed, in Brooks's view, were writers who could bridge this gap — Whitman, he thought, was one — by recognizing the realities of American life and conveying them through their art. In *The Pilgrimage of Henry James*, Brooks argued that James's renouncing of America for Europe cut him off from the realities of American society and politics. As an expatriate, James did not understand the country he had left; as an outsider, he did not understand Europe. His characters, therefore, were vapid, his plots contrived.

Writing in 1925, Brooks shared the opinion of other critics who called for more biting social commentary from fiction writers at a time of social and political unrest in America; Theodore Dreiser and Sinclair Lewis, it seemed to these critics, more forcefully met the needs of Americans facing urgent social and political problems. Readers should be encountering Sister Carrie, not Isabel Archer; Babbitt, not Lambert Strether. Even more than twenty-five years later, Brooks held to his earlier position about James. An adherent of "the so-called expatriate religion of art," Brooks says, James wrote as if his native land was not important. It was "disastrous," Brooks concludes, "for the novelist to lose his natural connection with an inherited world that is deeply his own, when, ceasing to be 'in the pedigree' of his own country, he is no longer an expression of the communal life" (Edel 62).

Brooks's assessment was shared by Vernon Parrington — like Brooks, educated at Harvard — who taught at the University of Oklahoma and later at the University of Washington. Parrington was at the end of a thirty-year career of teaching and writing when he published his three-volume study of literature and culture, *Main Currents in American Thought*. The book, which championed populist literature over what Parrington deemed highbrow works — and which devoted a mere two pages to James — won a Pulitzer Prize. Although decades later, Lionel Trilling castigated Parrington for his intellectual limitations, Trilling noted that *Main Currents* had become an unquestioned guide to literature for many readers and in many college classrooms. Parrington much preferred writers like Sherwood Anderson and James Branch Cabell to those who challenged him. "Whenever he was confronted with a work of art that was complex, personal and not literal," Trilling wrote, "that was not as it were, a public document, Parrington was at a loss" (4). James, of course, was just such a writer. Parrington calls him "a self-deceived romantic, the last subtle expression of the genteel, who fell in love with culture and never realized how poor a thing he worshiped." James, Parrington says, "romanticized Europe . . . Born of an unconscious inferiority complex in presence of a long-established social order to which he was alien, this romanticization of European culture worked to his undoing, for it constrained the artist to a lifelong pursuit of intangible realities that existed only in his imagination" (240). James was out of touch with America and even, Parrington, concludes, with the reality of European culture.

Many critics agreed. H. L. Mencken advised that "Henry James would have been vastly improved as a novelist by a few whiffs from the Chicago stockyards." James, Mencken said disparagingly, "died a sort of super-Howells, with a long row of laborious but essentially hollow books behind him" (500–501). Clinton Grattan, writing in the *Nation* in 1932, criticized James for identifying with the leisure class, individuals insulated from the economic pressures that affected so many others.

Yet within these negative assessments, there sometimes emerged a grudging admiration. Parrington, for one, noted James's "subtle psychological inquiries" into the landscape of an individual's mind (241), and other writers noted James's interest in spiritual life, and in the consequences of moral tensions. Because of James's mastery at probing an inner landscape, critics who shared with Brooks and Parrington a concern over the connection between art and politics were able to make a case for James's genius.

The Moralist

In an extended eulogy written two years after James's death, Ezra Pound made a claim that he believed no critic had made before: "that there was emotional greatness in Henry James's hatred of tyranny" (297). By tyranny, Pound meant both institutional oppression and "personal intimate tyrannies working at close range" (299). In the 1930s and '40s, many critics returned to this assessment and considered it James's great contribution to literature. Some of these critics saw that James, like his father, Henry, Senior, and his philosopher brother, William, was concerned with the consequences of beliefs and behavior. Whether or not he set his stories in American cities, whether or not his characters were working-class men and women, whether or not he dealt with class conflict or the pressures of immigration and poverty, James recognized that morality was located in individual sensibility and personal choices. He understood that experiences shaped sensibility, just as identity shaped one's perception of reality.

As Stephen Spender, writing in 1935, saw it, James's concern with the moral was always concern with the political. James, he wrote, recognized that he confronted "a world without belief" in which individuals had to invent their own ethical values (14). Spender, writing in what Joseph Warren Beach called "the full flood of Marxian hopefulness" (xli), acknowledged James's ability to identify significant social issues and show awareness of historical moments. James revolutionized the novel, Spender said, by shifting his focus from event to the mind, "from the scene to that intellectual and imaginative activity which leads to the scene. . . ." (16).

Like Spender, Yvor Winters also emerged as an influential voice in shaping James's reputation as a writer concerned with moral issues. Winters, writing in 1938, summarizes James's recurring theme: "that there is a moral sense, a sense of decency, inherent in human character at its best; that this sense of decency, being only a sense, exists precariously, and may become confused and even hysterical in a crisis; that it may be enriched and cultivated through association with certain environments; that such association may, also, be carried so far as to extinguish the moral sense. This last relationship, that of the moral sense to an environment which may up to a certain point enrich it and beyond that point dissolve it, resembles the ordinary relationship of intellect to experience, of character to sensibility" (300). Like other critics of the 1930s, however, Winters identifies a shortcoming in James's application of this theme to American culture. Although James was familiar with American tourists and expatriates, he had detached himself from the nation's economic realities, social classes, and contemporary manners, and therefore his insights about American moral choices were limited (308–9). Winters sees James as "an extreme development" of earlier American writing: his heritage from the Puritans, romantics, and transcendentalists, Winters asserts, stood in the way of James's apprehending concrete moral problems in his own time. Although Winters thinks James "certainly one of the five or six greatest writers of any variety to be produced in North America" because of the strength of his characterizations (336–37), still, because he was not immersed in American culture, James's consideration of moral problems could be nothing but abstract and theoretical.

To understand the context for critics' interest in James as moralist, an interest that peaked in the 1940s, we can look at the cover page of the *New Republic* for February 15, 1943, an issue that contained a special section "In Honor of William and Henry James," with articles by Alfred Kazin, Jacques Barzun, Philip Rahv, Irwin Edman, and William Troy. The topics discussed on this first page are instructive: "Hitler Has Lost the War," "Why Not a War Cabinet?" and "Army v. Civilians." Hitler's defeat did not mean the end of the war, and even the end of war did not mean the end of political turmoil around the world. The war effort, according to the magazine's writers, seemed hopelessly muddled and uncoordinated. The magazine urged the creation of a war cabinet, but one that contained a majority of civilians. War and its aftermath dominated this issue, even in advertisements. The publisher Little, Brown promoted two books: Herbert Agar's *A Time for Greatness*, which promised to point the way to a better nation; and Frederick Oechsner's *This Is the Enemy*, described as an up-to-date overview of the Third Reich. And then there was the section on the Jameses: inevitably, the writers asked about Henry James's relevance. This question, though, really has two interpretations: one way of thinking about James's relevance is by asking what James wrote about that resonated with readers of the 1940s. The other way of interpreting the question is to ask about James himself: as an artist, as a writer concerned with ideas, as a man who by his own admission set himself apart from his own tumultuous world — what can James's commitment to art teach us about how to live in our own tumultuous time? These two questions informed the writing of some of James's most ardent champions, Philip Rahv and Lionel Trilling, F. O. Matthiessen and F. R. Leavis.

The Champions

In the *New Republic* celebration of James, William Troy asserts that central to James's work is "something that corresponds to our deepest contemporary needs and hopes" (228). In the midst of war, people need to feel that violence and destruction have meaning, that the dead have not died in vain, that humanity can be redeemed and will flourish. Troy reads "The Altar of the Dead" as James's commentary "on the pathetic desolation of the individual in our society — a desolation shared by both the living and the dead" (230). James tells us, according to Troy, that the dead "enhance the state of the living"; by paying respects to the fallen we affirm "the whole tradition of civilized humanity of which we are a part and in terms of which we must ultimately be measured" (230). Although not a proponent of any particular theology, James, Troy tells us, conveys the humanism that underlies every religion.

Philip Rahv looks more broadly at the complexities and contradictions of James — the man, the artist, and the expatriate. Rahv set the groundwork for his *New Republic* piece in an essay published a few years earlier in the *Partisan Review* in which he calls James "revolutionary" in his mission, which, as Rahv sees it, was to liberate individuals to embrace personal freedom. Because of this aim, James did not need to concern himself with temporal problems; a much larger problem transcended those: a crisis, Rahv says, of the human spirit. "What James asks for, primarily, is the expansion of life beyond its primitive needs and elementary standards of moral and material utility; and of culture he conceives as the reward of this expansion and as its unfailing means of discrimination" ("Cult of Experience" 10–11).

The intellectual, Rahv laments, is missing from most American novels, but James's entire attention is focused on the minds of his characters, on how they perceive reality, on how they come to know, on how they think.

In his *New Republic* essay, Rahv sees James as a model of an intellectual so influential that his name "has of late been turned into the password of a cult" (220). The members of the cult have something in common: a frustration about their role in a society that asks for active participation to solve problems. In the midst of war, there seemed to be no role for men who did not go into combat; and even before the war, intellectuals wondered how they could contribute to urgently needed reform if they were not, so to speak, at the barricades and in the trenches, working for concrete change. To change minds by writing and teaching seemed effete. But James showed them otherwise: James was a writer immersed in contradictions, but from these contradictions of his personality and of his society, he created art. "In modern literature," Rahv writes, "which bristles with anxieties and ideas of isolation, it is above all the creativity, the depth and quality of the contradictions that a writer united within himself, that gives us the truest measure of his achievement . . . of his force and integrity in reproducing these contradictions as felt experience" (223). The most significant contradiction, according to Rahv, was James's simultaneous search for and withdrawal from experience: "The tension between the impulse to plunge into 'experience' and the impulse to renounce it is the chief source of the internal yet astonishingly abundant Jamesian emotion . . ." (223). For James, Rahv says, being an American of a privileged class was both "an ordeal and . . . an inspiration" (224). This sense of contradiction and doubleness felt familiar to Rahv, and James's ability to translate his tensions into art served as a model.

Like Rahv, Lionel Trilling celebrated James's interest in the intellectual, and he saw James as providing a much-needed counterpoint to Theodore Dreiser, the writer who had earned what Trilling calls the "doctrinaire indulgence" of liberals (10). For Trilling, however, James has much more to say to Americans in the 1940s than writers like Dreiser. Especially in *The Bostonians* and *The Princess Casamassima*, James seemed uncannily prescient of the world that was to come. In 1896, Trilling notes, James confessed to a friend, " 'I have the imagination of disaster — and see life as ferocious and sinister.' " James's conception of this disaster, Trilling says, "is what recommends him to us now" (60).

Trilling's assessment of James emerges most forcefully in an essay first published in *Horizon* in 1948, reprinted in that year as the introduction to a new edition of *The Princess Casamassima*, and then included in *The Liberal Imagination*. *The Princess Casamassima*, Trilling asserts, offers "an incomparable representation of the spiritual circumstances of our civilization" and an exemplary instance of James's moral realism (92). Although other critics complain that James represented a world where intellectuals could live insulated from violence and poverty, Trilling argues that James recognized fully the threat of anarchy in his own time. In letters to family and friends, James notes with alarm riots, unrest, and a sense of pervasive danger. The anarchist organization that he portrays in *The Princess Casamassima* seems to Trilling true to life. Most important to Trilling, James presented in this novel a vision of the artist not as "a subversive idler," innocent of connection to politics, but as an activist and as a powerful force in society (81).

Another strength of this novel, according to Trilling, is James's sensitive and, indeed, loving characterization of the poor. Unlike writers who treat underprivileged characters with condescension or pity, James recognizes their inherent humanity, in all of its ambiguity and contradiction. This "special moral quality" that James exhibits seems to Trilling exemplary for liberals and progressives, men and women Trilling knows well, who "know that the poor are our equals in every sense except that of being equal to us" (88). Trilling, disillusioned with the professed democratic views of his fellow liberals, certain that they embrace elitism and self-righteousness more than tolerance, sees in James a true "moral realist" (90).

F. O. Matthiessen came to the same conclusion from a different direction. A professor at Harvard, a scholar whose reputation already was established by his book *American Renaissance* (1941), Matthiessen was in the midst of preparing an edition of James's notebooks when he published his study of James's late novels. Building upon criticism by Spender, Winters, and Edmund Wilson, Matthiessen brought his understanding of James from the notebooks to his own close readings. In making a case for James's achievements, Matthiessen follows Joseph Warren Beach's formal analysis, published in 1918; yet his familiarity with the notebooks gave the analysis a richness that previous critics did not share. More forthcoming than James's prefaces, the notebooks allowed Matthiessen to trace a biography of each novel and to illuminate characters in ways that made them more nuanced and rounded than they ever seemed before.

At the same time that Matthiessen contributed to what Rahv and others called "the cult" of Henry James, he recognized James's stylistic and aesthetic weaknesses as well as strengths. But these weaknesses did not diminish his admiration for James as an engaged artist. Underlying Matthiessen's study was his abiding question of the relationship of literature to politics, and of a writer or an intellectual to the problems of his time. Matthiessen, who had been rejected as a soldier in the Second World War because of his height, struggled to justify his role as a professor when his students were going off to war. Yet when he told his undergraduates that his book on James "was to be my overaged contribution to the war effort" (he was forty-one in 1943), they responded that "in a total war the preservation of art and thought should be a leading aim. They persuaded me," he wrote, "to continue to believe it" (xvi). But not quite: Matthiessen, who defined his political affiliation as Christian Socialist and worked actively for the election of Progressive candidate Henry Wallace in 1948, felt an abiding urgency to contribute to society in a role other than curator or preserver of the past. We see evidence of that urgency in his last project, unfinished at the time of his suicide in 1950 — a study of the writer passionately defended by liberals and progressives, a writer whose aesthetic achievement Matthiessen sorely doubted, but whose social and political relevance seemed indisputable: Theodore Dreiser.

James's importance for such writers as Rahv, Trilling, and Matthiessen seemed to scholar Alfred Habegger a nostalgic predilection for a genteel culture that, as twentieth-century intellectuals, even as former radicals, they believed they should reject. These critics, Habegger wrote in *Gender, Fantasy, and Realism in American Literature* (1982), "loved James because his fiction supplied the ideal material prop — highbrow fantasy masquerading as realism — for mandarins on the margin of American political life" (295). James's renunciation of middlebrow society, his privileging of observing over acting, and his stance as an outsider, all fit these critics' model for how to justify themselves as morally responsible men.

British critic F. R. Leavis, writing in the journal *Scrutiny*, which he edited, also took up the theme of James's moral consciousness. He reprinted his several essays about James in *The Great Tradition* (1954), a book that took its place as one of the most influential critical works of the time. Leavis positioned himself against Matthiessen in arguing that James's later novels were weakest, and his early novels, such as *Roderick Hudson*, *The Bostonians*, and especially *The Portrait of a Lady* were more vigorous. While he acknowledges that James has weaknesses as a writer — some of his work, Leavis says, is "boring to the point of unreadableness" (17) — still "his registration of sophisticated human consciousness is one of the classical creative achievements" and allows us to rank him as a genius. His characters, Leavis writes, are rendered with such delicacy that "a nuance may engage a whole complex moral economy and the perceptive response be the index of a major valuation or choice" (16). Although Leavis distances himself from the "cult of James," he embraces James as an English novelist who was intimately knowledgeable about English manners and society. He had all the requirements for the kinds of cultural critique that he worked out in his fiction. But it was not merely cultural critique that interested James, according to Leavis, but rather a concern with the moral and spiritual choices of his characters.

Osborn Andreas offered a similar critical assessment in *Henry James and the Expanding Horizon*, also published in 1948, reflecting the anxieties of postwar America. Andreas identifies nine major themes in James's fiction, which can be distilled into a few assertions: individuals should live fully without being constricted by social proscriptions; individuals should be aware of their own motivations and identity; the sheltered life is to be shunned; each person should honor the integrity of another's life. What Andreas calls "emotional cannibalism" and "parasitism" are two forms of intrusion into that integrity. James's message seems to Andreas directly relevant to a world still shattered by the recent conflict. "Belief in the desirability of power over others — the core of nazi-fascist ideology," Andreas writes, "—has existed and grown side by side in recent centuries with the contradictory belief in the desirability of individual freedom" (162). James was acutely aware of the problem of modern life: "the problem of how to be free though organized, how to plan our economic life without destroying our personal liberties" and how to counter "the evils of power" whether that power is exerted by individuals or nations (163). As Andreas sees it, James urges us to look at the expansion of consciousness in his characters and in ourselves, and to consider ways in which a work of art helps to expand the reader's consciousness when we identify with feelings and actions of invented characters. James sought to liberate his readers to understand what Andreas calls "the mystery of personal identity" (124).

James's interest in his characters' inner life was met with — and perhaps inspired — critical interest in his own life. "The obvious constatation to start from, when the diagnosis of his queer development in is question," Leavis writes, "is that he suffered from being too much a professional novelist: being a novelist came to be too large a part of his living; that is, he did not live enough. . . . So we find him developing into something like a paradoxical kind of recluse, a recluse living socially in the midst of society" (163). Leavis points to a critical interest that paralleled examination of James's themes and literary strategies: a focus on James's life in an effort to probe his own inner landscape.

Senses of the Past

For about ten years, the most influential study of James's life was Anna Robeson Burr's *Alice James: Her Brothers — Her Journal*, which was published in 1934, and devoted more attention to the James family than did Pelham Edgar's *Henry James: Man and Author* (1927), a well-regarded study that focused more on James's fiction than his life, and drew for biographical details upon Lubbock's two-volume letters and James's autobiography. By bringing to light Alice James's journal, Burr, then, offered new information. Although Alice was central to Burr's study, Henry was a major figure, and seeing him grow up in the context of his eccentric family helped critics to understand his position as an outsider to mainstream American life. In his article "The Ambiguity of Henry James," however, Edmund Wilson hinted that more than his peripatetic upbringing separated James from others. Offering a Freudian reading of *The Turn of the*

Screw, Wilson argued that the governess suffered from sexual frustrations and neuroses, reflecting James's own. At the time, this radical reading of the novella seemed shocking, and it generated controversy among critics who balked at reading James's ghost story autobiographically. One critic, Edward Wagenknecht, writing in 1948, thought that Wilson's reading was disreputable and unsubstantiated; indeed, he added that reading sexuality into any of James's works — "The Pupil" and "The Middle Years," for example — was irresponsible (129). Many critics felt equally uncomfortable with Saul Rosenzweig's "The Ghost of Henry James" (1944), an examination of James's life through the lens of Freudian psychology; yet this critical perspective would attract many critics in the next few decades. In fact, Rosenzweig's *Partisan Review* article stood as an analysis that critics and biographers could not ignore.

Based on revelations in James's autobiography, Rosenzweig argued that what James described as an "obscure hurt" suffered while he attempted to put out a fire when he was eighteen, "was in some sense a repetition" of his father's injury while extinguishing a hayloft fire in his own youth. James, Rosenzweig conjectures, may have "suffered a lapse of attention or alertness, due possibly to some glimmering association about his father's accident on a so similar occasion; and that thus favored, the accident took effect" (440). Furthermore, Rosenzweig sees the injury as associated in James's mind with the Civil War and his guilt about not participating. But besides underscoring the theme of guilt in James's fiction, Rosenzweig uses the event also to explain James's characterizations and style: "The avoidance of passion and the overqualification in his later writings are largely traceable to such an implicit attitude of combined guilt and inferiority . . ." (440). According to his psychoanalytic reading, he explains, "the story just sketched could be retold as follows. The Oedipus situation of Henry James included a highly individualistic father — a cripple — and a gifted sibling rival (William) who together dwarfed the boy in his own eyes beyond hope of ever attaining their stature. A severe inferiority complex resulted. The problematic relationship to father and brother was solved submissively by a profound repression of aggressiveness" (453). The obscure hurt "now crystallized his early sense of inferiority into 'castration anxiety'. . . . The possible role of constitutional bisexuality should be noted in passing, even if only speculatively. Injuries like the one experienced by James may be conceived to subdue the more active and masculine components of personality and accentuate as a counterpoise the more passive and feminine ones. The creative drive of genius seems often to be enhanced even as its capacity is paradoxically also limited by such a destiny" (454). James's writing, therefore, became a way to escape from frustration and "a partial means of solving his problems through sublimation" (454).

Rosenzweig's Freudian reading of James's life and work hinted at a much more intimate form of biographical inquiry than that offered by

F. W. Dupee in his *Henry James* (1951), which focused mostly on setting James's work in biographical context; or by Matthiessen in *The James Family: Including Selections from the Writings of Henry James, Senior, William, Henry, and Alice James.* Matthiessen's book, published three years after his literary study of James's late novels, consists of excerpts from his subjects' writings, connected by his own narrative, a "life and letters" approach common in studies of nineteenth-century writers. In James's case, Matthiessen's contextualizing of his writing within his father's work helped critics to defend James's interest in religion and philosophy and therefore deepened their consideration of James's moral themes.

Quentin Anderson, for example, in *The American Henry James* (1957), argued that James continued "a mode of vision which had colored his childhood," inherited from his father's ideas about morality, consciousness, and identity (xii). Like the transcendentalists, Henry James, Senior believed that humans "collaborate to build moral reality" (20), but Emerson too forcefully celebrated individuality in an imperfect world, while Henry, Senior believed "that work, activity, is everything" (21). That work and activity, though, was not synonymous with business or the marketplace but referred to the moral choices that each individual made daily. Certainly Henry, Senior's admonition to his sons to "be," rather than to be a lawyer or an engineer, supports the idea that he defined achievement in special moral and ethical terms.

Besides setting the basis of James's interest in moral questions, Henry, Senior's work, as Anderson sees it, offered James metaphors that recur in his fiction: "emblems derived or borrowed from his father's system of universal analogies . . . The bowl, the house of life, the portrait, the rivers, and the sea have an importance in his work which quite transcends that ascribed to them by students of James's imagery." These emblems, according to Anderson, reflect "the principles which are thought to order consciousness itself" (xii). James's focus on individual consciousness does not support the idea that he believed humans are essentially isolated, nor that the artist necessarily is an outsider: "when one has a truly religious sense of consciousness, truly believes that it makes all the differences that matter," Anderson argues, "one is immune to the social malaise of the artist in a mass society" (350). In fact, the act of communication, Anderson says, "is the primary experience for him" (351).

Anderson believes that James's opposition of European to American sensibility was not "to furnish a moral guide book" (25). "The opposition of American spontaneity to institutionalized European manners is a way of figuring a conflict which all men must undergo, a conflict through which we may reach what the novelist calls (in another connection) a 'sublime consensus'. . . . The question for James was how to symbolize our relation to ourselves — how spontaneity in the given situation was related to righteousness or greed. European manners and artistic achievements came to stand for the particular; American spontaneity and good faith for that of the universal" (26). Certainly when one sees the significance of the European experience for Henry, Senior — as escape and refuge from an uncongenial American culture that did not celebrate his literary offerings — one can understand what Europe meant to James as well.

Novelist Graham Greene, writing in 1952, agreed that understanding James's family background — his father's religious fervor and William's youthful breakdown — is crucial to understanding James's theme of innocence, treachery, corruption, fear of spiritual evil, and moral anarchy. "James has been too often regarded as a novelist of superficial experience, as a painter of social types, who was cut off by exile from the deepest roots of experience . . . ," Greene writes. "But James was not in that sense an exile; he could have dispensed with the international scene as easily as he dispensed with all the world of Wall Street finance. For the roots were not in Venice, Paris, London: they were in himself" (22). James's realism, Greene says, had some sources in his father's and brother's sense of possession by spiritual evil; James, Greene writes, "had to show that a damned soul has its chains" (29).

Like other critics, Greene notes James's reticence in dealing with sex, although he admits that this attitude changed during his career. "In the early novels and stories," Greene writes, "with the exception of *The Princess Casamassima*, wherever James approaches the physical side of life he seems to draw on his gloves, and his nouns draw on their inverted commas . . . and if one tries to imagine his characters physically, one feels that one is lifting a veil which conceals something repulsive." Later, however, "his attitude to sex seems to have taken refuge in fantasy" (34). In trying to understand "the conflict" James felt about sex, Greene cites "rumors about castration" and the "obscure hurt" (36); even if these rumors prove founded, however, Greene does not think that the sexual problem explains everything about James's apparent obsession with renunciation and death, and with his abiding theme of betrayal and moral corruption.

Betrayal was also novelist and critic William Gass's focus in "The High Brutality of Good Intentions" (1958), an essay that became a touchstone for considering James's moral interests. Gass deemed James superior to his brother in exploring "the pragmatic ideal of the proper treatment and ultimate worth of man." Throughout his career, Gass says, James developed the theme of "the evil of human manipulation" (138). James did not concern himself with distinguishing good people from bad, but "is concerned with all of the ways in which men may be reduced to the status of objects." Furthermore, like his brother William, James believed there is no "single, universally objective reality. He is committed . . . to a standpoint philosophy, and it would seem, then, that the best world would be observed from the most sensitive, catholic, yet discriminating standpoint" (140).

Pure Critics

While James's reputation soared because of critics who explored connections between James's life and work, and who examined James's handling of moral themes, many writers — before and after the advent of New Criticism in the 1940s and '50s — offered attentive readings focused on form and craft. In 1918, Joseph Warren Beach's *The Method of Henry James* proved influential on other critics and unusual in its focus on James's literary strategies. When the book was reissued in 1954, Beach accounted for his own interest in method, inspired, he said by James's prefaces in the New York Edition, essays that illuminated the creative process as few writers had done before. Beach distinguishes between his attention to James's formal techniques — what he calls "pure" criticism — and the "biological-ideological" criticism practiced by other writers (xxiii).

Beach asserts that most critics were interested in James "as a revealer of ethical truth" rather than James "as a manipulator of the art of revelation" (lxii). Even Lubbock's *The Craft of Fiction* and Richard Blackmur's essays, some of which eventually were reprinted in *The Lion and the Honeycomb* (1955) and *Studies in Henry James* (1983), seem to Beach not focused attentively enough on technique, or what Beach called the "mechanics" of storytelling. In discussing point of view, for example, Beach says that he does not mean "the general outlook of the author," as Lubbock and other critics defined the term, but rather "the 'angle of vision' from which the scene is surveyed in a given chapter of a book, — whether that of an omniscient author ready to enter into the minds of all the characters at once . . . or, on the contrary, that of some person in the story who sees whatever is to be seen by him, and interprets all that he sees by the light of his own mind and vision" (xiv–xv). Beach examines James's development of characters, dramatic method, creation of suspense, point of view, dialogue, tone, and imagery: in short, the craft of storytelling, which Beach believes has not been given adequate attention.

In 1918, few critics engaged in this meticulous examination of formal strategies, and in the intervening years up to 1954, Beach counts few such studies: among them, Matthiessen's *Henry James: The Major Phase*, Pelham Edgar's *Henry James: Man and Author*, F. W. Dupee's *The Question of Henry James: A Collection of Critical Essays*, and Elizabeth Stevenson's *The Crooked Corridor: A Study of Henry James*. Most other critical works combined an aesthetic response to James with reflections on the biographical information that began to appear regularly — James's prefaces in 1934, his notebooks in 1947, and several biographical studies of James and his family. The publication of the notebooks was especially important since this document sometimes contradicted the assertions that James made in his prefaces; the creative process and the biographical context for James's work, then, became more complicated for critics to analyze. Moreover, they found that the prefaces were not so transparent, and so trustworthy, as they once believed.

With the advent of New Criticism, privileging text over context, articles appeared that furthered Beach's project of examining James's literary strategies. New Criticism, however, did not generate a spate of critical attention on James anywhere near as strongly as had been seen in the 1940s. Allen Tate examined tone and point of view in a 1950 article that considered James along with Edgar Allan Poe and James Joyce; Austin Warren, writing in 1948, considered symbolism; Leon Edel examined James's experiments with point of view. Some studies focused on James's literary influences — Balzac, Zola, Flaubert, George Eliot, and Hawthorne among them. But as time went on, critics saw that James usefully could be considered along with their own contemporaries: Faulkner, for example, or James Joyce.

Some critics saw James as being closer to modernists, such as Virginia Woolf and D. H. Lawrence, than to Dickens and George Eliot. Stephen Spender, for one, wrote that there was a greater gulf between James and his contemporaries than between James and Lawrence, Yeats, or Joyce. "His problems," Spender said, "were essentially those of writers that followed him, and not those of his contemporaries" (113). For these critics, then, James stood as a proto-modernist because of his interest in his characters' consciousness. Virginia Woolf, in an essay about James's ghost stories, agreed that the ghosts James created comes not from "bloodstained sea captains, the white horses, the headless ladies of dark lanes and windy commons" but "have their origin within us" in individuals' consciousness and conscience (Woolf 324).

If *cult* implies an elite club with secret knowledge, then James's champions should not be called a cult. They were widely published critics with a large readership of their own. Because of their interest, James's works became available in paperback editions for which they — Rahv, Trilling, Matthiessen, Edel, among others — provided introductions. James's novels and stories became staples of college English classes. Graduate students wrote dissertations about his fiction and essays, and these graduate students took their places as professors, continuing their scholarship and training others. Among these early dissertation writers were Quentin Anderson (Columbia, 1953), Maurice Beebe (Cornell, 1953), Robert C. LeClair (University of Pennsylvania, 1944), Donald Murray (New York University, 1951), Lyall H. Powers (University of Indiana, 1955), William T. Stafford (University of Kentucky, 1956), and Joseph Ward (Tulane, 1957), each of whom went on to become a noted James scholar. Through the efforts of some powerful critics, for twenty-five years, at least, James enjoyed the popular acclaim that had eluded him in his lifetime. Of all of his champions, none proved as powerful as Leon Edel.

Works Cited

Anderson, Quentin. *The American Henry James*. New Brunswick, NJ: Rutgers UP, 1957.

Andreas, Osborn. *Henry James and the Expanding Horizon*. Seattle: U of Washington P, 1948.

Beach, Joseph Warren. *The Method of Henry James*. Philadelphia: Albert Saifer, 1954 [1918].

Blackmur, Richard. "Henry James." In *Literary History of the United States*. Vol. 2, edited by Robert Spiller, et al., 1039–64. New York: Macmillan, 1948.

———. *The Lion and the Honeycomb: Essays in Solicitude and Critique*. New York: Harcourt, Brace and World, 1955.

———. *Studies in Henry James*. Edited by Veronica A. Makowsky. New York: New Directions, 1983.

Brooks, Van Wyck. *The Pilgrimage of Henry James*. New York: Dutton, 1925.

Burr, Anna Robeson. *Alice James: Her Brothers—Her Journal*. New York: Dodd, Mead, 1934.

Bynner, Witter. "On Henry James' Centennial: Lasting Impressions of a Great American Writer." *Saturday Review of Literature* 2 (22 May 1943): 23, 26, 28.

Calisher, Hortense. "A Short Note on a Long Subject: Henry James." *Texas Quarterly* (Summer 1967): 57–59.

Chesterton, G. K. *The Autobiography of G. K. Chesterton*. New York: Sheed and Ward, 1936.

Clemens, Cyril. "Bret Harte and Henry James as Seen by Marie Belloc Lowndes." *Mark Twain Quarterly* 2 (Fall 1937): 21–23.

———. "A Visit to Henry James' Old Home." *Mark Twain Quarterly* 5 (Spring 1943): 9.

Dupee, Frederick W. *Henry James*. New York: Sloane, 1951.

———, ed. *The Question of Henry James: A Collection of Critical Essays*. New York: Holt, 1945.

Edel, Leon, ed. *Henry James: A Collection of Critical Essays*. Englewood Cliffs, NJ: Prentice Hall, 1963.

Edel, Leon, and Gordon N. Ray, eds. *Henry James and H. G. Wells, A Record of Their Friendship, Their Debate on the Art of Fiction, and Their Quarrel*. Urbana: U of Illinois P, 1958.

Edgar, Pelham. *Henry James: Man and Author*. Boston: Houghton Mifflin, 1927.

Eliot, T. S. "Henry James." In *The Shock of Recognition*, edited by Edmund Wilson, 854–65. New York: Modern Library, 1943.

Fleet, Simon. "The Nice American Gentleman." *Vogue* (1 October 1949): 136, 183–85.

Gard, Roger, ed. *Henry James: The Critical Heritage*. London: Routledge, 1968.

Gargano, James W., ed. *Critical Essays on Henry James: The Early Novels*. Boston: G. K. Hall, 1987.

Gass, William. "The High Brutality of Good Intentions." In Gargano, *The Early Novels*, 136–44.

Gide, André. "Henry James." *Yale Review* 19, no. 3 (March 1930): 641–43.

Gosse, Edmund. *Aspects and Impressions*. New York: Scribner's, 1922.

Grattan, Clinton Hartley. "The Calm within the Cyclone." *Nation* 134 (17 February 1932): 201–3.

Greene, Graham. *The Lost Childhood and other Essays*. New York: Viking, 1952.

Habegger, Alfred. *Gender, Fantasy, and Realism in American Literature*. New York: Columbia UP, 1982.

Hound and Horn. 7 (April–May 1934). Special issue on Henry James.

James, Henry. *Literary Criticism: Essays on Literature, American Writers, English Writers*. New York: The Library of America, 1984.

Jordan, Elizabeth. "Mr. James and the London Season." *Three Rousing Cheers*, 195–221. New York: Appleton-Century, 1938.

LaFarge, John. "Henry James's Letters to the LaFarges." *New England Quarterly* 22 (June 1949): 173–92.

Leavis, F. R. "The Appreciation of Henry James." *Scrutiny* 14 (Spring 1947): 229–37.

———. *The Great Tradition: George Eliot, Henry James, Joseph Conrad*. Garden City, NY: Doubleday, 1954.

———. "Henry James." *Scrutiny* 5 (March 1939): 398–417.

———. "Henry James's First Novel." *Scrutiny* 14 (Spring 1947): 295–301.

Leslie, Shane. "A Note on Henry James." *Horizon* 7 (June 1943): 405–13.

Lubbock, Percy. *The Craft of Fiction*. New York: Scribner's, 1921.

———. *The Letters of Henry James*. 2 vols. New York: Scribner's, 1920.

MacKenzie, Compton. "Henry James." *Life and Letters* 39 (December 1943): 147–55.

Matthiessen, F. O. *Henry James: The Major Phase*. New York: Oxford UP, 1944.

———. *The James Family: Including Selections from the Writings of Henry James, Senior, William, Henry, and Alice James*. New York: Knopf, 1947.

Mencken, H. L. *A Mencken Chrestomathy*. New York: Knopf, 1920.

Parrington, Vernon. "Henry James and the Nostalgia of Culture." *Main Currents in American Thought*. Vol. 3, 239–41. New York: Harcourt, Brace and World, 1930.

Pound, Ezra. "Henry James." In *Literary Essays of Ezra Pound*, edited by T. S. Eliot, 295–338. New York: New Directions, 1968 [1918].

Rahv, Philip. "Attitudes to Henry James." *New Republic* 108, no. 7 (15 February 1943): 220–24.

———. "The Cult of Experience in American Writing" (1940). In *Essays on Literature and Politics, 1932–1972*, edited by Arabel J. Porter and Andrew J. Dvosin, 8–22. Boston: Houghton Mifflin, 1978.

Rosenzweig, Saul. "The Ghost of Henry James." *Partisan Review* 11 (Fall 1944): 436–55.

Smith, Logan Pearsall. "Notes on Henry James." *Atlantic Monthly* 172 (August 1943): 75–77.

———. "Slices of Cake." *New Statesman and Nation* 25 (1 June 1943): 367–68.

Spender, Stephen. *The Destructive Element*. Philadelphia: Albert Saifer, 1953 [1935].

Stevenson, Elizabeth. *The Crooked Corridor: A Study of Henry James*. New York: Macmillan, 1949.

Tate, Allen. "The Beast in the Jungle." In Vann, 75–78.

Trilling, Lionel. *The Liberal Imagination*. New York: Doubleday, 1950.

Troy, William. "The Altar of Henry James." *New Republic* 108, no. 7 (15 February 1943): 228–30.

Vann, J. Don, ed. *Critics on Henry James*. Coral Gables, FL: U of Miami P, 1972.

Wagenknecht, Edward. "Our Contemporary Henry James." *College English* 10, no. 3 (December 1948): 123–32.

Warren, Austin. "Henry James: Symbolic Imagery in the Later Novels." *Rage for Order: Essays in Criticism*, 142–61. Chicago: U of Chicago P, 1948.

Wilson, Edmund. "The Ambiguity of Henry James." *The Triple Thinkers*, 88–132. New York: Harcourt, 1938.

———. "The Pilgrimage of Henry James." *Shores of Light*, 217–28. New York: Farrar, Straus, and Young, 1952.

Winters, Yvor. "Maule's Well, or Henry James and the Relation of Morals to Manners." *In Defense of Reason*, 300–343. Denver: Alan Swallow, 1943 [1938].

Woolf, Virginia. "Henry James's Ghost Stories." In *The Essays of Virginia Woolf*. Vol. 3, *1919–1924*, edited by Andrew McNeillie, 319–26. New York: Harcourt, Brace, 1988.

4: A Life of the Master: Leon Edel's *Henry James* and Its Influence on Criticism

> *To render the expression of a soul requires a cunning hand....*
> — Henry James, "Middlemarch"

FROM 1953, WITH THE PUBLICATION OF *Henry James: The Untried Years*, until his death in 1997, Leon Edel dominated James studies. Besides his five-volume life of James (the last volume of which appeared in 1972), Edel edited James's notebooks and a four-volume selection of his letters, wrote essays and delivered lectures about James, reviewed books related to James's work and to the members of his family, and provided introductions for reprints of James's major works, including a twelve-volume set of *The Complete Tales of Henry James*. In short, for more than forty years, one hardly could read anything by or about James that was not touched by the hand of Leon Edel. Because of his prominence in shaping James's reputation for the last half of the twentieth century, Edel himself has become the subject of biographical inquiry and critical assessment.

Joseph Leon Edel was born in Pittsburgh in 1907 and at the age of three moved with his family to Saskatchewan, Canada; when he was five, his mother took him to her native Russia for just over a year before coming back to Canada, this time to the small town of Yorkton, where Edel spent the rest of his childhood. In 1923, when Edel was sixteen, the family moved to Montreal, where he attended McGill University. After graduating with a bachelor's degree in 1927, Edel decided to pursue a master's, hoping to write his thesis on James Joyce, the writer who had most captivated his interest. But McGill forbade a study about a living writer, and a professor suggested that Edel instead explore Henry James, the progenitor, according to the professor, of such modernists as Joyce and Woolf.

At the time, Edel had not yet read Henry James, but *The Wings of the Dove* enticed him, and he saw in James's focus on the inner lives of his characters the precursor of Joyce's stream of consciousness. Edel's master's thesis was titled "Henry James and Some Recent Psychological Fiction." After McGill, Edel won a scholarship that enabled him to study abroad; because he had worked as a copyboy at the *Yorkton Press* and as a reporter for the *Montreal Herald* and *Daily Star*, he chose to study French journalism in Paris. Once there, however, his interests took a different direction: he decided to pursue a degree, and also to continue his work on

Henry James, this time investigating James's plays and their relationship to his fiction. Edel's work resulted in a thesis, *Henry James: Les Années Dramatiques* (1931). In the same year, he published a study of James's prefaces, grounding his future portrayal of James as an observer.

One crucial event of his European study occurred during a trip to Vienna. Through friends, he met the psychoanalyst Alfred Adler, attending a seminar that Adler gave for visiting students. As Edel recalled this episode in his life, Adler welcomed him warmly, singling him out for special attention. Adler invited the twenty-three-year-old Edel to his special table at a local café, seated the young man next to him, and listened thoughtfully to Edel's description of his work on James. "I remember his saying to me that if I were interested in biography, I should look very attentively at the relations of the two brothers," Edel told James William Anderson in an interview more than fifty years later. "It's extraordinary how this casual and unexpected encounter with one of Freud's early disciples bore such profound fruit in my life. Adler said to me there was every reason to bring together the disciplines of literature and psychology and I have been doing this ever since" (19). Besides emphasizing the importance of psychology to the biographer, Adler also convinced Edel of the prevalence of power struggles within the family, particularly between siblings. Adler "evolved a belief that humans strive for some kind of superiority, some manner of power, some way of self-exaltation; anonymity is a kind of death . . ." (Edel, *Stuff*, 9). And not least, Adler explained his theory of "the inferiority complex," in which low self-esteem "breeds anxiety, fear, excessive timidity, and a burden of guilt; it fosters rage and frustration, exaggerated competitiveness, and often concomitant violence" (*Stuff* 10). Edel was much impressed by Adler's ideas, especially his interpretation of Freud, and also by his urbanity. With Adler, Edel admitted, he suddenly felt "in the midst of a high civilization" (11). When he returned to Paris, he began to read Freud. "After a while," he said, "I came to believe that we can hardly write a line without informing ourselves of the promptings unveiled for us in the psychoanalytic study of the imagination" (*Stuff* 11).

In all of his writings about biography, Edel asserted that the "relation of the biographer to the subject is the very core of the biographical enterprise" and, borrowing a Freudian term, called this emotional involvement "transference" (*Writing Lives* 4). A biographer chooses his subject, Edel said, by feeling a sense of identification with him. "Freud long ago described this as a latching-on to some aspect of the subject that has belonged to one's earlier years," Edel explained; "the subject may have a familiar smile, or a facial resemblance, or offer some hint of some likable person in the past, a parent, a favorite uncle, a nanny, some figure of our schooldays" (McCulloch 174). For Edel, this "latching-on" that he felt toward James was generated both by biographical facts and what he perceived was a shared sensibility of the power struggles that characterized their respective families. Indeed, in most articles about Edel's life, writers repeat the phrase "like James." Like James, Edel had a brother fifteen months apart in age, with whom he felt intimacy and rivalry. He described his mother as strong-willed but cold and distant, and his father as emotionally weaker, a man who doted on his children and was also something of a dreamer; Edel ascribed these traits to James's parents as well.

Like James, Edel grew up feeling that he was an outsider to his society — in James's case, caused by his father's refusal to participate in the world of business; in Edel's, caused by his Jewishness. "From the beginning," Lyall Powers noted in a biographical sketch, "Leon Edel's life has been that of the outsider, of the alien unsure of his identity, deprived of his roots, lacking a place distinctively his own" (Powers, "Leon Edel," 598). Because his parents were Russian-Jewish immigrants, they fostered a home atmosphere "rife with nostalgia and elegies to lost homelands, a sense of exile and disinheritance," that Edel saw as analogous to James's exaltation of European culture (Powers 598). Perhaps Edel's most intense feeling of identification with James was in his desire for recognition of his talents and even for fame. Edel had noted that Adler "was interested — no doubt out of deep personal experience — in the universal struggle of men and women to escape from an anonymous world" (*Stuff* 9); James, Edel believed, enacted this struggle, and so did Edel.

His appropriateness as James's biographer was clear to Edel not only because he identified with James, but also because James told him so. In a dream, Edel confessed, he revealed to James that he was having trouble "establishing the hierarchies" of his friendships. "You know, I never got them sorted out myself," James replied. "I think what I did in that dream was to give myself James's blessing," Edel concluded. "The dream also enunciated a biographical truth. The subject of a biography has never had a chance to bring order to a life so constantly lived and involved in action. It is the biographer who finds the frame, sorts things out, and for better or worse tries to bring order into a life story . . ." (McCulloch 199). The biographer, Edel claimed, "gets to know a subject better than the subject ever knew himself or herself, because the biographer has read everything" (McCulloch 181).

Possession

Because he gained the trust and cooperation of Henry James III, Henry's nephew, William James's son, and executor of the family papers before his death in 1947, Edel did seem to have access to "everything" that survived James's own purging of his papers. During the time he worked on the biography, and even afterward, Edel kept this material sequestered, frustrating generations of scholars. Pierre Walker has given a detailed account of Edel's efforts to keep any James letters from publication during the period from 1958, when he signed a contract with Harvard University Press to publish four volumes of Henry James correspondence, until 1974, when the first volume finally appeared. Not only did he object to anyone else's publishing James's letters, but he even minimized quoting from them in his own biography, explaining in his introduction to the second volume that he was reserving those documents for his forthcoming edition of James's letters (Walker "Leon Edel"). Walker's interest in James's correspondence goes beyond that of historian: he and Greg Zacharias have tracked down, edited, and annotated more than ten thousand letters — four thousand at Harvard, one thousand at Yale, and the remainder in 130 different collections — that are being published, as of fall 2006, by the University of Nebraska Press (Walker "Seeing a Life"). This project will have a huge impact on James scholarship and, of course, on scholars' assessment of Edel's work. Certainly the publication of the correspondence between Henry and William, three volumes edited by Ignas Skrupskelis and Elizabeth Berkeley, has caused scholars to question Edel's interpretation of that relationship as rivalrous and Henry as victimized by his more aggressive brother. "What is clear," Robert Davidoff wrote in an introduction to the last of these three volumes, "is that Henry was in effect William's equal and that he as well as William acknowledged this" (xxxi). What is clear, besides, is the deep love and concern that the brothers showed for one another throughout their lives.

When asked late in his career if he ever felt possessive of James, Edel replied that he had not, but "I was committed to a long-range project. I had devoted years to it and it had cost me a great deal. In simple business terms, I wasn't going to tolerate trespassers. There were plenty of other subjects in the world open to them; the old frontier spirit of my childhood asserted itself. I had established my territory. I didn't see why I shouldn't exercise my rights. There were times when the academics were like a bunch of little nibbling mice and if one allows them to nibble away, your work is endangered, the best gets eaten up" (McCulloch 199). It is no wonder that Geoffrey T. Hellman's 1971 profile of Edel in the *New Yorker* was titled "Chairman of the Board."

Edel was a savvy businessman even before the first volume of his biography appeared, positioning himself into prominent visibility as an authority on James some fifteen years earlier, and setting his own authority against that of Percy Lubbock, Richard Blackmur, F. O. Matthiessen, and especially against that of a growing number of scholars newly interested in James. Beginning in 1939, Edel contributed articles and reviews to such publications as the *University of Toronto Quarterly, Times Literary Supplement, Poetry, Atlantic Monthly, Harvard Library Bulletin, New England Quarterly, American Imago,* and the *New York Times Book Review,* where in 1951 alone he published three reviews of books related to James, including F. W. Dupee's biography. In addition, Edel edited and contributed introductions for *The Complete Plays of Henry James* (1949) and *The Ghostly Tales of Henry James* (1950), which were both reviewed in prominent magazines and journals. In the same year that the first volume of his biography was published, Edel also published his edition of James's *Selected Fiction* and *The Sacred Fount*. In many of these pieces, Edel made a case for the need for a biography. Reviewing Simon Nowell-Smith's *The Legend of the Master: Henry James*, in 1948, Edel wrote that "the absence of a biography and the unbalanced picture of [James's] life emerging from Percy Lubbock's collection of but a small portion of his correspondence . . . has contributed to a considerable body of critical speculation and a super-abundance of specious anecdote" (Edel, Review, 545).

Once Edel corrected the "unbalanced picture" by publishing his five-volume biography over twenty years, he released his own collection of James's letters, selected, critics asserted, to support his own conclusions about James. Edel denied that "soft impeachment," defending his choices by pointing out "that a biographer most certainly uses important letters for the light they throw on a life and work and if they have this importance they obviously deserve inclusion in any subsequent collection of letters." To those who accused him of trying "to suppress sides of James's life," he replied tersely, "This is fantasy" (*Selected Letters* xvi–xvii). Yet Edel made it clear that his collection of letters was intended for "a reader who is not necessarily a scholarly specialist or a student researcher, or a Jamesian initiate, but who has read some of James's fiction and may want to know what sort of letter-writer he was" (xvi). Choosing letters that showed James in the best literary light was one guide to selection; another, Edel admitted, was a "less obvious reason": the psychological undercurrent of "stance and strategy behind the veiled politeness, and even lovingness, of a letter" (xviii). But this justification for choosing letters was precisely the criticism leveled by scholars: Edel was annotating his biography.

Philip Horne, among other scholars, could not make sense of Edel's principle of selection and complained that he neglected the needs of scholars for publication of the complete letters — Edel had read some fifteen thousand he said — in favor of a selection of several hundred. Responding to Edel's professed aim to publish only letters of literary interest, Horne wondered if his editing was "regrettably overprotective, unnecessarily distrustful of the reader's sense of proportion" (128). Although Edel said he intended his volumes to supplement Lubbock's earlier two-volume selection, Horne noted that sometimes Edel chose to reprint Lubbock's selections, and sometimes, inexplicably, to omit particular letters. Furthermore, Horne, like many others, noticed that the letters Edel chose to publish tended to validate his own biography: "the collection gives priority to certain relations in James's life at the expense of others and . . . its emphases tend to corroborate the controvertible interpretation of his life embodied in Professor Edel's biography" (132). Horne notes with some incredulity that Edel decided to edit the letters single-handedly, even though scholars who had worked on James manuscripts knew how difficult James's handwriting was. Edel's smooth transcriptions — his "elegant pages of confidently definitive print" — lead Horne to question the reliability of his decisions. "It gives some pause," Horne notes, ". . . that in the four volumes there are *so* few occurrences either of '[illegible]' or '[*sic*]' . . ." (134). In short, Horne concludes that the "far-reaching unreliability" of Edel's collection "makes a comprehensive scholarly edition, daunting project as it is, an urgent necessity . . ." (141). That scholarly edition, however, was not possible during Edel's lifetime. Horne's own collection, *Henry James: A Life in Letters* (1998) contributes several hundred hitherto unpublished letters to James scholarship.

Since Edel's death, other collections of correspondence also have been published, including Susan E. Gunter's *Dear Munificent Friends: Henry James's Letters to Four Women* (1999), Gunter's and Steven H. Jobe's *Dear Beloved Friends: Henry James's Letters to Younger Men* (2002), and Rosella Mamoli Zorzi's *Beloved Boy: Letters to Hendrik C. Anderson, 1899–1915* (2004). These collections, as we will see in chapter 7, have contributed to scholarship concerning James's friendships, and his intimate and possibly sexual relationships.

Rivals

Edel's rivalry with other critics emerged in his introduction to his edition of critical essays on James, published in 1963. Here, he derided F. O. Matthiessen, who had been a major James scholar at the time that Edel was beginning to publish his own works. Referring to Matthiessen's "brief and busy excursion into James," Edel reminds us that Matthiessen was a "critic and explicator of poetry" rather than fiction, who was drawn to study James after he discovered the archive of papers and letters recently deposited at Harvard. In other words, Matthiessen's decision was based on convenience rather than passion. Matthiessen, Edel wrote, "plunged into a type of scholarship which involved him with literary history as much as with criticism. He worked through the archive I think with a certain impatience, recognizing in James a kindred spirit in the aesthetic world, but feeling also an estrangement from him, for Matthiessen was too much a rebel to be at ease with a novelist who took the world as he found it." Matthiessen's criticism, Edel decided, was weakened by "an irrelevant use of the historical materials" and "the irrelevant use of criticism in their editing" (7). Furthermore, Edel argued, Matthiessen's criticism was derivative of previous writers; and besides, his reputation depended largely on a burgeoning interest in James around the time of his centenary. That

Matthiessen was a primary factor in sustaining that interest was a notion that Edel would not admit.

Edel selected essays that supported his own view of James; he omitted such major writers as Morton Zabel, Blackmur, Trilling, or Alfred Kazin because he thought they were sufficiently known; F. R. Leavis because he was "too opinionated and too autocratic." He omitted what he called "source-hunting studies," deeming them "least relevant when we deal with an imagination as creative as James's, an imagination so saturated with literature that all the writings of the past may be said to have provided the soil for his own work" (9). He excluded any leftist criticism, and any "examples of the exegetes and the allegory seekers, since these tell us less about James than about the critics themselves" (10). By the time this collection was published in 1963, Edel already was the most visible authority on James: in 1957, he coauthored *A Bibliography of Henry James*; in 1958, he coedited *Henry James and H. G. Wells: A Record of Their Friendship, Their Debate on the Art of Fiction, and Their Quarrel*; in 1960, he published *Henry James* for the University of Minnesota Press's Pamphlets on American Writers series; in 1962, the second and third volumes of his biography appeared; and during this period, also, he wrote introductions for many reprints of James's fiction, as well as articles for magazines and scholarly journals.

Each volume of Edel's biography received respectful critical attention. The first volume, published in 1953, was reviewed in the *New York Herald Tribune*, the *New York Times*, the *Nation*, the *New Republic*, the *Christian Science Monitor*, the *New Yorker*, the *Saturday Review*, the *Chicago Tribune*, and the *San Francisco Chronicle*, among many other newspapers and magazines. Most reviewers praised the biography: compared with previous portraits, Edel's work appeared thorough and detailed. Reviewers noted that Edel had a flair for narrative and anecdote; the books, structured in short, climactic chapters, were interesting to read. Although Alfred Kazin remarked that "his interpretation of the James family strife is far too psychological and à la mode"; although Edward Wagenknecht agreed that "Edel, in my judgment, overdramatizes the tensions which existed in the James household and, I think, seriously maligns and misinterprets the novelist's mother," reviewers on the whole felt that James emerged from Edel's book as a palpable and rounded individual, far different from the ruminating intellect portrayed in previous studies. In general interest magazines, especially, reviewers praised the biography; the second volume won a National Book Award and a Pulitzer Prize.

Writers in scholarly journals, however, were less generous. Although Edel noted that he received "cautious reviews from the academics," he believed that he had earned a reputation "as the ranking Jamesian expert" (McCulloch 169). Scholars criticized him, he said, because they "felt shortcomings in their own works, [and] when they saw what I had done and what I demonstrated, faulted me. But most of my readers," he noted, "reacted quite differently. You must remember there's still a great resistance to certain simple truths about the human animal.... Academe hates what it calls 'psychologizing'" (McCulloch 188). But Edel adamantly defended his approach. In his preface to volume 4, which he called "The Treacherous Years," he insisted that in the 1890s, James's stories about children were actually "the case history of the growth of a single child. By offering us the inner history of his little Maisie or of his young governess, James was in reality re-dreaming and using for art the essential materials of his own childhood; and in turn, using art as a form of catharsis for the lingering wounds within his psyche. He performed self-therapy rather than self-analysis," Edel argued; "but he offered us the material by which we can glimpse his extraordinary private history" (vol. 4, 15). Responding to the incredulity of some of his critics, "chiefly those in the academic world," he explained that he had "accepted the axiom of modern psychology that there is a sequence and consistency in the stuff of man's imagination; that an artist's work is less accidental than it has seemed; and that even as a form and discipline represent conscious effort on the part of the artist, there exists an equally consistent unconscious effort — an inescapable use of the buried materials of life and experience — to which the artist constantly returns." Edel delved in search of "personal parables" about James. "All the rest," he said, "is gossip and anecdotage" (vol. 4, 16–17).

Academe, though, objected to more than Edel's psychologizing; certainly many scholars were uncomfortable with his insistence on certain Freudian interpretations throughout; but they also criticized his refusal to consider scholarly articles; his selection of material that supported his psychoanalytic interpretation when other material might contradict it; his assumption that all James's creative work was a reflection of his unconscious needs to work out a few psychological problems that Edel argued persisted throughout James's life: his rivalry with his brother William, for one; his psychological castration by his domineering mother, for another. "Given this much analysis, we have the right to more," wrote J. C. Levenson in a review of the first volume; "along with the id behind the ego, we want the man behind the art. James himself argued that to be a good novelist, a man had to be not only a psychic phenomenon, but also a poet, a painter, an historian, and a philosopher. Really good fiction is not accounted for in terms of morbid thought.... Nor is good fiction simply a pastiche of recollections...." (535–36). "If too narrow a focus on James is sometimes a defect, so too is the biographer's determination to present his own view as unique" and to manipulate the writings of others so that they support the biographer's own views, using partial quotations, for example (536). Lyon N. Richardson noted of the first three volumes: "One quality usually supplied in some measure in a scholarly study of large dimensions is completely lacking: Mr. Edel has chosen to refrain from mentioning the many insights, perceptions, and comments in scholarly articles and books by students of James, even the most outstanding" (379).

Reviewing *The Treacherous Years*, Kenneth Graham pointed to what he called the "essential preposterousness" at the heart of Edel's project: "it is Mr. Edel's commitment to 'psychobiography,' with its lurid cast of sibling rivals, transvestite personae, amputated fathers, Gorgon mothers, and Napoleon" (236). Graham objected to seeing James's themes as merely "a re-dreaming and a catharsis of childhood's psychic wounds" (236). "It becomes more and more difficult to take Mr. Edel's Henry James seriously as the profound creative artist he was: there is always the trouble with the naive reductivism, the domination of aesthetic effect by hypothesized cause, of the older psychological criticism. When Mr. Edel discusses the novels as literature he is pleasant but on the whole exiguous: what really seizes him, and is meant to seize his reader, is speculative myth" (236). Edel, Kenneth S. Lynn wrote in the *New England Quarterly*, "is generally unwilling to translate his easy familiarity with these texts into significant interpretation. Nor does he show much concern for the over-all logic of James's creative life, how and why James's vision developed as it did, with the result that he is forced again and again to resort to two or three basic Freudian propositions about James's relationship to his family in order to lend his narrative some semblance of motivation" (262). Yet Lynn did concede that Edel offered a new and complex view of James. "From beneath Mr. Edel's shaping hand there emerges a new figure, more formidable, more magnificent — and far less sympathetic — than the one we were accustomed to" (263).

Other scholars took the opposite view entirely: far from making James more complex, Edel had reduced James's complexities by ascribing all his motivations to an attempt to heal psychic wounds, offering a reductionist reading of James's fiction, and misreading letters and notebook entries to fit his own argument. Martha Banta's review of Edel's one-volume revision of his biography was unequivocally damning: "What causes pain," she wrote in *American Literature*, "is the realization that this massive record of that most fastidious of men and writers is a rather vulgar book: vulgar, and misleading in the maladroit manner it interprets his life and art" (639). Although she did not deny that James may have suffered from psychological problems and pressures, she objected to the insistent interpretation that Edel offered: "Give us James as neurotic, surely," she conceded, "but not as he is portrayed here: a prosaic case-study of sibling rivalry and sexual anxiety. What Edel gives us as literary criticism is a set of pat readings which reduce the subtleties of James's fiction to little more than an encoding of a man's secret life. Give us, of course, James with a complex psyche that encourages us to reexamine the narrative themes to which he returned throughout his writing career, but not the coarsely rendered figure we receive here: every stroke of James's pen converted into projections of a man recumbent upon a couch" (640). Although Edel may convince his readers that James did have a secret life, Banta believed that the richness of James's fiction is evidence of wider and deeper sources of inspiration than simply his own traumas. "It is a pity that readers of Edel's version of James's career are continually coerced into peering in upon James in the act of literary masturbation . . .," she argued. "We are left with a man whose sole source for creative force was the inward turning of his solipsism. Edel never suggests that James was capable of imagining *what he was not*; or that James worked hard to appeal to his diverse audiences by calculating *their* imaginative needs; or that he experimented with existing literary formulas while adding ever new streaks to his narrative tulip" (641).

In a lengthy consideration of Edel's biography after the last volume appeared in 1972, Millicent Bell concurred that Edel's approach was reductionist and often simplistic. Edel, she wrote, "extracts James's psyche almost entirely from his fiction considered as evidence of suppressed and persistent obsessions and fantasies. A very large number of the little chapters is concerned with speculative deductions about James's unconscious life and identifications with fictional character and situation with family figures whose images, Edel thinks, were imprinted on his traumatized consciousness in early childhood" (395). In no way, she concluded, can his biography be called definitive. Although Edel accounted for James's comings and goings, presenting daily events in a readable narrative, he failed on many counts to consider the context of James's life and the breadth of his interests. He ignored James's political and social views; nor did he deal "with James's relation to the sense of the ideal, the moral and the social-utopian" ideas that flourished as he grew up because of his father's interest in Emmanuel Swedenborg and the family's friendship with Emerson. "Edel's approach to James," Bell argued, "is decidedly unphilosophic and offers no clues to the intellectual roots of his style and aesthetics" (393). Instead, she wrote, Edel's "biographic ransacking of the works" generated a view of James's writings "drained of their variety of theme" and reduced to "a series of tedious repetitions" (395–96).

The James Industry

Equally distressing to Bell was Edel's hold over the primary material. While it is not unusual for a scholar to have exclusive use of letters and papers during the time he or she is researching and writing, the length of Edel's project meant that scholars did not have access to the material for more than two decades. Frustrated, scholars interested in studying James were forced to concentrate "on the inner aesthetics of the fiction" rather than to consider, as well, the connection of the fiction to James's life. As Bell sees it, Edel's proprietary hold on James's archive undermined his own project as much as it did the work of others. "For Mr. Edel himself," she writes, "this situation has meant an excess of freedom to shape and interpret, to indulge speculation without curb or self-criticism. The active attention of other scholars able to refer to his sources with equal authority or publish alternative or contrary readings of James's life might have made a difference" (414).

Bell encountered Edel's influence directly when she was about to publish *Edith Wharton and Henry James: The Story of Their Friendship* (Braziller, 1965), in which she quoted from some of James's letters. When the book was still in galleys, Edel found out about the excerpts and directed the literary agency that handled the James estate to insist that the quotations be cut. This time, however, Edel was thwarted: Bell and her publisher had received permission from Harvard's Houghton Library to publish, based on Percy Lubbock's typescripts of the letters that had been deposited there by the James family, along with publication rights. Because in this case Harvard College owned publication rights, the institution, and not the literary agency representing the estate, had the legal right to allow Bell to proceed. But the conflict with Edel caused Bell to give up archival research on James, and to advise her graduate students to work on projects that did not depend on unpublished material. Although her book appeared as she intended, Edel had succeeded in limiting James scholarship (Walker, "Leon Edel," 281, 284).

Rayburn Moore saw that even in the annotations to the biography, Edel made sure that scholars would be frustrated. The notes, Moore said, "seldom afford specific help to anyone working on the same problem; they infrequently mention secondary sources; and they are difficult in some instances to verify. . . . Altogether it may be commendable to avoid 'sowing footnotes,' but in a work of five volumes fuller and more thorough citation from the author's prodigious research would have been of great value to others working on James" (263–64). But Edel was defiantly ungenerous about helping other scholars.

Herschel Parker echoed Bell's and Moore's complaints, regretful, especially, that many scholars and critics did not examine biographical evidence in their studies analyzing James's revisions. That perspective is understandable, Parker admitted, because "for biographical research James is a special case, a major writer on whom the biographical materials were, to an extraordinary degree, monopolized by one man, Leon Edel. The inherent danger in the decision of James's heirs to invest exclusive privilege in one person was infinitely compounded when the man so privileged came to be jealous of his territory and rather idiosyncratic in his literary judgments" (89–90).

Certainly Edel's idiosyncratic interpretations partly were a product of his own cultural context. As Fred Kaplan noted in an essay explaining his motivation to write a new biography of James (*Henry James: The Imagination of Genius* was published in 1992), Edel was "a scholar/writer whose basic literary and cultural values were formed between 1920 and 1940. That is the date of the glass slide in which Edel's James exists; his biography tells us as much about the cultural moment that created it as it does about the subject" (2). Kaplan noted that Edel's relationship with the subject "whom he unironically called 'The Master' was tainted by a myopic hero-worship," a perspective that by the 1990s made the biography outdated. To Kaplan, the biography was "distancing" in its "coziness, its assumptions about cultural contingency, its psychological formulas, its high journalistic version of James as modern artist, its intellectual thinness, its absorption in social surfaces, its absence of dialectical tensions, its tone being overly familiar and at-home with its subject" (3). In addition, Kaplan identified one important weakness in Edel's "reticence about James's sexuality" (6). Although Edel allowed for homoeroticism, he refused to consider the possibility of homosexuality, which did not fit the identity of the Henry James whom Edel had created. "Somehow," Edel told an interviewer for the *Paris Review*, "homosexuality in James's mode of life seems out of character. He was too fastidious, too afraid of sex altogether — and contented himself by being publicly affectionate, giving his friends great hugs and pats on the back. That was why I use the term homoerotic" (McCulloch 194). Yet even Edel knew that his conclusion about James might well be questioned, and even contradicted, by future writers: "We can foresee great changes as a result of the sexual revolution," he said in 1985. "The biographer can now write with greater openness.... The problem will be how and where the lines will be drawn between privacy and the unbuttoned self" (McCulloch 194). Those lines, as chapter 7 will show, have become barely perceptible, as scholars who do not share Edel's fastidiousness inquire into the intimate corners of James's experience.

Although other writers — Virginia Woolf, Emily Dickinson, Walt Whitman — have spawned their own literary "industry," the Henry James legacy is unique in its ownership, for many decades, by a single writer. No doubt the future of James studies will reveal both the illumination that Edel offered and what Pierre Walker calls the "dark side" of Edel's wide influence ("Leon Edel" 279).

Works Cited

Anderson, James William. "An Interview with Leon Edel on the James Family." *Psychohistory Review* 8, no. 1–2 (1979): 15–22.

Banta, Martha. Review of *Henry James: A Life*. *American Literature* 58, no. 4 (December 1986): 639–43.

Bell, Millicent. "Henry James: The Man Who Lived." *Massachusetts Review* 14 (Spring 1973): 391–414.

Edel, Leon. "Confessions of a Biographer." In *Psychoanalytic Studies of Biography*, ed. Moraitis and Pollock, 3–27.

———. *Henry James*. Pamphlets on American Writers, no. 4. Minneapolis: U of Minnesota P, 1960.

———. *Henry James*. Vol. 1, *The Untried Years, 1843–1870*. Philadelphia: Lippincott, 1953.

———. *Henry James*. Vol. 2, *The Conquest of London, 1870–1883*. Philadelphia: Lippincott, 1962.

———. *Henry James*. Vol. 3, *The Middle Years, 1882–1895*. Philadelphia: Lippincott, 1962.

———. *Henry James*. Vol. 4, *The Treacherous Years, 1895–1901*. Philadelphia: Lippincott, 1969.

———. *Henry James*. Vol. 5, *The Master, 1901–1916*. Philadelphia: Lippincott, 1972.

———, ed. *Henry James: A Collection of Critical Essays*. Englewood Cliffs, NJ: Prentice Hall, 1963.

———, ed. *Henry James: Selected Letters*. Cambridge, MA: Belknap Press of Harvard UP, 1987.

———. *Literary Biography*. London: Rupert Hart-Davis, 1957.

———. Review of *The Legend of the Master: Henry James*. *New England Quarterly* 21, no. 4 (December 1948): 544–47.

———. *Stuff of Sleep and Dreams*. New York: Harper & Row, 1982.

———. *Writing Lives: Principia Biographica*. New York: Norton, 1984.

Edel, Leon, and Dan Laurence. *A Bibliography of Henry James*. 3rd ed. Oxford: Clarendon Press, 1982.

Edel, Leon, and Gordon Ray, eds. *Henry James and H. G. Wells: A Record of Their Friendship, Their Debate on the Art of Fiction, and Their Quarrel*. Urbana: U of Illinois P, 1958.

Graham, Kenneth. Review of *Henry James: The Treacherous Years, 1895–1901*. *Review of English Studies*, New Series 22, no. 86 (May 1971): 235–37.

Gunter, Susan E., ed. *Dear Munificent Friends: Henry James's Letters to Four Women*. Ann Arbor: U of Michigan P, 1999.

Gunter, Susan E., and Steven H. Jobe, eds. *Dear Beloved Friends: Henry James's Letters to Younger Men*. Ann Arbor: U of Michigan P, 2002.

Hellman, Geoffrey T. "Chairman of the Board." *New Yorker*, 13 March 1971: 46+.

Horne, Philip. "The Editing of James's Letters." *Cambridge Quarterly* 15 (1986): 126–41.

———. *Henry James: A Life in Letters*. New York: Viking, 1998.

James, Henry. *Literary Criticism: Essays on Literature, American Writers, English Writers*. New York: The Library of America, 1984.

Kaplan, Fred. *Henry James: The Imagination of Genius*. New York: Morrow, 1992.

———. "James Without Beret." In *Biography and Source Studies*, edited by Frederick R. Karl, 1–8. New York: AMS Press, 1996.

Kazin, Alfred. Review of *Henry James: The Untried Years*. *New York Herald Tribune Book Review*, 3 May 1953: 1.

Levenson, J. C. Review of *Henry James: The Untried Years, 1843–70*. *New England Quarterly* 26, no. 4 (December 1953): 533–37.

Lynn, Kenneth S. Review of *Henry James, The Conquest of London: 1870–1881; Henry James, The Middle Years: 1882–1895*. *New England Quarterly* 36, no. 2 (June 1963): 260–63.

McCulloch, Jeanne. "The Art of Biography I: Leon Edel." *Paris Review* 98 (Winter 1985): 157–207.

Moore, Rayburn S. "'The Full Light of a Higher Criticism': Edel's Biography and other Recent Studies of Henry James." *South Atlantic Quarterly* 63 (1964): 104–14.

———. "Henry James Ltd., and the Chairman of the Board: Leon Edel's Biography." Review of *The Life of Henry James*. *South Atlantic Quarterly* 73 (1974): 261–69.

Parker, Herschel. "The Authority of the Revised Text and the Disappearance of the Author: What Critics of Henry James Did with Textual Evidence in the Heyday of the New Criticism." *Flawed Texts and Verbal Icons: Literary Authority in American Fiction*, 85–114. Evanston, IL: Northwestern UP, 1984.

Powers, Lyall. "Leon Edel, The Life of a Biographer." *American Scholar* 66 (Autumn 1997): 598–607.

Richardson, Lyon N. Review of *Henry James: The Conquest of London, 1870–1881; Henry James: The Middle Years*. *American Literature* 35, no. 3 (November 1963): 377–79.

Skrupskelis, Ignas, and Elizabeth Berkeley, eds. *The Correspondence of William James*. Vol. 3, *William and Henry, 1897–1910*. Introduction by Robert Davidoff. Charlottesville: U of Virginia P, 1994.

Wagenknecht, Edward. Review of *Henry James: The Untried Years*. *Chicago Sunday Tribune*, 3 May 1953: 2.

Walker, Pierre A. "Leon Edel and the 'Policing' of the Henry James Letters." *Henry James Review* 21, no. 3 (2000): 279–89.

———. "Seeing A Life through Biography, Letters, and Fiction." *Chronicle for Higher Education (The Chronicle Review)*, 12 November 2004: 11.

Zorzi, Rosella Mamoli, ed. *Beloved Boy: Letters to Henrik C. Andersen, 1899–1915*. Charlottesville: U of Virginia P, 2004.

5: Critical Revisions: James in the Academy

> *When you re-read coldly and critically a book which in former years you have read warmly and carelessly, you are surprised to see how it changes its proportions.*
>
> — Henry James, "George Eliot"

BEGINNING IN THE 1960s, interest in James shifted to the academy, and those writing about James increasingly were scholars trained in literary analysis and theory. Biographical information emerging from Leon Edel's study inspired a Freudian reading of some of James's fiction, but other critical perspectives also informed James studies, including feminist, Marxist, and reader-response criticism; semiotics; the psychoanalytic criticism of Jacques Lacan; and the cultural criticism of Michel Foucault. Dorothy McInnis Scura's *Henry James, 1960–1974: A Reference Guide* and Judith Funston's *Henry James, 1975–1987: A Reference Guide* show that James studies has developed into a major scholarly industry, with around 150 and sometimes over two hundred articles and books published yearly, for a total of more than 4,500 items to date. Sarah B. Daugherty's overviews of criticism that appear annually in *American Literary Scholarship* testify to continuing productivity. Besides critical articles appearing in already established scholarly journals, in 1979 the Henry James Society inaugurated the *Henry James Review*, edited by Daniel Mark Fogel; and several publishers — notably Norton in its Critical Edition series and Bedford/St. Martin's in its Case Studies — reprinted James's work with appended contemporary and current criticism.

Although Philip Rahv remarked that James's reputation waned after its peak in the 1940s, in fact, James's reputation was maintained by a new set of academic readers: the Master joined the American literary canon, heir to Emerson, Hawthorne, Melville, and Poe. If any writers were lost from that canon, it could be argued that William Dean Howells, once the reigning representative of American realism, and Theodore Dreiser, once the main proponent of American naturalism, were not as likely to be found on American literature syllabi. James, though, often was represented by some perennial favorites: *Daisy Miller, The Portrait of a Lady, The Ambassadors, The Turn of the Screw,* "The Jolly Corner," and "The Beast in the Jungle." Not surprisingly, scholarship became focused on the same texts: for example, Scura notes that besides a plethora of critical articles on the short and melodramatic *Turn of the Screw*, five collections of critical essays appeared between 1960 and 1974. Scholarship responded to the marketplace created by the academy.

This scholarship did not always win the approval and cooperation of Leon Edel, who saw himself as an outsider to the academy, even after he took a faculty position. As a self-appointed gatekeeper to the James legacy, he encouraged some scholars just as he discouraged others. Fogel noted that prior to 1979, Robert Gale, William Stafford, and Maurice Beebe each had wanted to create a publication that could serve as a forum for James scholarship, but Edel quashed their efforts. Only with the help of Adeline Tintner, a tireless researcher on James and a friend of Edel, did Fogel manage to win Edel's approval and cooperation, enabling the Henry James Society and its journal to become established. Tintner, trained as an art historian, stands as one of the most prolific writers on Henry James, contributing more than two hundred publications from 1963 until her death in 2003. She reveled in research and annotation, such as documenting works of art, books, literary allusions, and references to other authors in James's work. As an independent scholar, untainted by the academy, she was just the kind of James devotee that Edel admired and valued. He encouraged Tintner to resume her interest in James when he decided to include her 1946 essay, "The Museum World," in the collection of critical essays that he published in 1963.

In his own essay for that collection Edel allowed himself the last word: that James endures as "the historian of manners, the psychologist, the civilized mind, and the profound moralist. . . . A single reading never exhausts the richness of his prose or the detail of his observation" (178). Edel's characterization of James indicates the focus of much scholarship from the 1960s through the 1980s: critics focused on James as historian of late-nineteenth-century society, American and European; as psychologist interested in the consciousness of his characters and the process of knowing and perceiving reality; and as moralist, interested in power, the condition of women, and the possibility of evil. Scholars also focused on James's aesthetics and literary strategies, with some, such as Lyall Powers and Fogel, exploring James's connection to his literary forebears; and others, such as Oscar Cargill, Robert Gale, and Edward Wagenknecht, offering overviews of James's major works, no doubt helpful for a new generation of readers.

Essay collections abounded, bringing together articles published in disparate journals or, sometimes, inviting new essays from prominent scholars. Several publishers began to issue volumes of criticism about novels that proved to be popular texts in literature courses: for example, *The Ambassadors* (Norton, 1964; Prentice Hall, 1969); *The Turn of the Screw* (Norton, 1966; Prentice Hall, 1970; St. Martin's, 1995); *The Portrait of a Lady* (New York University Press, 1967; Prentice Hall, 1968); *Washington Square* (Crowell, 1970); *The American* (Merrill, 1971); *The*

Tales of Henry James (Norton, 1984). Most of these collections have been revised since their first editions to include more recent criticism and new perspectives.

As for general collections of criticism, John Goode's *The Air of Reality: New Essays on Henry James*, published in 1972, brought together British scholars to consider James's insights into his culture. The following year, Lyall Powers released his collection of essays entitled *Henry James's Major Novels*. James Gargano edited two volumes, both of which appeared in 1987 — one on James's early novels and the other on the late novels. Ruth Bernard Yeazell edited a collection of criticism in 1994 that included contributions from such notable scholars as Carolyn Porter, Jonathan Freedman, Eve Kosofsky Sedgwick, and Jean-Christophe Agnew. One collection that aims at accessibility for nonspecialized readers is Jonathan Freedman's *The Cambridge Companion to Henry James* (1998), with essays specially commissioned for the volume by Philip Horne, Hugh Stevens, Millicent Bell, and Martha Banta, among many others.

Setting Forth Problems

Much criticism in the 1960s and early 1970s offered close readings that complicated ways of understanding the polarities that earlier critics had identified in James's work: America versus Europe, innocence versus experience, observation versus action. Although some scholars took up a formalist defense of James as a literary master, most took for granted James's eminence and focused on a few significant issues — morality, power, and the acquisition of knowledge — that remain abiding interests of James criticism. During these decades, scholarship often was not grounded in theory, but can be considered largely belletristic. Perhaps the most eloquent example appears in Kenneth Graham's *Henry James, The Drama of Fufilment* (1975), which presents itself modestly as "an approach . . . and only an approach . . . a limited attempt towards reappropriating the novels to our sympathetic imagination and to our full sense of life . . ." (ix). Graham wrote the book, he said, because he felt increasingly "estranged" from the desiccation of current criticism, the insistence of Leon Edel's Freudian reading, and the hermeticism of formalist criticism. Graham quite simply wanted to revive the joy of personal encounter with James and to argue, in addition, that James's novels are able to "involve us in many of the rhythms and contradictions of our common experience, and that his dominating vision of the struggle for fullness and reality is not one that leads only to the ivory tower and to the 'religion of consciousness' " (xv). Graham's generous reading of seven of James's major works (including *The Aspern Papers, The Spoils of Poynton,* and *The Wings of the Dove*) places him among the ranks of James's champions.

Moral questions occupied Frederick Crews in his influential book *The Tragedy of Manners: Moral Drama in the Later Novels of Henry James* (1957). Like many critics before him, Crews believed that James's later period was his greatest because his characters became more complex, not easily divided between heroes and villains (8). Moral conflict in any Jamesian novel, Crews argued, comes from "philosophical differences of opinion among the principal characters" because of their "differing social background" (7). James is interested not only in abstract moral questions, then, but in the way that society constructs an individual's ethics and the way that individuals shape a community's shared values. Looking at *The Ambassadors, The Wings of the Dove,* and *The Golden Bowl,* Crews concludes that Jamesian heroes have in common "a selfless passion for knowledge, an awareness of life-as-a-whole . . . rather than an endorsement of one way of living against another . . . [The hero] will look for a measure of validity in every attitude that he meets, including those of his worldly enemies" (32–33). In *The Ambassadors,* for example, Crews sees Strether's decision not to marry Maria Gostrey not as a renunciation of love, but as a recognition that any choice would be limiting. Marriage would not take away his freedom, but "it would be a symbolic avowal that her world, the European one, corresponds to what he wants" (56). Crews finds *The Golden Bowl* the most ambiguous of James's tales because James keeps his own moral position hidden. As he presents his characters, "James refuses to imply that one point of view is more valid than the others. In order to arrive conclusively at one set of moral insights we must therefore deny three other sets. James is scrupulous to divert us from such rashness" (82). Reality consists of clashing interests and worldviews, James implies, as each individual constructs a world through his or her own choices. Crews, then, set forth ideas that would be taken up by critics connecting James's fiction to his brother's writing about pragmatism.

The problem of narration occupied Wayne Booth in *The Rhetoric of Fiction* (1961), a wide-ranging study of many British, American, and European writers that included a consideration of James's observer-narrators. Booth recognizes that for James, the observer "can 'reflect' the story to the reader." But in many tales, Booth says, that observer is "a profoundly confused, basically self-deceived, or even wrong-headed or vicious reflector" (340). These "unreliable narrators," as Booth calls them, may have arisen because James first created a narrator to reflect one theme, and when that theme changed, James failed to change the narrator's perspective. The result, then, is perplexity for the reader over ambiguity that, Booth suggests, may have been unintentional. James, Booth says, needs "a reader so flexible and so thoroughly attuned to James's own values that he could shift nimbly from stance to stance, allowing the narrator to shift his character from moment to moment" (363). Commenting on the enormous contrasts among critics about interpretations of James's work, Booth believes part of the problem stems from the unreliability of the narrator through whom the reader comes to perceive the story.

Apparently, Ora Segal felt that she was a more nimble reader than Booth. Several years after Booth's book appeared, Segal took up the problem of James's observer-narrator in *The Lucid Reflector* (1969), asserting that the Jamesian narrator "is a most flexible and complex functional character" who performs "important authorial functions" (xi). Each narrator, Segal says, shares certain qualities: "reflective nature, sensitivity to impressions, analytical turn of mind, speculative propensities, and, above all, insatiable curiosity and capacity for appreciation" that make them a controlling intelligence in the story (xii). As James matured as a writer, Segal decides, his observer-narrator became more refined, subtle, and complex. Unlike Booth, who thinks James may not always have exerted control over this character, Segal believes that what others see as unreliability is caused instead by the fictional universe in which the narrator functions. "He is not omniscient, and his moral and epistemological perspectives are necessarily limited," but James uses this limited perspective to present the "complicated, groping processes of observation and evaluation" (233). For James, the observer — what Segal calls the "author's deputy" — served as "the right reflector or perfect mirror of the case he observes and interprets" (234). James privileged the observer, Segal argues, because he believed that seeing "could be an authentic rather than merely a vicarious form of 'being' — a form more intense and more valuable than any other" (xii). The relationship of seeing to being would engage future scholars, such as Carolyn Porter, who examined the observer not only in his impact on the reader's understanding of fiction, but in his connection to the moral questions that the fiction explores. What, these scholars ask, does the observer see, and why?

The complexity of James's later fiction attracted many scholars, as it did Segal, but controversy persisted about whether James's reputation should rest on his early or late works. Richard Poirier, for one, believed that James became increasingly abstract, and therefore less successful, as his career progressed. In his surprising focus on humor in *The Comic Sense of Henry James* (1960), Poirier admits that previous criticism ignored, or even denied, the existence of comedy in James's fiction; he believes, however, that examining "comic expression" in the early novels can illuminate "some of the psychological identity of the author" (7). Poirier argues that James felt "a very painful moral scrupulousness" toward his characters, striving to allow them freedom of expression while conscious of the possibility that he might exploit them as merely conveyers of his ideas. Comedy, according to Poirier, proved a way for James to relieve the tension of authorship. Central to Poirier's analysis is attention to the reader's experience of apprehending meaning in fiction. For Poirier, this experience involved not only "what we figure out after we are through," but, just as important, our immediate personal reaction to a tale. Meaning, he says, "is apprehended only by our whole sensibility, including the simplest forms of excitement and amusement" (10). Poirier, then, anticipates the perspective of reader-response criticism that would follow.

Despite a general consensus in the academy about James's stature, in the early 1960s a few writers enjoined the long-standing controversy about the value of fiction that focused on a world past and on characters apparently unconnected to American life in the second half of the twentieth century. Even James's former champion Richard Blackmur came to believe that James held a narrow conception of the possibilities for an individual's life. Because James saw himself as an outsider who never could participate fully in experience, he doomed his characters to that very position. By the early 1960s, in his introductions to some of James's late novels, Blackmur concurred with other critics who saw in James a "feeling of human belittlement" (*Studies* 238); he believed that James, especially at the end of his career, was devoted exclusively to aesthetics and to honing his identity as an artist. Blackmur regrets the "great gestures of repudiation" that are the fate of James's characters — characters, Blackmur asserts, who "do the wrong things for the right reasons" (224). Wherever this instinct for renunciation originated — perhaps "in some layer of the psyche much deeper than the imagination" — Blackmur sees James's choices as dehumanizing his characters by limiting their freedom and thwarting their desires (225).

Even more damning, Maxwell Geismar, in *Henry James and the Jacobites* (1963), a book dedicated to Van Wyck Brooks, reprises Brooks's criticism of James as vastly overrated and irrelevant. Calling James a "romantic medievalist," Geismer argues that "the real world of the Jamesian yearning was the semifeudal and pictorial amalgam of French and English nobility . . ." (413). Yet in the 1940s and '50s, James fit the needs of many American intellectuals — Geismar cites Matthiessen, Dupee, Trilling — who refused to deal with "all the hard, unpleasant, dangerous or threatening facets and facts of the 'real world' " and preferred "the high, pure, weightless outer space of pure esthetics and pure fairy tale" (439). These critics lauded James's identity as an "aristocratic Anglo-American artist — with his elaborate rationalizations of his own work and temperament; with his non-political (well, royalist), non-social, non-economic and non-historical sense of 'history' " because, Geismer asserts, they were trying to obliterate their own identities as radicals, perhaps with "subversive" ties, and to refashion themselves as artists. Jamesian aesthetics, Geismar says, "was the perfect register, reverberator, mirror, reflector for changing and distorting, or for eliminating, the realities of world history which a large sector of the American intellectuals no longer wished to understand and deal with. Henry James was a symbol of national make-believe on the highest level of intellectual or cultural status and respectability" (443). In an age that needed an Emerson or Thoreau, a Melville or a Dreiser, James's reputation, lamentably for Geismer, was soaring.

Most scholars contributed to enhancing that reputation. Dorothea Krook, in *The Ordeal of Consciousness in Henry James* (1962), argued against critics such as Geismer who dismissed James as irrelevant; she explains that because James was interested in the moral aspect of power, he necessarily focused on "the moneyed classes" who wield the greatest power in society. Because he was interested in the way the mind perceives and interprets reality, he necessarily created intelligent and sensitive characters who are "full vessels of consciousness" (12, 17). Krook asks us to think about the great tragedies — Greek and Shakespearean — that also consider "the rise and fall of great spirits, of personages endowed with gifts and graces, weaknesses and vices, far above the common level." The desires and passions of these characters, she says, are "truly exemplary and instructive" for readers (17). James is not privileging these characters, but rather uses them for trenchant, if subtle, cultural criticism. Throughout her attentive study of James's major novels, Krook is always aware of James's detractors and offers counterarguments to some of their assertions. She calls F. R. Leavis, for example, "sweeping and inaccurate" in his denigration of the imagery of *The Golden Bowl* (391); she assesses Edmund Wilson's Freudian interpretation of *The Turn of the Screw* as provocative but incomplete; she defends Isabel Archer against critics who deemed her frigid. Krook's study proved influential for other critics focusing on both James's rendering of his characters' consciousness and on those characters' struggles for power.

Although Laurence Holland, in *The Expense of Vision: Essays on the Craft of Henry James* (1964), argued that Krook overemphasized James's "rigor of moral judgment" (x), he agreed that James's fiction does focus intently on moral problems. According to Holland, James created what he calls "the intimate novel," by which he means that James deliberately used formal strategies "to arouse interest, to woo the reader, to make the reader believe or entertain the fiction and be entertained by it"; these strategies, Holland says, have "all the contingencies and resonance of intimacy" (x). Holland examines James's major novels, including *The Portrait of a Lady*, *The Spoils of Poynton*, *The Ambassadors*, and *The Wings of the Dove*, to show how form contributes to the reader's understanding of James's major themes: "the courtships and marriages, the exploitation and the deceptions which are practiced on some of his characters, the endowments of money and the acquisition of possessions which move his plots, the sacrifices exacted in the very process of transformation" (xi). Certainly these themes had been identified in the past; Holland contributes by linking them to rhetorical strategies: the architectural metaphors in *Portrait*, for example; the shifting verbal tenses in *The Ambassadors*; the intrusion of the narrator's "I" in *The Wings of the Dove*. James's manipulation of the reader would prove a fertile area of examination for other critics as well.

Taking up the theme of polarities that characterize Jamesian fiction, Sallie Sears, writing in 1968, explored what she calls James's "negative imagination" and "its literary consequences. Each of the last novels," she writes, "can be looked upon as an unresolved debate about the promise and meaning of life, a debate between a voice of yearning and a voice of restriction" (xii). James, she says, devises choices for his characters that never will work. "He is the most unsentimental of our great romanticists" (151). But it is not as a romanticist that James interests Sears. She sees him as a transitional figure whose writing straddles the nineteenth-century novel and modernist fiction, especially in "his use of the controlling 'point of view' " and his use of multiple vantage points, none of which reveals an objective truth (46). Unlike Virginia Woolf, James does not aim for a synthesis of perspectives that brings readers closer to apprehending reality; on the contrary, Sears says, "one of the characteristics of James's sensibility is precisely the *inability* to engage in a real dialectical process or to reconcile conflicting if partial points of view." Instead, James opposes "mutually exclusive possibilities . . . each of which furthermore is attended by a negative consequence" (38–39). As even his contemporaries noted, James depends on his readers to make sense of the inherent ambiguity of his tales: "what is problematic," Sears writes, "is not what is going on, but how we are to take it and to which category, moral or otherwise, it belongs" (25). What James's books are about, Sears concludes, is not the fate of one or another character, but the clashes of perspective (31). Sears's focus on the ambiguities in James's novels, on the multiplicity of viewpoints, and on the shifting possibilities of the readers' interpretation grounds future critical work that considers James in the context of pluralism.

Before 1974, when Richard Hocks published *Henry James and Pragmatistic Thought: A Study of the Relationship between the Philosophy of William James and the Literary Art of Henry James*, the major figures in William and Henry James scholarship — Ralph Barton Perry, F. O. Matthiessen, and Leon Edel — resisted the idea that Henry responded in his fiction to his brother's philosophy. Yet Hocks, and others who followed him, saw strong evidence to the contrary. After reading *Pragmatism* in 1907, for example, Henry announced to William that he was "lost in the wonder of the extent to which all my life I have . . . unconsciously pragmatised" (Skrupskelis and Berkeley, vol. 3: 347). And two years later, after reading *A Pluralistic Universe*, Henry wrote, "As an artist and a 'creator' I can catch on, hold on, to pragmatism, & can work in the light of it & apply it; finding, in comparison everything else . . . utterly irrelevant & useless . . ." (Skrupskelis and Berkeley, vol. 3: 391–92). In arguing for Henry's connection to pragmatism, Hocks, besides illuminating the philosophical underpinnings of James's fiction, also attempted to refute some of the negative criticism that had recently appeared — from Wayne Booth, for example, who felt that James was not in complete control of his narrator, or Sallie Sears, who felt that James imposed negativity on his characters' fates.

Hocks defines pragmatism as "an attitude at odds with assuming knowledge from concepts apart from their unfolding consequence in sensory and perceptual life" (60). When T. S. Eliot remarked that James's mind was " 'so fine that no idea could violate it,' " he was pointing exactly to James's "acute sense of the fallacy of profundity." James's task, according to Hocks, was "to become involved with his little 'percepts,' to show how interesting *they* are, and how they can even have surprisingly broad dimension" (71). Hocks argues that James always began with a "germ" of a tale that transformed itself during the writing. James's "fluid reading of experience," therefore, emerged in his themes: the expression of genuinely "humane sensibility" (126, 133). For Hocks, James used polarity not to point up an opposition of points of view, but to demonstrate "interpenetration" of perspectives "rather than juxtaposition." Readers would do well, Hocks suggests, to consider that when one "pole" dominates, the other has the potential to do so. James does not want us to choose sides on moral questions, but to recognize how all perspectives are interdependent (174).

The philosophical questions inspired by James's works inevitably connect to questions of knowing. Ruth Bernard Yeazell considered how a character's perspective informs his or her knowledge of the world in *Language and Knowledge in the Late Novels of Henry James* (1976), a study that responds to the arguments of several previous scholars, especially Dorothea Krook and Sallie Sears. Yeazell focuses on the late novels because, she says, James's style generates "uneasiness" in the reader, creating as it does "a world where the boundaries between unconscious suspicion and certain knowledge, between pretense and reality, are continually shifting . . ." (3). Unlike critics who feel that this shifting reflects James's inadequate control over his characters, Yeazell argues that for James, point of view does not imply consistency. A mind, she says, may be "deeply and mysteriously in conflict with itself" (9). In James's fictional worlds, characters may act like artists, creating their reality with a logic that may defy convention, but may appeal to irrational needs and deep desires. Their intelligence, then, is not amputated from their full consciousness, but constantly buffeted by other elements of their consciousness. As readers, however, we may naturally identify with those characters whose interpretation of reality comes closest to our own; we see such characters as intelligent, reliable, sympathetic. Yet do they have the clearest vision of reality or, even more crucial, are they the most virtuous or moral? Questions such as the ones Yeazell brings to her work — and which James E. Miller echoes in his 1976 essay "Henry James in Reality" — about the connection between seeing and being, between intelligence and morality, served as a springboard for future scholars.

Feminist Criticism

Among the critical issues gaining prominence during this period, what came to be known as "the woman question" inspired much scholarship, especially beginning in the late 1970s. The growing field of feminist criticism focused on James's female characters, the extent of his sympathy with women, his privileging of a feminine point of view, and his interest in women's minds. As with most questions concerning James, this one resulted in debate, with some scholars arguing that for James, women were more liberated than men to know themselves and to reflect on the ways that social constraints shaped them, and others arguing that James demeaned women, circumscribed their choices, and repeatedly undermined their freedom.

In *A Woman's Place in the Novels of Henry James* (1984), Elizabeth Allen built upon the work of Judith Fryer, who identified several categories of James women in the 1976 volume *The Faces of Eve: Women in the Nineteenth Century Novel* — the American Princess, the Great Mother, and the New Woman; and Judith Fetterly, who argued for James's belief in women's powerlessness in *The Resisting Reader: A Feminist Approach to American Fiction* (1978). Allen, taking a structuralist perspective, looked at James's use of women as signs and as consciousness. As sign, representative of a type, women are visible objects of interpretation for other characters; this process of interpretation enhances the contrast between appearance and essence. Because women are open to interpretation according to others' expectations, they may manipulate their appearance so as to exert some control over what others conclude about them. In considering a woman's consciousness, James asks how she interprets her own experience, constructs herself in the contexts of others, and has the potential for power in her world. According to Allen, James saw the type of the American girl particularly useful for his explorations of consciousness because the American girl signified for him "the individualistic spontaneity, freedom and innocence of the New World," while at the same time she exhibited the contradictions of spirit and a vulnerability to misinterpretation that made her complex and that ensured her plight would create tension (10). As James sees them, women are necessarily outsiders to a culture in which men by virtue of their gender are able to wield more power even — as in *The Portrait of a Lady* — when a woman can match a man's wealth. There is a disparity between the apparent opportunities and actual choices available to Isabel Archer, "a disparity," Allen says, "which suggests a fundamental failure in the conception of the freedom of the American girl" (83). In *The Golden Bowl*, Allen argues, as in other novels, women's function "is to mediate experience for those in control; to order either by representation, or by arranging existing appearances and making sense of them" (185–86).

Much feminist criticism focused on *The Bostonians*, in which aspiration to power is starkly visible in the struggle between Basil Ransom and Olive Chancellor for domination of the passive Verena Tarrant. Allen, like Judith Fetterly and other feminist critics, maintains that James is not validating masculine power and portraying Olive as perverse, but rather opposing two powerful figures to Verena's submissive identity, her willingness to be interpreted, and her lack of self-reflection about her own potential to signify or her creativity as an interpreter of her own experiences.

According to Nina Auerbach, writing in 1978, *The Bostonians* was part of a tradition with antecedents in Louisa May Alcott's *Little Women* and Elizabeth Gaskell's *Cranford*, novels that celebrated the strength of communities of women. "Olive," Auerbach maintains, "is echoing Alcott's faith that a solitary woman is a fragment of a greater female whole, an irresistible mystical body with the power to cleanse history" (191). James identified the new American girl with America's nationhood; in Auerbach's view, James's works "abound in obsessive references to the domination of America by women," yet she admits that these references are "oddly insistent but uncertain" in tone (192) as James explores the possibility and implications of this new power.

Virginia Fowler, in *Henry James's American Girl* (1984), argued that James creates a "central paradox": a woman's "innocence, spontaneity, and purity . . . offers an alternative to the old corruption of Europe and the rampant materialism of America," but the nineteenth-century American girl has been nurtured in a culture that has blighted and weakened her (8). Bringing Jacques Lacan's theory of psychological development to her consideration of James's women, Fowler believes that James confronted his American girls with the challenge of becoming a subjective "I" — "to be an agent of action rather than simply a receiver or object of action" (33). According to Lacan, existing within the subjective "I" means to accept ambiguity and to recognize that a fully unified self is not possible. This recognition, which shattered his heroines' psychological provincialism, occurred when they encountered the foreign, the Other, and saw themselves in a vastly new way. Although James's women failed to completely achieve selfhood, at least they lost some debilitating illusions about themselves and their culture.

Alfred Habegger offered a dissenting view in his two considerations of gender in James's works: *Gender, Fantasy, and Realism in American Literature* (1982) and *Henry James and the "Woman Business"* (1989). According to Habegger, James "grew up a genderless man with a dark suspicion that all sexual roles and functions are sinister." As a writer, he created fictions that centered on "sensitive, genderless minds, usually devoid of desire, who discover the secret shameful facts of life about a species essentially alien" (*Gender* 255). That "species," whether American or European, male or female, is alien because it consists of humans who are actors in, and not merely observers of, society. Not only does Habegger refute the idea that James admired women because they were outsiders and potentially more sensitive and empathic than men, but he also refutes other critics' arguments that seeing is a more intense and significant activity than acting: indeed, that seeing equals being. Habegger believes that James encountered the world with eyes shut, that he retreated into his own consciousness and created characters who withdrew into themselves as well. James could do nothing more than chronicle "the varied movements of the searching but still innocent mind" (*Gender* 280–81).

James focused on the female mind, according to Habegger, largely because women novelists and their women-centered plots dominated popular fiction in the mid-nineteenth century. James read these novels, reviewed many of them, and drew on their conventions in his own fiction. Repeatedly, his heroine is a young woman yearning to be independent who eventually pairs herself with a much older lover. In fiction by women writers, this alliance gives the young woman love and protection; in James's retelling, the older lover undermines the young woman's freedom. In this way, Habegger says, James "betrayed" women's fiction, insisted that the American girl could not handle too much freedom, and caused her to be defeated in the end (*Woman Business* 26).

In the 1990s and after, feminist criticism became integrated into, and for some critics subsumed by, gender studies and queer studies, with scholars focusing pointedly on sexuality and power. Chapter 7 takes up these critical perspectives for which writers in the 1970s and '80s laid the groundwork.

James and Culture

Besides feminist criticism, cultural criticism also energized scholars during the 1960s through the 1980s. Scholars investigated the scope of James's imagination in the context of his autobiographical writings, nineteenth-century history, and literary precedents. To what extent was James intellectually embedded in his own time? And to what extent did he offer a cultural critique through his fictions? Writing in 1972, Martha Banta, for example, examined James's interest in the occult. Contemporary thinking about the supernatural inspired that interest, Banta argues, but James cannot be counted among the spiritualists of his time although, like many of his contemporaries, he shared an interest in the ineffable. James, Banta says, focused on the psychological effect of believing in the supernatural; he acknowledged the existence of inexplicable forces and the possibility of the uncanny that could generate a sense of anxiety for his characters and for the reader.

Certainly some of the works that Banta considers in her study of the occult raise the question of evil, which Peter Brooks, writing in 1976, examined in the context of Balzac and French drama. Brooks focuses on the conflict of good and evil, arguing that James's use of melodrama stemmed from "his desire to make ethical conflict, imperative, and choice the substance of the novel, to make it the nexus of 'character' and the motivation of plot" (159). Focusing on *The Turn of the Screw*, the work that overtly questions the possibility of evil, Brooks thinks both Edmund Wilson and Dorothea Krook took too limited a view. According to Wilson, Brooks writes, "if there is no objective evidence of the presence of evil at Bly and of the corruption of the children," then evil must lie in the consciousness of the person who perceives it; and here, Brooks says, "he finds hints enough to establish a plausible, if extrapolated, case" (167). Brooks thinks Krook was "excessively theological" because she sees the tale as "a Faustian struggle of corruption and attempted salvation. . . ." For Brooks, betrayal is James's central theme. "Evil is treacherous in that its darkest intent is dissimulated under layers of good manners or even beneath the threshold of consciousness in the evildoer himself; and evil is treachery in that it means denying to someone the means to free realization of his (or so much more often in James, her) full potential as a moral being." Treachery is opposed not by innocence, "but more forcefully loyalty, what might best be characterized in James's own terms as 'kindness': the refusal to do hurt, the refusal to betray, a full awareness of the independence of other beings" (169). As Brooks sees it, James did not define "good" as innocence or purity; a good person is aware of evil — even within himself or herself — but nevertheless is able to make ethical choices that insure another's integrity.

The problematic theme of evil arises in Shoshana Felman's Lacanian reading of *The Turn of the Screw*, "Henry James: Madness and the Risks of Practice (Turning the Screw of Interpretation)," first published in 1985 and reprinted many times since, which asks about the reader's relationship to and participation in a work that presents us with the uncanny and immoral, a work that James's contemporaries saw as scandalous. Like Brooks, Felman sees Edmund Wilson's Freudian reading as reductive, contrived to provide too simple an answer to a question about the governess's reliability, sexuality, or even sanity. Wilson, according to Felman, took psychoanalysis to mean a literal transformation of one text — James's language, symbols, allusions — into another: a Freudian revision, a simple equation. Felman, though, argues that Wilson's effort to interpret the text according to Freudian psychoanalysis ensnares him in a trap of misinterpretation and the very atmosphere of suspicion that the governess herself enacts. Besides presenting her reading of *The Turn of the Screw*, Felman offers a self-reflective analysis of the critical process itself, questions the perspective of the critic ostensibly outside of the text under analysis, and asserts that literature does not allow a place outside the text but by its very nature involves a reader within the workings of the text.

It is no wonder that the entwinement of author, text, and critic became increasingly visible in the last quarter of the twentieth century, with the author's relationship to the marketplace in a commodity culture emerging as a fertile area of criticism. William Veeder set the stage for this work in his *Henry James — the Lessons of the Master: Popular Fiction and Personal Style in the Nineteenth Century* (1975). Dissatisfied with New Criticism's wresting works from their historical context, Veeder examines James's early works, from *Watch and Ward* (1871) to *The Portrait of a Lady* (1881), to show, as he puts it, "how Victorian scribblers and young James used hallowed stylistic techniques," and how, by the time he wrote *The Portrait*, James "transformed the conventional materials of his genre . . ." (8). James learned these conventions, Veeder argues, from a wide range of authors, not limited to such major writers as Dickens and Trollope, and including the "fashionable trash" of the "scribbling women" that James derided (8). James, Veeder says, was an omnivorous reader who became well aware of what the Victorian reader wanted from fiction: "Primarily, the Victorian reader wants security, wants reassurance that God is in His heaven or at least that order remains on earth. Popular fiction provides this security by replacing 'things as they are' with idealized situations and happy endings." Assured of a happy resolution, the Victorian reader delighted in violence: "hairbreadth escapes, touching deaths, violent confrontations" (18). In addition to considering James in the context of Victorian fiction, Veeder also discusses the profound cultural, industrial, and technological changes that occurred in this decade, and their effect on James's intellectual life.

Veeder's historical and literary contextualization of James offered a model for other scholars such as Marcia Jacobson, Jean-Christophe Agnew, and Jonathan Freedman. In *Henry James and the Mass Market* (1983), Jacobson agreed with Veeder that James, in an effort to please a large readership, incorporated styles of popular genres into such works as *The Bostonians* and *The Tragic Muse*. Agnew, in "The Consuming Vision of Henry James" (1983), identified James as an early critic of America's consumer culture and examined the role of commodities in *The American Scene*, the autobiography, and several works of fiction, discovering a new polarity: between what James calls "privacy," or resistance to the marketplace, and "publicity," by which he refers to "the traffic in commodities, the habit of display, the inclination to theatricality, the worship of novelty and quantity" (76). Agnew cites what James calls his "visionary ache," a longing for impressions that began when he was a boy and, as Agnew describes him, "window-shopped his way through Europe" (81). Especially after 1886, Agnew sees, the consuming vision was central to James's fiction, especially in such works as *The Aspern Papers, The Spoils of Poynton, The Sacred Fount,* and *The Golden Bowl*. The latter novel, Agnew argues, "offers itself as the first fully achieved literary expression of an American culture of consumption" (91) because it best demonstrates the Jamesian polarity of possession of commodities or renunciation.

By the time Jonathan Freedman took up a similar question in *Professions of Taste: Henry James, British Aestheticism, and Commodity Culture* in 1990, cultural critique itself, and the idea of commodity culture in particular, was raising theoretical questions that inspired in Freedman the kind of self-consciousness that Felman also manifested. Acknowledging James's professed resistance to a culture in which he energetically participated, Freedman nevertheless thinks it important to situate James in the context of British aestheticism to deal with the recurring accusation of James's "withdrawal from the soil of social reality . . . into the never-never land of art" (xiii). To counter assertions by such critics as Brooks, Parrington, and Geismer, James's champions in the 1940s and '50s sought to erase any connection between James and British aesthetes, and thereby to argue for James's passionate engagement in real life. Freedman sees this defense as contributing to a mistaken definition of British aestheticism, much as James himself made when he defined the aesthete on the model of Oscar Wilde. As Freedman sees it, "both Jacobite and anti-Jacobite understandings of aestheticism seem remarkably reductive" (xviii). The aesthete claimed to be "the consummate professional," possessing special knowledge about the "mysterious entity" of the aesthetic and imparting that knowledge to the public. This rarefied professionalism was supposed to place the aesthete outside of consumer culture, and yet, Freedman argues, "the aesthete both enacts and represents the commodification of art" (xix). According to Freedman, James's views on British aestheticism shaped his own fiction and his understanding of himself as an artist; in addition, James helped to redefine aestheticism itself, which entered cultural life, Freedman says, "under the sign of modernism" (xxvi). James took a prominent role in training his reading public "to expect its writers and artists to be alienated, self-satisfied, and flamboyant; to expect their discourse to be hermetic, privatized, and self-referential; and, at the same time, to instruct these writers and artists to walk the delicate line between insulting and indulging the middle-class audience who patronized their work with increasing avidity" (xxiv–xxv).

Scholars claimed James as a cultural critic in other ways too. Fogel, for example, reads "The Jolly Corner" as James's exploration of the potential of American identity, basing his interpretation, in part, on an entry in James's notebooks that Dorothea Krook also cited — a note about recovering a dead self. In this entry of 5 February 1895, James returned to an idea that had intrigued him a year before: a Dead Self that "lives for him still in some indirect way, in the sympathy, the fidelity (the relation of some kind) of another . . . and what I wanted not to let slip altogether was simply some reminder of the beauty, the little tragedy, attached perhaps to the situation of the man of genius who, in some accursed hour of his youth, has bartered away the fondest vision of that youth and lives ever afterwards in the shadow of the bitterness of the regret." This protagonist, James said, would recover "a little of the lost joy, of the Dead Self, in his intercourse with some person, some woman, who knows what that self was, in which it still lives a little" (Edel and Powers, *Notebooks*, 112–13).

Fogel argues that if this dead self is Spencer Brydon's worst self, the theme becomes more interesting than merely the hackneyed theme of a man's regret over lost chances. As Fogel sees it, Brydon's worst self is not only the shortcomings he tried to slough off, but the worst that he became, "particularly his isolating egotism" (Gargano 199). Noting that other critics have found biographical parallels between James and Brydon, Fogel cautions against a too easy equation of author and character who both left America and lived in Europe as expatriates for several decades. Fogel focuses on James's numerology in the story and argues that the centennial aspect of the story is significant: Brydon would have begun his expatriation in America's centennial year, which suggests to Fogel that Alice Staverton embodies the old New York for which James was nostalgic. Alice "represents the best American spirit," and therefore the tale is not anti-American, as some critics have called it. "Brydon, then, accepts the best in his American identity when he is reborn to reciprocal love with Alice," and he rejects the worst, which is America's insistence on participation in a fiercely competitive marketplace (196). Brydon's "hunger for an expanding consciousness, the very appetite for perception that makes him seek his alternative self so steadfastly and at such manifest risk, is superior to the mere 'rank money passion' and appetite for power of the worst self" (198).

In exploring James's interest in cultural criticism, scholars often questioned his place in literary history. Tracing James's connection to literary antecedents, Lyall Powers makes a case for James as naturalist, influenced by such writers as Gustave Flaubert, Edmond de Goncourt, Ivan Turgenev, Emile Zola, Alphonse Daudet, and Guy de Maupassant. These realist and naturalist writers, themselves heirs of Balzac, came to James's attention in 1875 and, Powers argues, caused a significant change in his subject matter and literary technique. In such later novels as *The Bostonians, The Princess Casamassima*, and *The Tragic Muse*, James moved out of the milieu that characterized his earlier work to focus on the lower classes and some volatile social issues. Powers is careful to assert that James was not translating the concerns of the naturalists into his own fiction, only that "the aesthetic principles of the Flaubert group" inspired him to experimentation and a widening of his scope (2).

In *Henry James and the French Novel* (1973), Philip Grover focuses on Balzac and Flaubert as particularly pervasive influences on James's themes and techniques. Grover offers a useful chronology of James's life and work, citing James's readings and responses to French literature as they appear in his correspondence and autobiographies. Building upon Powers, Grover, and other scholars, Pierre Walker, in *Reading Henry James in French Cultural Contexts* (1995), expands an inquiry about James's connection with French fiction by considering how French popular literature, including experimental and sentimental novels, influenced *The Princess Casamassima, The Ambassadors, The Awkward Age, Washington Square,* and *The Tragic Muse.*

Fogel cites Tintner's discovery of allusions to Keats in James's work as inspiration for his argument about James's inheritance of Romantic tradition in his themes and structures. Romanticism concerned itself with the quest for experience and an ensuing evolution of consciousness as a character moves toward insight. The structure of the quest, as Fogel sees it, involves a "spiral dialectic . . . a motion from 'innocence' through 'experience' to 'organized innocence' ": that is, a "synthesizing, circular ascent" (4). James begins with what Fogel calls "bipolar" oppositions — American/European, innocence/experience, idealism/pragmatism, appearance/reality — that create the essential tension of his fictions and which James explores through a dialectic structure. Fogel examines this structure in some of James's tales and four novels, *The Awkward Age, The Ambassadors, The Wings of the Dove,* and *The Golden Bowl,* to argue that the structure itself reflects not the dual nature of James's own mind — which he believes Edel reductively asserts — but rather the literary influences of such writers as Goethe, Coleridge, Keats, and Blake.

John Carlos Rowe explores James's anxiety of influence by Hawthorne, Trollope, and other nineteenth-century writers in his first chapter of *The Theoretical Dimensions of Henry James* (1984). This chapter grounds Rowe's consideration of some of James's major works through the lens of feminist, psychoanalytic, Marxist, phenomenological, and reader-response criticism. His study, then, serves as an overview of James criticism up to the early 1980s, and therefore is useful not only for Rowe's measured reading of such fiction as *The Bostonians, The Aspern Papers, The Turn of the Screw,* and *The Princess Casamassima,* but also for his synthesis of critical perspectives. As he says, he proposes "to read the theoretical potential of Henry James" (xiii): that is, to show how different perspectives can illuminate James's works, and also to "evaluate the respective limitations of those theoretical positions" (24). Rowe's study has endured as one of the most incisive and careful investigations of both James and the theoretical perspectives applied to his works.

In the last few decades, James scholarship has garnered considerable attention especially in two areas: questions about Jamesian consciousness, and issues of gender. Certainly other questions have also generated interest, as a glance at any issue of the *Henry James Review* can attest. But because writing on consciousness and on gender has been so prolific and controversial, I devote the following two chapters specifically to these issues.

Works Cited

Agnew, Jean-Christophe. "The Consuming Vision of Henry James." In *The Culture of Consumption: Critical Essays in American History, 1880–1980*, edited by Richard Wightman Fox and T. J. Jackson Lears, 65–100. New York: Pantheon, 1983.

Allen, Elizabeth. *A Woman's Place in the Novels of Henry James*. New York: St. Martin's, 1984.

Auerbach, Nina. "*The Bostonians*: Feminists and the New World." In *American Novelists Revisited: Essays in Feminist Criticism*, edited by Fritz Fleishmann, 189–208. Boston: G. K. Hall, 1982.

Banta, Martha. *Henry James and the Occult*. Bloomington: Indiana UP, 1972.

Blackmur, Richard P. *Studies in Henry James*. Edited by Veronica A. Makowsky. New York: New Directions, 1983.

Booth, Wayne C. *The Rhetoric of Fiction*. Chicago: U of Chicago P, 1983 [1961].

Brooks, Peter. *The Melodramatic Imagination: Balzac, Henry James, Melodrama and the Mode of Excess*. New Haven, CT: Yale UP, 1976.

Cargill, Oscar. *The Novels of Henry James*. New York: Macmillan, 1961.

Crews, Frederick C. *The Tragedy of Manners: Moral Drama in the Later Novels of Henry James*. Hamden, CT: Archon Books, 1971 [1957].

Edel, Leon, ed. *Henry James: A Collection of Critical Essays*. Englewood Cliffs, NJ: Prentice Hall, 1963.

Edel, Leon, and Lyall H. Powers, eds. *The Complete Notebooks of Henry James*. New York: Oxford UP, 1987.

Felman, Shoshana, "Henry James: Madness and the Risks of Practice (Turning the Screw of Interpretation)." In *Writing and Madness (Literature/Philosophy/Psychoanalysis)*, translated by Martha Noel Evans, Shoshana Felman, and Brian Massumi, 141–247. Ithaca, NY: Cornell UP, 1985.

Fetterly, Judith. "*The Bostonians*: Henry James's Eternal Triangle." *The Resisting Reader: A Feminist Approach to American Fiction*, 101–53. Bloomington: Indiana UP, 1978.

Fogel, Daniel Mark. *Henry James and the Structure of the Romantic Imagination*. Baton Rouge: Louisiana State UP, 1981.

———. "A New Reading of Henry James's 'The Jolly Corner.'" In Gargano, *The Late Novels*, 190–203.

Fowler, Virginia C. *Henry James's American Girl: The Embroidery on the Canvas*. Madison: U of Wisconsin P, 1984.

Freedman, Jonathan, ed. *The Cambridge Companion to Henry James*. Cambridge: Cambridge UP, 1998.

———. *Professions of Taste: Henry James, British Aestheticism, and Commodity Culture*. Stanford, CA: Stanford UP, 1990.

Fryer, Judith. *The Faces of Eve: Women in the Nineteenth Century American Novel*. Oxford: Oxford UP, 1976.

Funston, Judith E. *Henry James, 1975–1987: A Reference Guide*. Boston: G. K. Hall, 1991.

Gale, Robert. *Plots and Characters in the Fiction of Henry James*. Hamden, CT: Archon Books, 1965.

Gargano, James W., ed. *Critical Essays on Henry James: The Early Novels*. Boston: G. K. Hall, 1987.

———, ed. *Critical Essays on Henry James: The Late Novels*. Boston: G. K. Hall, 1987.

Geismar, Maxwell. *Henry James and the Jacobites*. Boston: Houghton Mifflin, 1963.

Goode, John. *The Air of Reality: New Essays on Henry James*. London: Methuen, 1972.

Graham, Kenneth. *Henry James, The Drama of Fulfillment*. Oxford: Clarendon Press, 1975.

Grover, Philip. *Henry James and the French Novel*. New York: Barnes & Noble, 1973.

Habegger, Alfred. *Gender, Fantasy, and Realism in the American Novel*. New York: Columbia UP, 1982.

———. *Henry James and the "Woman Business."* Cambridge: Cambridge UP, 1989.

Hocks, Richard A. *Henry James and Pragmatistic Thought: A Study in the Relationship between the Philosophy of William James and the Literary Art of Henry James*. Chapel Hill: U of North Carolina P, 1974.

Holland, Laurence B. *The Expense of Vision: Essays on the Craft of Henry James*. Princeton, NJ: Princeton UP, 1964.

Jacobson, Marcia. *Henry James and the Mass Market*. University: U of Alabama P, 1983.

James, Henry. *Literary Criticism: Essays on Literature, American Writers, English Writers*. New York: The Library of America, 1984.

Krook, Dorothea. *The Ordeal of Consciousness in Henry James*. New York: Cambridge UP, 1962.

Miller, James E. "Henry James in Reality." *Critical Inquiry* 2, no. 3 (Spring 1976): 585–604.

Poirier, Richard. *The Comic Sense of Henry James: A Study of the Early Novels*. New York: Oxford UP, 1960.

Powers, Lyall. *Henry James and the Naturalist Movement*. East Lansing: Michigan State UP, 1971.

———. *Henry James's Major Novels; Essays in Criticism*. East Lansing: Michigan State UP, 1973.

Rowe, John Carlos. *The Theoretical Dimensions of Henry James*. Madison: U of Wisconsin P, 1984.

Scura, Dorothy McInnis. *Henry James, 1960–1974: A Reference Guide*. Boston: G. K. Hall, 1979.

Sears, Sallie. *The Negative Imagination: Form and Perspective in the Novels of Henry James*. Ithaca, NY: Cornell UP, 1968.

Segal, Ora. *The Lucid Reflector: The Observer in Henry James' Fiction*. New Haven, CT: Yale UP, 1969.

Skrupskelis, Ignas, and Elizabeth M. Berkeley. *The Correspondence of William James*. Vol. 3, *William and Henry, 1897–1910*. Charlottesville: U of Virginia P, 1994.

Tintner, Adeline. *The Book World of Henry James*. Ann Arbor, MI: UMI Research Press, 1987.

———. *The Museum World of Henry James*. Ann Arbor, MI: UMI Research Press, 1985.

———. *The Pop World of Henry James*. Ann Arbor, MI: UMI Research Press, 1989.

Veeder, William. *Henry James — The Lessons of the Master: Popular Fiction and Personal Style in the Nineteenth Century*. Chicago: U of Chicago P, 1975.

Wagenknecht, Edward. *Eve and Henry James: Portraits of Women and Girls in His Fiction*. Norman: U of Oklahoma P, 1978.

———. *The Novels of Henry James*. New York: Ungar, 1983.

———. *The Tales of Henry James*. New York: Ungar, 1984.

Walker, Pierre A. *Reading Henry James in French Cultural Contexts*. DeKalb: Northern Illinois UP, 1995.

Winner, Viola Hopkins. *Henry James and the Visual Arts*. Charlottesville: U of Virginia P, 1970.

Yeazell, Ruth, ed. *Henry James: A Collection of Critical Essays*. Englewood Cliffs, NJ: Prentice Hall, 1994.

———. *Language and Knowledge in the Late Novels of Henry James*. Chicago: U of Chicago P, 1976.

6: Jamesian Consciousness: Mind, Morality, and the Problem of Truth

> *The novel is of all pictures the most comprehensive and the most elastic. It will stretch anywhere — it will take in absolutely anything. . . . For its subject, magnificently, it has the whole human consciousness.*
>
> — Henry James, "The Future of the Novel"

IN HIS OWN TIME, James's interest in his characters' minds seemed a shortcoming to readers who failed to identify with men and women who intellectualized — felt and observed — rather than acted. During the James renaissance of the 1940s, however, critics increasingly focused on James's attention to the mind. Osborn Andreas, for example, in *Henry James and the Expanding Horizon* (1948), called James "the novelist of consciousness," for whom thinking was an act of freedom and creativity. Indeed, Andreas wrote, "creative awareness of things" was, for James, the greatest good (1). By the 1960s, many scholars decided that James's preoccupation with consciousness ranked him with such modernists as James Joyce, Samuel Beckett, William Faulkner, and Virginia Woolf. If James had been a writer ahead of his time, as H. G. Dwight had asserted in 1907, then by the middle of the twentieth century, his time had come. In the past few decades, as critical perspectives increasingly have drawn upon philosophy, psychology, and cultural studies, a focus on consciousness has become central to James scholarship.

A few questions recur to inform this scholarship: How do we know reality? What of reality can we know? Is the self a transcendent entity or is it socially constructed? Some scholars explore these questions in the context of nineteenth-century psychological theories, asking, for example, about the relationship between perception and identity, and about the existence of a stable, unified self. To what extent is it possible to know the self? Does self-knowledge afford freedom? Is the self mutable, malleable, adaptable? To what extent is it possible to know another? Scholars extend these questions when they explore the relationship of knowing to morality. How, they ask, does knowledge affect ethical decisions? What does James mean by "moral consciousness?" Does James have faith that truth is discoverable, or does he believe that truths are various and created by individuals?

Investigating the connection of knowledge to ethics has suggested to many scholars, not limited to those with affinities to Michel Foucault, that there exists a connection of knowledge to power. As Jonathan Freedman noted in a review of Mark Seltzer's *Henry James and the Art of Power* (1985), such scholarship reveals "a James more fully practiced in his deployment of the tactics of power, a James more fully enmeshed in the social circumstance, and a James more cannily uncanny in the ghastly mildness with which he encounters both his own powers and those of the social formations in which they are embedded" (329–30). Seltzer and scholars interested in how James interprets pragmatism explore ways in which the self is socially and culturally constructed — and not only the self, but the genre of the novel as well.

In his prefaces to the New York Edition, James points to consciousness as a central element in literary fiction. "The great chroniclers," he wrote in his preface to *The Princess Casamassima*, ". . . have at least always placed a mind of some sort — in the sense of a reflecting and colouring medium — in possession of the general adventure . . . or else paid signally, as to the interest created, for their failure to do so" (67). The more we know of characters' minds, James said, the more "their emotions, their stirred intelligence, their moral consciousness, become . . . our own very adventure" (70); we share in the perspective of characters able to serve as "intense *perceivers*, all, of their respective predicaments" (71). In his much-quoted preface to *The Portrait of a Lady*, James was explicit about his focus on the mind of Isabel Archer: " 'Place the centre of the subject in the young woman's own consciousness,' I said to myself, 'and you get as interesting and as beautiful a difficulty as you could wish. Stick to *that* — for the centre; put the heaviest weight into *that* scale . . . of her relation to herself. Make her only interested enough, at the same time, in the things that are not herself, and this relation need n't fear to be too limited' " (51). As this chapter demonstrates, scholars look at not only the consciousness of James's characters, but at those of the author and his readers as well; not only at what characters see but what James chose to see; not only at what characters discover but how James manages to lead readers to make their own discoveries.

Consequences of Seeing

The act of seeing in Jamesian fiction offers both opportunity and danger. For example, Isabel Archer's sudden glimpse of Madame Merle standing while Gilbert Osmond is seated when alone in a room together reveals to her an undeniable truth about their intimacy. Seeing may generate knowledge, but knowledge may erode comforting assumptions or change one's sense of identity. Moreover, one character's knowledge may undermine another's freedom and certainly may invite manipulation. In "The Jamesian Lie," published in the *Partisan Review* in 1969 and reprinted in *A Future for Astyanax* (1984), Leo Bersani focused particularly on "the confrontation in nineteenth-century works between a structured, socially viable and verbally analyzable self and the wish to shatter psychic and social structures [that] produces considerable stress and conflict" (x). He argues that James's recurring project was to explore the limits of freedom, and the connection of freedom to seeing. For James's characters, "nothing is more stimulating, more exhilarating . . . than that of recognition which they constantly and somewhat breathlessly confirm" (133). Through seeing, they sometimes are shocked so profoundly from their accustomed and comfortable worldview that they reach a crucial revelation, often of betrayal, that changes their perception of their own reality.

If freedom may be won through seeing, that achievement is not always positive. Bersani notes that some characters try to escape from seeing by what he calls "a luminous blindness," or "a radical casting of doubt on the objects of vision" (136). Bersani recognizes that James imposed restraints on seeing. Characters cannot see everything available to them, but only what they select to see; and what they select "invents and satisfies desires which meet only a minimal resistance from either the external world or internal depths" (146). Furthermore, whatever is seen becomes transformed into language, which itself limits understanding. Language, Bersani writes, "promotes new versions of being. . . . Nothing impedes the play of the Jamesian 'I' — but the 'I' itself has become merely the neutral territory occupied by language, that is, by a system which is by nature always 'outside' any particular self" (146).

Like many other scholars, Bersani connected seeing to power over others. Seeing may involve usurping others' realities, turning them into texts open to interpretation or misinterpretation. When this act compels characters to revise their understanding of reality, that revision may prove "agonizing," Bersani says; it may destroy their "taste for life," as it does with Isabel Archer and Lambert Strether (148).

Carolyn Porter further explored the connection of freedom to power in *Seeing and Being: The Plight of the Participant Observer in Emerson, James, Adams, and Faulkner* (1981), where she applied Georg Lukacs's term *reification* to her Marxist reading of James. As Porter explains, "reification refers to a process in the course of which man becomes alienated from himself" in a world of commodities. Whatever humans create appear "as a given, an external and objective reality operating according to its own immutable laws," and each individual "assumes a passive and 'contemplative' stance in the face of that objectified and rationalized reality — a man who stands outside that reality because his own participation in producing it is mystified" (xi). Porter sees James as heir to Emerson, revising Emerson's transparent eyeball as a lucid reflector, but, Porter cautions, "the lucid reflector serving as a narrative lens is not transparent and cannot blithely float in the 'currents of Universal Being'" (40). James's seer participates in the world that he confronts and creates. James's problem, as Porter conceives it, is "to account for the seer's agency without forfeiting his status as seer" (41). The result, which Porter sees most evident in *The Sacred Fount*, is the conflation of a "visionary poet" with a "capitalist entrepreneur" who reveals a commodified society in which an individual is both consumer and consumed (41).

The seer provoked a narrative problem for James. According to Porter, James could not allow his seers to speak in the first person, functioning as the narrators of their own stories because to do so would contradict their place as outsiders. Instead, James created a third-person center of consciousness that preserved "the contemplative stance of the visionary seer without thereby running the risks entailed by according the seer power to speak directly to the reader" (125). In *The Ambassadors*, for example, Strether is both passive and impotent; he can see, but that is all he can do. In *The Portrait of a Lady*, Isabel can see, but only to "survey her prison walls" (126). Still, even the most powerless seer proved to be "inevitably complicit in the events he serves to record," a complicity that raises a moral problem. In *The Portrait of a Lady*, James solves the problem by giving the seer Ralph Touchett god-like, and therefore artist-like, powers over other characters; in *The Sacred Fount*, Maggie becomes the seer who wields power by exploiting "her own bewilderment," her own lack of knowledge (134).

James's narrative problems were taken up by Adré Marshall in *The Turn of the Mind: Constituting Consciousness in Henry James* (1998), a formalist reading focused on the literary strategies James employs to depict thinking. Marshall notes that "figural narration" is evident in James's later works: in figural narration "the omniscient narrator is suppressed; the narrator becomes invisible or inaudible and his or her place is taken by a figural medium or reflector character" who, "tainted with subjectivity," may or may not be reliable (18). In order to bridge the intellectual or ethical gap between narrator and reflector, James used the mode of free indirect discourse (31). Marshall grounds her study in the theoretical work of Dorrit Cohn, who posited three features that characterize the narrating consciousness: "psycho-narration: the narrator's discourse about a character's consciousness"; "quoted monologue: a character's mental discourse"; and "narrated monologue: a character's mental discourse in the guise of the narrator's discourse" (45). These three techniques, Marshall argues, result in a more complex depiction of character than does the deployment simply of an omniscient narrator. Marshall's taxonomy responds to the question of how James conveys meaning, but her largely descriptive study does not suggest the implications of his narrative technique for our understanding of the reader's role in creating meaning nor, really, what it is that James means to convey.

Whether seeing is truly an engagement in experience — the question that continues to beset critics — concerned Carren Kaston in *Imagination and Desire in the Novels of Henry James* (1984). Kaston notes recurring instances of renunciation of experience and power "for the solitary pleasures of consciousness, vision, and memory" (ix). According to Kaston, critics have understood the seer as synonymous with the artist, concluding that the artist or writer renounced living in the world in favor of living in the mind. "Renunciation," Kaston writes, "may be regarded as the gesture of both an empathic self, which registers and identifies with the feelings and points of view of other characters, and an evacuated self, which has abandoned its 'center' to the fictions or versions of life created in it by the other points of view that it contains" (2). Each character invents a fiction that becomes his or her own story. Kaston argues further that James invented some characters, such as Fleda Vetch in *The Spoils of Poynton* or Lambert Strether in *The Ambassadors*, who act as representatives for others, interrupting their own selfhood to become a "socialized or domesticated" version of Emerson's "visionary eyeball self. Being visionary now meant floating out over other characters' consciousness, becoming a medium of reception capable of registering what it was like to be them, at the risk . . . of making the personal self tenuous" (69). For James, Kaston says, this empathy was a supremely moral act, since it meant that an individual transcended his or her own needs and desires to imagine another person's experience. But transcending one's desires, in Jamesian fiction, often does not lead to liberation, but rather to renunciation.

Surely the most insistent and controversial study of the connection of selfhood to power appears in Mark Seltzer's *Henry James and the Art of Power* (1984). Seltzer notes that past critics — James's champions in mid-century, for example — agreed with James that desiring power was scandalous, claiming that James had never been "tempted by the political and always resisted the exercise of power" (13). Although in the 1970s many feminist critics focused on power dynamics between men and women, Seltzer does not refer to these studies, but instead grounds his work in the cultural theory of Michel Foucault. Seltzer concedes that Bersani rightly identified James's central theme as freedom, but Seltzer believes that this concern with freedom urges scholars to look closely at "all that is seen to constrict freedom . . . law, power, and authority." For Seltzer, power and authority are not "external interventions in the novel but are already immanent in the novelist's policies of representation" (15–16). The literary cannot be seen as opposed to the political, but inextricably bound to it.

Seltzer, therefore, sets himself the task of examining such themes as surveillance and supervision in *The Princess Casamassima*; the social policies of control in *The Golden Bowl*; and James's critique of the structures of power in *The American Scene*. Far from arguing that James resisted exercising power, Seltzer argues that power is the overriding theme in James's fiction and, indeed, in the genre of the novel: "the manner in which the novel at once acts as a relay of social mechanisms of regulation and lays claim to an autonomy and difference from the political, a claim to autonomy that may ultimately support these mechanisms" (192). Other scholars, such as Paul Armstrong, Winfried Fluck, and Colin Meissner, take issue with Seltzer's portrayal of James as a conspirator in the manipulation of his characters and his readers, even going so far as to accuse Seltzer — in his standing as an academic scholar — of being caught up in the very hierarchies of power that he notes in James's work.

Although such critiques as Seltzer's testify to the importance of cultural studies in James scholarship, this perspective has not effaced psychoanalytic criticism, as can be seen in Beth Sharon Ash's reading of *The Golden Bowl* entitled "Narcissism and the Gilded Image" (1994). Ash argues that Maggie Verver's motivation is desire, not only for power, but "in terms of an archaic structure of both oedipal and preoedipal narcissistic wishes" (55). Although Ash agrees with Mark Seltzer that in the novel "love and control coincide," Seltzer, Ash believes, does not help us understand why this is so. Leo Bersani, too, does not consider Maggie's motivation, but explains her behavior as pure intelligence, mind without self. Ash contends that the oepidal relationship is not resolved for Maggie, but her wishes "continue to exert a powerful regressive pull" (57). Ash says that her perspective is "post-Freudian" since she sees the self as socially constructed, whose "central psychological struggle . . . is between the powerful need to protect bonds with internalized others and various efforts to escape the pains, dangers, and anxieties of those bonds" (58).

In another psychoanalytic reading of James, Donna Przybylowicz, writing in 1987, applies the concept of narcissism to "The Beast in the Jungle," a work she sees as exemplary of the theme of the unlived life. John Marcher does not inhabit the past or present, but a "self-reflecting universe" on which he narcissistically projects his needs and desires. Marcher's narcissism makes him incapable of loving May unless she mirrors his own desires. As Pryzybylowicz reads the tale, although Marcher's is the central consciousness, May's point of view is evident throughout, allowing the narrator to imbue the story with irony.

Despite these various critical perspectives, and the feminist and queer theorists that emerged contemporaneously, aesthetic interpretations also have persisted, notably by Millicent Bell in *Meaning in Henry James* (1991). Bell gently brushes away "a too-literal psycho-historical interpretation" of such works as "The Beast in the Jungle" and *The Turn of the Screw* offered by Eve Sedgwick and Edmund Wilson. She applauds Shoshana Felman's exhaustive refutation of Wilson's Freudian reading of *The Turn of the Screw* in the essay "Henry James: Madness and the Risks of Practice (Turning the Screw of Interpretation)," a study originally published in 1985 and frequently excerpted in critical collections about the work; and Bell cautions against making assumptions about James's sexuality. Instead, Bell argues that James was an impressionist who conveys meaning through "the 'look' of things'. . . . James's impressionism," Bell writes, "is an attitude toward experience and a principle of composition that can be felt throughout his work" and contrasts him with naturalists (5). Bell concedes, along with many of her contemporary critics, that James believed meaning "is not to be imposed upon experience but, problematically, discovered in it," and he is cognizant of the reader's collaboration in interpreting the impressions gleaned from a work of fiction (6–7). If Bell's reading of James may seem blinkered to some scholars, still there emanates from her book a refreshing sense of joy in reading James's fiction that seems to elude other scholars.

Psychologies and Pragmatisms

Inquiries into the theme of power have led some scholars to examine James's understanding of pragmatism, which they take to involve testing ideas through experience within a community. Truths, then, are what ideas become when they prove socially and personally useful for the good of the community and the individual. Henry's access to William's ideas about pragmatism occurred much earlier than 1907, when *Pragmatism* was published, since William had been developing his theories for decades before. In *Henry James and Pragmatistic Thought: A Study in the Relationship between the Philosophy of William James and the Literary Art of Henry James* (1974), Richard Hocks argued that Henry intuitively understood his brother's writings, and created characters who, faced with a plurality of truths, acted pragmatically, rather than according to a prescribed ethical system. Later, in "Multiple Germs, Metaphorical Systems, and Moral Fluctuation in *The Ambassadors*" (1997), Hocks reconsidered Strether's consciousness and, building on the scholarship of Susan Griffin and Paul Armstrong, among others, Hocks argued that Strether's "moral fluctuations" result from a narrative epistemology that does not "rest on the laurels of the transcendent absolute," but instead responds to "a universe both plural and in constant flux, where ideas, even the most profound and useful ones, are 'transitional'" ("Germs" 55).

Exploring intellectual convergences between Henry and William inevitably brought many scholars to consider William's writings on psychology. In her well-regarded study "The Selfish Eye: Strether's Principles of Psychology" (1984), Susan Griffin argued that seeing is not passive, nor does observation oppose experience. Indeed, seeing is part of a complex process whereby characters adapt to the world. In establishing James's connection to his brother's psychological principles, Griffin offers an overview of the two prominent schools of nineteenth-century psychology: associationist, which saw the mind as a blank slate and sensations as discrete units; and functionalist, which saw the individual as actively selecting perceptions from the environment. The passive associationist model contrasted with the active functionalist model. Griffin concludes that Henry James, like his brother, adopted the functionalist model: "What the Jamesian eye sees," Griffin writes, "is always in the interest of the Jamesian 'I'" (398). Although the individual's environment necessarily limits what can be perceived, individuals "survive in their environments by directing their attention towards those perceptions that interest and benefit them" (404). The relationship between an individual and his or her environment, then, is reciprocal: the environment alters needs, the individual sees differently, actions follow new perceptions. Griffin elaborated on the role of the visual in the construction of identity in *The Historical Eye: The Texture of the Visual in the Late James* (1991), which considers seeing in *The Golden Bowl*, *The American Scene*, and the autobiographies.

A provocative dissenter to such views as Hocks's and Griffin's, Sharon Cameron, in *Thinking in Henry James* (1989), argued that consciousness can be understood as disconnected from any individual character's psychology in James's fiction. James "isolated consciousness from realistic considerations of it," Cameron asserts, to reveal it as a force "outside of psychological confines: able to have a life, to be as if embodied, divorced from the strictures of situation and character, made sufficiently independent of these" (2). Although in his prefaces to the New York Edition, James presented consciousness as "centered, subjective, internal, and unitary," Cameron finds that in the novels, "consciousness is not stable, not subjective, not interior, not unitary . . . not in persons; it is rather between them" and "disengaged from the self" (77). In *The American Scene*, for example, Cameron finds consciousness "all-pervasive. . . . Disparate points of view are not significant because they exemplify conflicts in consciousness." Instead, James demonstrates that consciousness is omnipresent, "that there is no place in the book where consciousness has not been made to penetrate" (5). In *The Portrait of a Lady*, Cameron claims that "significant moments in the novel contest the autonomy of Isabel Archer's consciousness," showing it "disrupted and broken into" by a pervading consciousness. As much as James, in his preface, deflects our attention to Isabel as the central consciousness of the novel, Cameron sees instances of Isabel connecting with Madame Merle's thought and even vision.

Although other scholars found Cameron's work original and, as Hocks put it, "bracing," he, for one, maintains that it has some important shortcomings: for one, a few misreadings of certain key passages; for another, "Cameron," Hocks writes, "never bothers to explain *why* James so misconstrued the nature of his artistic consciousness time and again in the Prefaces. Certainly these days we doubt many of James's explanations in the Prefaces about his 'germs' or, say, his judgments of a novel's success or failure, but it is rather different to deny his very conception of consciousness without further explanation of why he made the mistake"

(Review 391). Similarly, Ruth Bernard Yeazell, reviewing the book in *Modern Philology*, praised Cameron for questioning why James's late novels result in "a peculiarly disquieting experience" for readers, and for refusing to treat those novels "as far more conventional than they are." But like Hocks, Yeazell differs with some of Cameron's key readings, and believes that her "rigid distinction between problematic and plot — and her implicit contempt for the latter — also produces some strikingly oversimplified accounts of what in fact happens in late James . . ." (305).

Cameron represented a growing interest among many scholars writing in the late 1980s and 1990s, who engaged themselves in the philosophical issues raised by James's fascination with the mind. One of the most influential and well-respected studies of the similarities and differences between the two famous Jameses is Ross Posnock's *The Trial of Curiosity: Henry James, William James, and the Challenge of Modernity* (1991). Influenced by New Historicism's project of examining texts in their literary, philosophical, political, and sociological contexts, Posnock looked at James's late works, notably *The Ambassadors, The American Scene*, and the autobiographies, to make a case for James's modernism.

Posnock rejects the dualism that has characterized assessments of William and Henry — William as active and manly, Henry as passive and effeminate; both men responded to their shared "cultural moment" that generated "anxiety about and fascination with forms of being that resist normalization, the obedience to social techniques of domination that produce the subject" (29). In that anxious time, Posnock sees the two as "simultaneously interlocked and decisively different" (6). One of the differences lies in their conception of the cognitive possibilities resulting from human relationships; here Posnock offers a characterization of the two men that contradicts popular portraits of William as gregarious and generous, Henry as reclusive. Instead, Posnock argues that unlike William, who believed in the unbreachable separateness of each individual, Henry, especially in his memoirs, seeks "an alternative to an atomized self" (6). Both men resisted authorities, both demonstrated an intensely energetic curiosity, which Posnock defines as "a concept and stance toward the world that is being perennially contested," or, more attractively, as an energy similar to play. For Henry, this curiosity resulted in a "passion for difficulty" and complexity in his writings (54); curious and passionate, Posnock's James is vastly different from the "Olympian formalist and aesthetic idealist" who emerged from earlier critical accounts (80). In fact, in Posnock's view, Henry is the more aggressive modernist, engaging in such "major intellectual debates" as "the philosophical opposition to identity logic" by offering "a way to loosen emotional and sexual constrictions and abandon oneself to the shocks of experience" (81–82).

Posnock believes that Henry revised William's pragmatism by seeing it as more fluid and experimental; William, for his part, pushed pragmatism toward a pluralism that, according to Posnock, "radically narrows our sphere of activity by stripping us of the tools of intellectual experience, relieving us of language, the instrument of intersubjectivity, and deracinating us to float in the flux" (110). Unlike Henry, who was, Posnock argues, a better sociologist than his brother, William did not recognize that "the violence of control is not externally imposed (that is, something one can choose to escape) but rather internalized as the condition of social life" (115). Posnock's revisionist portrait of the two Jameses enhances Henry's reputation as the enactor of a spirit of pragmatism more fully developed, and more philosophically humanistic, than his brother's.

As part of a larger study of the confluences between turn-of-the-century psychology and literature, Judith Ryan, in *The Vanishing Subject: Early Psychology and Literary Modernism* (1991), examined the Henry-William connection by looking first at Henry's ideas about consciousness in the context of nineteenth-century psychology, noting his increasing interest in the mind after William's *The Principles of Psychology* published in 1890. She believes that Henry was interested especially in "the gaps and limitations of consciousness" (76), exemplified in *What Maisie Knew*, where he "was able to explore the relationships between perceptions, verbalization, and intellect" because the young Maisie perceives more than she can communicate (76–77). "The Figure in the Carpet," in Ryan's view, reflects William's notion "that thoughts were just as real as things" because the tale shows "what happens when something that may or may not exist is presumed to do so: what we have is not an empty space, not 'nothing,' but an imaginary object that functions just like a real one in the world of real people and real things." The figure, after all, is a powerful image that sets real events in motion (78). *The Turn of the Screw* also shows how the imaginary, in this case the visions experienced by the governess, "bursts in upon the real" (79).

Ryan says that William's conception of pragmatism also influenced Henry, and she sees evidence of this interest most clearly in *The Ambassadors*, which she calls "an empiricist quest" that reveals the "essential instability" of reality "and validates those components of it which seem most thoroughly mental" (80). Yet rather than portray pragmatism as an optimistic project in which one could "banish (or attempt to banish) troublesome thoughts" and proceed cheerfully by testing ideas in experience, Henry "more often than not reveals the 'pragmatistic' solution as ambiguous and in some sense deeply unsatisfactory" (84). She shows that pragmatism involves "closing one's eyes to complexities one is, on some other level, also constrained to admit" (88). The endings of Henry's novels point to the ambiguity of a pragmatic resolution and the loss that resolution may entail. His characters never attain certainty, but do make moral choices that satisfy them.

Like Porter and other scholars, Ryan connects James's interest in consciousness to the convoluted and difficult style of his late fiction: his "hesitations, parentheses, and constant modifications of what is being said," she writes, "is an attempt to render the elusiveness of experience while also coming to terms with it." In the late fiction, "not only children, like Maisie, but ordinary sensible grown-ups wrestle with the fragmentariness of their perceptual fields and try to find ways to compensate for it" (80).

In writing about Henry's connection to William's ideas, the very definition of the term *pragmatism* often seems slippery and protean. In "Jamesian Pragmatism and Jamesian Realism" (1997), philosopher Harvey Cormier aimed at clarification by distinguishing between two meanings of "truth": one to define the essence of something, and the other to describe the importance of something. Truth, as William James saw it, is "the stuff that's good for intellectual, spiritual, and emotional headaches. It solves problems" (292). He is interested, Cormier says, in "what truth really and contingently *does*" (294). Like William, Henry too was interested in the ways that we come to know the self through action. Without seeing what the self does, we cannot know what it is. Cormier cites Henry James's dissatisfaction with *The American*, which he saw as a romance because it failed to show how selves develop through experiences. For Cormier, Henry James's sense of realism equaled William James's concept of pragmatism.

Cormier's suggestion that both men took a perspective of "literary realism" prompted a conversation, published in the *Henry James Review* in 1997, between Jonathan Levin and Sheldon Novick about Kant's legacy in the works of William and Henry. Levin and Novick agree that the two shared "a belief that the data of material perceptions and the knowledge of moral or spiritual entities both have a kind of objective reality" (303). Both men also recognized two views of how writers reflect experience: William distinguished between idealism and empiricism, Henry between realism and romance. Yet even when creating fiction embedded in material reality, Henry seemed to believe in a separate faculty of the imagination that allows experience to take a coherent shape. William, on the other hand, in his repeated repudiations of Kant, rejected the idea of a separate faculty of imagination. Although Levin and Novick come to no consensus about the influence on Henry of Kant's belief that moral judgments result from a priori, transcendent ideas, they agree that James, as Levin puts it, "is a profoundly moral novelist" (306).

Living Morally

On a parallel track with investigations into Henry's interpretations of pragmatism and pluralism, semiotics, structuralism, phenomenology, and heuristics have focused recent scholarship on Jamesian ways of knowing, scholarship in which Paul Armstrong has become an important voice. "The modern epistemological crisis," Armstrong wrote in *The Phenomenology of*

Henry James (1983), "is also a moral crisis." How, Armstrong asks, are we to "justify our purposes and values in a world of signs that, when interpreted, seem to lead only to other signs and not to any ultimate truth" (210). If, as James's works suggest to many contemporary scholars, the universe does not contain any transcendent truth, how can we live morally and ethically? According to Armstrong, James believes that through experience we can "discover and justify purposes and values to guide our lives" (211). Although experience involves risk, although we may fail at our quest for these values, James nevertheless suggests "that a dialectic of belief and doubt is necessary to realize the potential values intrinsic to existence" (211). We can lead a moral life "by taking seriously the work of expanding what we know, enhancing our sphere of possibilities, and narrowing the gap between the Self and others. On these terms, morality for James is never finally achieved but is always still to be won . . ." (213).

In *The Challenge of Bewilderment* (1987), Armstrong furthered his analysis by arguing that through bewilderment — disorientation and confusion — characters "acquire a new understanding of oneself and one's world" (3). He examines James's narrative strategies, noting "the function of the manner of narration in controlling a work's perspectives and the problem of adjudicating the validity of opposing interpretations." Armstrong also asks about the influence of the reader's expectations on interpretation, and on "the relation between the reader and the world offered by the work and the dilemma posed by the gap between the self and others, the basis of much if not all misunderstanding" (17). For Armstrong, perspectives themselves become James's theme. "Because the limits to our perspectives both compel and entitle us to project guesses about hidden selves," Armstrong writes, "James believes that an active imagination can be rewarded with powerful insights. But it may also trick the observer, he fears, into placing excessive confidence in fanciful suppositions" (29).

Armstrong thinks *The Ambassadors* is "a classic example of the interdependence of James's hermeneutic exploration and his experiments with narrative structure" because besides revealing to us what Strether comes to know about Chad's behavior, James explores how Strether comes to understand what he sees (63). Given the multiplicity of interpretations of reality, James asks if it is possible "to develop an ethics that is not undermined by its relativity. . . . Interpretation is itself a moral activity for James because understanding others can lead to ethical self-awareness (as it does for Strether) and to a justifiable moral choice (although perhaps not a necessary and certain one)" (64). All ethical choices, James suggests, are debatable in a universe in which there is no transcendent truth.

Unlike Seltzer, Armstrong gives a generous reading of James's own moral sense. Armstrong sees that although James believes we can never know anything with certainty, still we can engage in the goal of discovering reality. James himself has "faith in the real" and faith, too, in the possibility of discovering "purposes and values to guide our lives" (*Phenomenology* 209, 211).

Responding to the work of Seltzer, Armstrong, and Posnock, Colin Meissner, in *Henry James and the Language of Experience* (1999), argued that James does not reproduce existing power structures within his fiction, but instead "frees the subject by making that subject aware of the economies of power which exert influence at culture's visible and invisible levels" (7). He disagrees with Seltzer that James is a "genteel aesthete" who is complicit with his culture's social control by enacting "a strict management of reality" in his fiction (6). He extends Armstrong's investigations by applying the theories of Hans-Georg Gadamer, who "sees understanding . . . as an event in which we come to understand how we stand in relation to other people, to ourselves, and to our immediate historical situation" (11). According to Meissner, experience, for James's characters, urges them to reflect on their own ideologies and revise them. Meissner also sees this revision in James's autobiography: "For James," he writes, "the autobiography becomes the creation, not the accounting of, a life . . . nothing less than an exemplary mode of self-construction which fuses the human and the aesthetic. . . ." (195).

Meissner identifies in James's work two theories of experience: one, which Meissner calls a "cumulative theory," sees experience as something simply to be acquired; the other requires that characters be immersed in an alien culture, the better to question their own assumptions about what experience illuminates for them — and for his readers as well. "It is not by accident then," Meissner writes, "that in forcing interpretive engagement on his readers James subtly and significantly changes the reading event from a passive enterprise to an active process in which the reader is initiated into the very processes of artistic production which lead to a heightened ability to understand" (20). James wants to make readers conscious of the "machinery of interpretation" as much as "interpretation's final product" (21). Experience, then, does not affirm beliefs held by an individual, but has the potential to change those beliefs and to change even the process through which one arrives at beliefs. "I want to underscore the idea," Meissner writes, "that Jamesian hermeneutics accentuates the fundamental tension or dialectic between private and public versions of the self, between a subject's private consciousness and social construction, between bewilderment and enlightenment" (27).

Several recent studies on Jamesian consciousness point to the diversity of scholarly interests that continue on this topic. In *The Figure of Consciousness: William James, Henry James, and Edith Wharton* (2002), Jill Kress examines how James used metaphors to represent the layered structures of the mind, including in her study not only Henry James, but also William and Wharton. According to Kress, these writers understood the limitations of language to represent the ineffable, and the metaphors they chose constructed their implicit or, in the case of William James, explicit arguments about how the mind works. Besides considering the Jameses and Wharton, Kress also looks at the figurative language used by Darwin, Lewes, and Spencer, among other nineteenth-century writers.

Andrew Taylor, in *Henry James and the Father Question* (2002), revisited territory investigated by Quentin Anderson and Alfred Habegger, who also asked how James's thinking about consciousness and identity reflected, responded to, or interpreted his father's ideas. Taylor believes that Anderson and Habbeger both limited our understanding of those ideas, offering a "blinkered and dehistoricised reading" of James Senior (15). Instead, Taylor argues that Henry needs to be contextualized in his own cultural and social milieu, which shaped his interests differently from those of his father. He also seeks to distance himself from Edel's Freudian insistence on repression and sublimation. Taylor sees an intellectual correspondence between James and his father that can be found in themes of religious sensibility, spiritual regeneration, and redemption. "James Senior's preoccupations," Taylor writes, "were essentially religious ones: his abiding concerns were with the nature of evil, the process of conversion and redemption, and the final restoration of man within a Christianized universal brotherhood" (201). Writing a generation later, Henry James secularized those preoccupations and tested them "within the often unpredictable and untidy world of rendered human experience. . . . James's employment of narratives of conversion, those charting the changed state of consciousness of his fictional characters and of the character of 'Henry James' in the autobiographies, illustrates the extent to which the religious cast of mind, although diluted through secularisation, retained a potent residual force" (202).

Sami Ludwig's *Pragmatist Realism: The Cognitive Paradigm in American Realist Texts*, published in 2002, considered James as part of a larger study of the connection of realist fiction to pragmatism. Ludwig sees realist fiction as interested in "the generation of representation by human beings in a pragmatic context — rather than starting out from signs, it is interested in how signs come into being" (4). "Placing James in a cognitive context makes it possible to reclaim him as a realist from poststructuralist and psychoanalytical appropriations, and it even offers a way to reconcile him with a particular view of Christian empathy that is by nature fundamentally cognitive" (8). Ludwig gives readings of *The Portrait of a Lady*, "The Real Thing," and *The Turn of the Screw*, in each concentrating on ways that characters construct reality. He sees *Portrait* as exemplary of a text focused on the transition of a personality. "What is the new definition of a good human being? Which are the qualities that turn an average woman into a 'lady,' when social superiority is no longer defined by a given aristocracy of status or at least of fixed values? What is 'the good' that takes the place of a sanctified order? How would a new standard of excellence have to be defined pragmatically?" (154). He argues that James places Isabel in "a narrative laboratory" where she "navigates among multiple allegories and becomes independent of any single underlying system that would predetermine her identity" (154).

Ludwig argues that realists as well as pragmatists assume an animate relationship between people and objects and an interactive relationship between people. Knowledge about reality "is learned through human interaction with reality. This interaction implies agency and cognitive construction" (213). Because this construction is social — that is, shared and negotiated — it has an ethical dimension.

This ethical dimension informs Gert Buelens's collection of essays, *Enacting History in Henry James* (1997), containing studies that consider "questions of knowability, performance, responsibility and narrative empowerment or disempowerment" in James's fiction and nonfiction (8). Winfried Fluck provides a useful overview of how critics have assessed James's treatment of moral issues from the 1940s to the 1990s. As Fluck sees it, James has been embraced by some critics who wish to see him as enacting a politically liberal agenda, by others who argue that he suffered "unwitting complicity with a social system which his work claims to distance or even transcend by art," and by still others who wish to portray him "in the grasp of hidden anxieties about his lack of success in the market-place, his masculinity, or his class status. . . ." James has been called a poststructuralist, a feminist, or a latent Marxist (Buelens 16). All of these interpretations, Fluck asserts, result from an examination of the way power is exerted in James's works. Among his contemporaries, James is the most cognizant "of the permanent presence of manipulation and the constant re-emergence of social asymmetries in relations" (23). His victimized characters transcend this manipulation through a "painful process of growing awareness" that results in a triumph of self-consciousness (25).

Considering the connection between consciousness and power necessarily leads scholars to the question of race and ethnicity in James's fiction and especially nonfiction. *The American Scene*, in particular, has become a central text in James criticism; and the publication of James's essays on politics and American social life in Pierre Walker's edited volume, *Henry James on Culture* (1999), has contributed further to this critical examination. In *Black and White Strangers: Race and American Literary Realism* (1993), Kenneth W. Warren focused on fiction as well, including *The Bostonians* and *Portrait of a Lady* to support his argument that writers such as James failed to further the cause of black civil rights. Although James concerned himself with characters who can be considered outsiders to established communities, he perpetuated the idea that blackness, because of its association with vulgarity, made inclusion impossible.

Surely one of the most respected works on this topic is Sara Blair's *Henry James and the Writing of Race and Nation* (1996), which begins with James's *A Small Boy and Others* and considers such fiction as *The Princess Casamassima* and *The Tragic Muse* along with essays such as "The Art of Fiction," "Trollope," and, of course, *The American Scene*. Blair argues that issues of race, ethnicity, gender, and nationality had a central place in James's project of representing and shaping a transnational, multifarious culture; and furthermore, that he brought a perspective of openness and civic consciousness to his representations.

In "Affirming the Alien: The Pragmatist Pluralism of *The American Scene*" (1998), Ross Posnock sees James enacting a liberal politics, hoping "to disrupt our propensity to arrest meaning in identity" and protesting "American simplicity" (Freedman 225). "The project of *The American Scene*," Posnock writes, "might be summed up as the effort to foster active democratic citizenship and the messy heterogeneity of what I call a pragmatist pluralism" (229). In other words, exposure to the realities of American life caused James to revise his own conclusions about his native land, as well as to revise his identity as an American and expatriate. Like his fictional characters, James experienced "shocks, contingencies, and the attractions of transitory urban moments of fugitive communion" (231). These experiences, Posnock believes, caused James to conceive of the "endless possibilities" of a future in which "a Victorian culture of hierarchy and homogeneity" is transformed into "a more unsettling urban modernity." Posnock admits that James may be "mired in the nativist prejudices of his class" — prejudices that critics agree includes racism — and yet "he complicates his snobbery with sympathy" (227).

Although he does not overtly condemn racism, James expresses ambivalence in his writing about African Americans and deems the Southern hierarchy to be based on delusions. Posnock sees James allied with W. E. B. DuBois — himself a student of William James — in his questioning of American identity and his belief in the potential of multiple perspectives. Both men, Posnock asserts, attacked "America's mania for invidious classification and its refusal to face up to its own hybridity" (241).

In a special 1995 issue of the *Henry James Review* devoted to the topic of race, Beverly Haviland argues that when James returned to America in 1904, he himself was the alien in a culture that had changed dramatically during his years of expatriation, a position that James's contemporary reviewers were quick to note. Haviland argues, however, that this position as an outsider was not a shortcoming in his ability to perceive the realities of early-twentieth-century America, but rather gave him a special insight. Because he felt a "bond of solidarity with all those who have been dispossessed of their heritage," James was able to think concretely about the formation of racial and ethnic identities (257). Haviland is more generous than other scholars, who note James's apparent anti-Semitism, when she writes that James deemed Jews most able to preserve their ethnicity because they had done so for much of their history, living as they did at "the margins of the mainstream" (259).

James does not emerge as tolerant in studies by Walter Benn Michaels and Leland S. Person, who consider James's attitude toward blacks. Michaels, taking evidence from *What Maisie Knew*, asserts that James connected blacks with vulgar behavior; and Person, drawing on *The Bostonians*, sees that James portrayed the power struggles in a changing America by blurring boundaries between racial and gender identities and heterosexual and homosexual desires. The mind, as Person rightly argues, has a body, and the body has a gender. This statement, applied to James's writing, is not simple. Probing the mind-body-gender connection in James's work has become the project of queer theory and gender studies, a huge and energetic segment of the James critical industry, and the focus of chapter 7.

Works Cited

Andreas, Osborn. *Henry James and the Expanding Horizon*. Seattle: U of Washington P, 1948.

Armstrong, Paul B. *The Challenge of Bewilderment: Understanding and Representation in James, Conrad, and Ford*. Ithaca, NY: Cornell UP, 1987.

———. *The Phenomenology of Henry James*. Chapel Hill: U of North Carolina P, 1983.

Ash, Beth Sharon. "Narcissism and the Gilded Image: A Psycholanalytic Reading of *The Golden Bowl*." *Henry James Review* 15, no. 1 (1994): 55–90.

Bell, Millicent. *Meaning in Henry James*. Cambridge, MA: Harvard UP, 1991.

Bersani, Leo. *A Future for Astyanax: Character and Desire in Literature*. Ithaca, NY: Cornell UP, 1984.

Blair, Sara. *Henry James and the Writing of Race and Nation*. New York: Cambridge UP, 1996.

Buelens, Gert. *Enacting History in Henry James: Narrative, Power, and Ethics*. Cambridge: Cambridge UP, 1997.

———. "Possessing the American Scene: Race and Vulgarity, Seduction and Judgment." In Buelens, 166–92.

Cameron, Sharon. *Thinking in Henry James*. Chicago: U of Chicago P, 1989.

Cormier, Harvey. "Jamesian Pragmatism and Jamesian Realism." *Henry James Review* 18, no. 3 (1997): 288–96.

Felman, Shoshana. "Henry James: Madness and the Risks of Practice (Turning the Screw of Interpretation)." In *Writing and Madness (Literature/Philosophy/Psychoanalysis)*, translated by Martha Noel Evans, Shoshana Felman, and Brian Massumi, 141–247. Ithaca, NY: Cornell UP, 1985.

Fluck, Winfried. "Power Relations in the Novels of James: The 'Liberal' and the 'Radical' Version." In Buelens, 16–39.

Freedman, Jonathan, ed. *The Cambridge Companion to Henry James.* Cambridge: Cambridge UP, 1998.

———. Review of *Imagination and Desire in the Novels of Henry James; Henry James and the Art of Power.* *New England Quarterly* 58, no. 2 (June 1985): 323–30.

Griffin, Susan. *The Historical Eye: The Texture of the Visual in Late James.* Boston: Northeastern UP, 1991.

———. "Seeing Doubles: Reflections of the Self in James's *Sense of the Past.*" *Modern Language Quarterly* 45, no. 1 (March 1984): 48–60.

———. "The Selfish Eye: Strether's Principles of Psychology." *American Literature* 56, no. 3 (October 1984): 396–409.

Haviland, Beverly. "The Return of the Alien: Henry James in New York, 1904." *Henry James Review* 16, no. 3 (1995): 257–63.

Hocks, Richard A. *Henry James and Pragmatistic Thought: A Study in the Relationship between the Philosophy of William James and the Literary Art of Henry James.* Chapel Hill: U of North Carolina P, 1974.

———. "Multiple Germs, Metaphorical Systems, and Moral Fluctuation in *The Ambassadors.*" In Buelens, 40–60.

———. Review of *Desire and Love in Henry James: Study of the Late Novels; Thinking in Henry James. Nineteenth Century Literature* 45, no. 3 (December 1990): 338–91.

James, Henry. *Literary Criticism: Essays on Literature, American Writers, English Writers.* New York: The Library of America, 1984.

Kaston, Carren. *Imagination and Desire in the Novels of Henry James.* New Brunswick, NJ: Rutgers UP, 1984.

Kress, Jill M. *The Figure of Consciousness: William James, Henry James, and Edith Wharton.* New York: Routledge, 2002.

Levin, Jonathan, and Sheldon M. Novick. "Realism and Imagination in the Thought of Henry and William James: A Conversation." *Henry James Review* 18, no. 3 (1997): 297–307.

Ludwig, Sami. *Pragmatist Realism: The Cognitive Paradigm in American Realist Texts.* Madison: U of Wisconsin P, 2002.

Marshall, Adré. *The Turn of the Mind: Constituting Consciousness in Henry James.* London: Associated Universities Press, 1998.

Meissner, Collin. *Henry James and the Language of Experience.* New York: Cambridge UP, 1999.

Michaels, Walter Benn. "Jim Crow Henry James?" *Henry James Review* 16, no. 3 (1995): 286–91.

Person, Leland S. "In the Closet with Frederick Douglass: Reconstructing Masculinity in *The Bostonians.*" *Henry James Review* 16, no. 3 (1995): 292–98.

Porter, Carolyn. *Seeing and Being: The Plight of the Participant Observer in Emerson, James, Adams, and Faulkner.* Middleton, CT: Wesleyan UP, 1981.

Posnock, Ross. "Affirming the Alien: The Pragmatist Pluralism of *The American Scene*." In Freedman, 224–46.

———. *The Trial of Curiosity: Henry James, William James, and the Challenge of Modernity*. New York: Oxford UP, 1991.

Przybylowicz, Donna. "The 'Lost Stuff of Consciousness': The Priority of Futurity and the Deferral of Desire in 'The Beast in the Jungle.'" In *Henry James's Daisy Miller, The Turn of the Screw, and Other Tales*, edited by Harold Bloom, 93–116. New York: Chelsea House, 1987.

Ryan, Judith. "Henry James." *The Vanishing Subject: Early Psychology and Literary Modernism*, 75–88. Chicago: U of Chicago P, 1991.

Seltzer, Mark. *Henry James and the Art of Power*. Ithaca, NY: Cornell UP, 1984.

Taylor, Andrew. *Henry James and the Father Question*. Cambridge: Cambridge UP, 2002.

Walker, Pierre A, ed. *Henry James on Culture: Collected Essays on Politics and the American Social Scene*. Lincoln: U of Nebraska P, 1999.

Warren, Kenneth W. *Black and White Strangers: Race and American Literary Realism*. Chicago: U of Chicago P, 1993.

Yeazell, Ruth Bernard. Review of *Thinking in Henry James*. *Modern Philology* 89, no. 2 (November 1991): 302–6.

7: Gender, Sexuality, Intimacy

> *Humanity is immense, and reality has a myriad [of] forms.... It is equally excellent and inconclusive to say that one must write from experience.... What kind of experience is intended, and where does it begin and end?*
>
> — Henry James, "The Art of Fiction"

THE EXTENT TO WHICH JAMES WROTE from his own experiences has long been an important question for James scholars. What kind of experiences did he have? Did his range of experiences go beyond observation and contemplation? What was the quality of his closest friendships? Did he ever have a physical relationship with anyone? These questions concerning James's experiences urge scholars to focus on his capacity for intimacy, and that focus has led, in the last few decades especially, to the fraught and controversial topic of sex. As Hugh Stevens remarked in a 1998 essay about "In the Cage," "The story of Henry James's sexuality has certainly held us sufficiently breathless round the fire, yet it remains as elusive and difficult (and as compelling and disturbing) as James's own *Turn of the Screw*" ("Queer Henry" 120).

The reticence with which most critics and scholars dealt with the subject of homosexuality in James's life and work changed significantly after the publication of Eve Sedgwick's "The Beast in the Closet: James and the Writing of Homosexual Panic" in 1986. Sedgwick argued that in "The Beast in the Jungle," John Marcher's secret is his absence of heterosexual desire and terror of homosexual desire; May Bartram, rather than recognizing and hoping to liberate Marcher's heterosexuality, sees that "what needs to be liberated is in the first place Marcher's potential for homosexual desire . . ." (177). Sedgwick's analysis, a much-cited text in queer studies, proved controversial, provocative, and certainly challenging to other scholars. Although in the 1980s, James had been the subject of feminist criticism by such writers as Nina Auerbach, Judith Fryer, and Alfred Habegger, the widening perspective afforded by gay, lesbian, and queer studies inspired scholars to ask new questions about gender, intimacy, and sexuality in James's work. "What was once celebrated as the aesthetic indeterminacy of James's modernism," John Carlos Rowe wrote in *The Other Henry James* (1998), "must now be interpreted in relation to James's ambiguities regarding the gender and sexual identification of his most compelling characters and, of course, himself" (101).

Queer studies inextricably contextualized James's work historically, culturally, and biographically as scholars explored such issues as James's characterization of men and women, his redefining of manhood for his characters and for himself, the ways that his characters experience love and intimacy, and the relationship of sex to power. As Wendy Graham described her approach in *Henry James's Thwarted Love* (1999), hers is "a hybrid study — part cultural history, part textual analysis, and part biography" (2). This summary could well describe most work in queer studies. Scholars have complicated our understanding of the events of James's life and of his relationships with men and women; in doing so, they also have complicated our understanding, more generally, of gender, sexuality, and emotional intimacy. Just as queer studies is shaping our reading of James, the problems James presents to scholars are shaping the scope and focus of queer studies.

Queer, gender, and feminist critical perspectives have reinvigorated James criticism, but as Richard Henke argued in "The Man of Action: Henry James and the Performance of Gender" (1995), gender also played a crucial role in what he calls James's "redemption" in the 1940s. Countering assaults from critics who denigrated James for being fussy, passive, and effete, F. O. Matthiessen, in his 1944 study, *Henry James: The Major Phase*, maintained that for James, writing was a strenuous, virile activity — James likened writing to going into battle — that required courage. Selectively reading James's notebooks and essays, Matthiessen portrayed James as a man of action — assertive and aggressive (Matthiessen 7). Henke, though, reads Matthiessen's sources through the lens of queer theory to create a diametrically different portrait. James, Henke argues, "challenges the notion of a universal, ungendered 'experience' for his characters," and, Henke suggests, for himself (236). James acknowledges stereotypical masculine and feminine identities, but asks, through his characters, what it must feel like to apprehend the world through the sensibility of another, even someone of another gender. As Henke sees it, James's belief in the continuity of experience extended to gender; "even to attribute gender 'identities' is to categorize too violently, to separate what is really continuous" (238). Furthermore, Henke says, far from being determinedly aggressive, James saw the aesthetic usefulness of passivity; in order to fully know the world, one must allow reality to wash over one, to be someone so observant that "nothing is lost." If passivity suggests femininity, Henke concludes that for James, "perception enables us to transgress the arbitrary boundaries of gender" (236). Just as Matthiessen saw gender identity as crucial in rehabilitating James's image for mid-twentieth century readers, Henke sees gender identity as equally crucial for justifying James's significance in our own time.

Questioning binary constructions of gender has generated a critique of Sedgwick's notion of homosexual panic and has urged scholars to consider more nuanced implications of James's sexuality. Lynda Zwinger, in "Bodies that Don't Matter: The Queering of 'Henry James'" (1995), criticized

Sedgwick's methodology as decoding rather than reading. "As a necessary consequence," Zwinger writes, "it leaves narrative out: cryptography is a one-to-one translation. . . . *Reading* is messy, layered, distracted, peripatetic . . ." (668). Reading, then, has led some scholars away from a focus on homosexual acts to consider, more broadly, cultural constructions of sexuality. Rowe, for example, argues that James's early fiction recognizes the ideology of patriarchy, but offers no solution for how individuals can wrest themselves from patriarchal constrictions (105). In his middle period, James was interested in the "New Woman," and created characters, such as Isabel Archer and Daisy Miller, modeled on this type; but, Rowe concludes, none of these characters achieved the degree of liberation supposedly in reach of the New Woman; "no feminine character in his fiction of the 1880s," Rowe says, "succeeds in approaching the complexity, cultivation, and self-reliance of his own narrative voice" (105). In the 1890s, "James's ironies bespeak his deep conflicts regarding his changing attitudes toward same-sex relations and to the general issue of sexual propriety in early modern culture" (106). In the fiction of this period, Rowe argues, James pitted his male protagonists against "'dangerous' women characters" — dangerous because of the ways they undermine James's own values — and he invented homosexual or homoerotic temptations "by setting male friends in opposition to socialite women, often also represented as couples" (105–6). As James created these relationships, he found the freedom to explore roles and identities that transgressed contemporary models.

Like Rowe, other scholars also argue for James's changing interest in gender throughout his works; one way to consider this shift is by recognizing that queerness affects more than sexual behavior. Hugh Stevens, for example, in his essay "Queer Henry *In the Cage*," found the term *queerness* useful in his consideration of ways in which James's "erotic exploration" in fiction was not merely an expression of his own sexuality, but a creation of "charged moments when subjectivity is formed through negotiation with social stigmas, with the taboo." Rather than reducing the fiction to biographical evidence, as he believes Edel did, Stevens holds that "sensitivity to the historical conditions of James's writing, and to the social setting this writing addresses, can only enhance our sense of how very daring this fiction is." In *Roderick Hudson*, for example, Stevens believes that queerness "might be thought of as a highly private, heroic mode of suffering" ("Queer Henry" 123, 124). In other words, queerness, as it pertains to James, suggests idiosyncrasy and perhaps discomfort with prescribed modes of thinking and feeling.

Although the enigma of James's own sexual identity is a recurrent focus in queer studies, many scholars recognize the risk of reading James's fiction as autobiography. Nevertheless, scholars rarely fail to comment on James's own characterization of himself in 1914, in a letter to Henry Adams, as "that queer monster, the artist." The context of the letter shows that James was using the adjective to refer to an artistic, rather than sexual, identity: as he put it, "an inexhaustible sensibility" (Monteiro 89). This use of *queer* is consistent with the popular sense of the term at the time; as Alfred Habegger noted in " 'What Maisie Knew': Henry James's *Bildungsroman* of the Artist as Queer Moralist," *queer* was used "to invoke an oddness that is not felt to be desirable and that surpasses harmless eccentricity" (94). The first citing of *queer* to mean homosexual occurred in 1922. Yet the "oddness" that the term suggests transcends what Stevens sees as James's "stable, identifiable sexual identity" and urges "a certain boldness in reading his fiction" ("Queer Henry" 124).

Certainly, as Stevens notes, James was fascinated by the fluidity and multiplicity of identity, and Stevens admits that "any reductive interpretation," such as a purely "gay" reading of a text, would deny manifold possible readings ("Queer Henry" 132). Wendy Graham agrees, and refuses to label James as " 'celibate,' 'repressed,' or 'closeted' " (1). Still, scholars such as Sedgwick, Rowe, Stevens, Eric Haralson, Helen Hoy, Eric Savoy, and many others, find a "gay" reading irresistible. In fact, James seems to invite such a reading. As Stevens noted in "Homoeroticism, Identity, and Agency in James's Late Tales," James's choice of names for his male characters — Prodmore, Puddick, Pappendick, Bender, for example — often are "overflowing with innuendo.... The sexual connotations of such names create an erotic register which subverts the text's genteel veneer, and suggest multiple possibilities which remain unconfirmed (but no less radical for their uncertainty)" ("Homoeroticism" 127). "Are we to understand," he asks, "that a writer whose work simply overflows with double entendres — whose prose is an extraordinarily erotically charged vehicle — was simply unaware of this fact?" (121).

James's reticence in "describing any genital activity," Stevens adds, should not restrict our interpretation, but on the contrary allows us more freedom of interpretation. Especially in the late fiction, Stevens believes, James explored "new possibilities for eroticism.... Across the late tales, James develops an erotic lexicon, invents a discursive eroticism in which sexual tensions and connections between fictional characters are not contained by a heterosexual frame. If the stories avoid description of sexual activity [as any fiction contemporary to James also does], the genitality of their language and of the erotic spaces they describe ironizes and critiques the standards of literary gentility to which they ostensibly conform" (130). According to Stevens, James uses puns, double entendres, and references "to the spectres of homosexual blackmail, scandal, and suicide" (130). He plays with words that have sly meanings, or that shimmer with a subversive aura. His recurrent use of the word *queer* in many tales suggests that he was aware that it was tinged with, at the least, a connotation of naughtiness.

Manhood

Besides James's tantalizing reference to himself as queer, critics also have focused on his autobiographical disclosure of the "obscure hurt" that he suffered during the time of the Civil War. As other young men around him rushed to help put out a fire, James realized that "to have trumped up a lameness at such a juncture could be made to pass in no light for graceful." He ran to join the others, and soon found himself caught between two high fences, "where the rhythmic play of my arms, in tune with that of several other pairs, but at a dire disadvantage of position, induced a rural, a rusty, a quasi-extemporised old engine to work and a saving stream to flow"; but in the process of helping, he had suffered, he said, "a horrid even if an obscure hurt . . ." (*Autobiography* 415). When his father took him to an eminent surgeon for a diagnosis of the injury, the doctor, to James's mystification, uttered "a comparative pooh-pooh" (416), leaving the young man with the impression that there was nothing, really, the matter with him. This anecdote, written for *Notes of a Son and Brother* in 1913, led to conjecture that the injury involved the genitals, perhaps even castration. As Paul John Eakin explained in his detailed consideration of the injury, "Henry James's 'Obscure Hurt': Can Autobiography Serve Biography?" (1988), this speculation was elaborated on by Saul Rosenzweig, in his 1944 essay on James, and thereafter, the incident "has been treated as a major biographical event, both determining and determined by the larger context of James's life history — his unconscious psychic identification with his injured father (Rosenzweig, Edel), his repressed incestuous love for his brother (Hall), and so forth" (677). Certainly the possibility of genital injury has sustained the assertion that James was impotent and therefore sexually inactive for the rest of his life. Even after Edel traced the veracity of the episode to show that James's chronology of events was inaccurate, the connection of the injury — perhaps psychosomatic — to James's sexuality persisted.

In addition to thinking about the alleged injury in the context of the Civil War, Eakin considers James's motivation to make sense of his life fifty years later. The story about the injury, Eakin suggests, served James's need for a "metaphorical substitute early and late for his failure to serve in the war" (689). Eakin, then, connects "the hurt" to James's manhood, but not limited to sexual performance, as did Susan Griffin in "Scar Texts: Tracing the Marks of Jamesian Masculinity" (1997). Besides offering a more wide-ranging metaphorical reading of scars in James's fiction, Griffin suggested ways that queer theory and gender studies can embrace inquiry that goes beyond proving or disproving James's homosexuality. As Griffin sees it, wounds and scars, which recur in James's work, "represent, and sometimes substitute for, masculine interiority" (62). Yet wounds do not necessarily represent trauma, but "the marks of self-making, of the entanglements of sexuality" (74). Furthermore, as Eakin also suggests, for James reviving the story of his "obscure hurt" decades after it occurred was a way of revising the past, of affirming an interpretation that offered consolation. James defines "scar," Griffin writes, "as an injury not fully healed, a continuation of the past into the present by means of difference. . . . Yet, a scar is not an opening through which we can see the past intact; instead, it is the past as it now exists in the present" (76). The scar is visible evidence able to be interpreted: in the case of James's wound, what does it tell us about his identity as a male living in a certain time and place?

Pamela Thurschwell revisited James's Civil War experiences in her 2001 study of the intersections between literary works and new technologies entitled *Literature, Technology and Magical Thinking, 1880–1920*. Thurschwell agrees with other scholars that shame is apparent in James's presentation of his injury, but she goes further to suggest that for James, shame is associated also "with attempting to love, have, encompass, sympathize with, be, a larger collective. . . . The threat of being transparent, of being penetrable, provokes both joy and shame" in James's fictional characters, and for James himself (69–70). Besides considering the wartime injury, Thurschwell investigates the problem of intimacy in the context of new technologies of communication, such as the telegraph and typewriter. Here, she sees James's "In the Cage" as exemplary of how the telegraph became "instrumental in creating transgressive fantasies of access to others who would be otherwise inaccessible to the fantasizing operators of these technologies, because of gender and class barriers, or that even more difficult to negotiate barrier between the living and the dead" (87). James confronted barriers between the living and dead when he appropriated his brother's letters, revising them, for his own autobiography. In doing so, Thurschwell argues, James fantasized his ability to channel William's spirit, to establish intimacy with the dead, which did not carry the risk of exposure and shame. For James, however, barriers between living individuals and himself were fraught with those risks.

Like Eakin and Thurschwell, Eric Haralson, in *Henry James and Queer Modernity* (2003), was drawn to the enigmatic obscurity of James's "hurt," maintaining that James sought to find an alternative to culturally validated male identities. The injury, after all, made it compulsory for James to rest and withdraw from exertion. It permitted him to read, and, most important, to write. "For Henry James," Haralson argues, "the struggle to articulate a modern manhood — apart from the normative script of a foxed national identity, a vulgarizing, homogenizing career in business and commerce, a middle-class philistinism and puritanical asceticism in the reception of beauty, and crucially, a mature life of heterosexual performance as suitor, spouse, physical partner, and paterfamilias — resulted in his valorizing the character of the disaffiliated aesthete" (3). James, then, was compelled more by a desire to create an identity as an artist rather than a "masculine desire" to enter into the "homo-sexual discourse" of his times (24). In this view, Haralson differs from such biographers as Fred Kaplan and Sheldon Novick, who portray James as beset, and sometimes roiled, by homoerotic feelings throughout his life.

Haralson focuses on *The Ambassadors* to support his argument. Although he acknowledges Strether's homoerotic attraction to young men, Haralson argues that in this novel, "the 'belated man of the world' and bachelor-aesthete Lambert Strether [emerges] as a culminating figure in James's quest to imagine a sympathetic masculinity whose bearings are homosexual, whose own sex appeal is significantly ambivalent, and yet whose affective complexities are not easily reducible to the rigidifying grids of the modern sex/gender system" (25). Strether, along with John Marcher in "The Beast in the Jungle," becomes the central focus of many other scholars as well, all of whom explore the meaning and implications of homoeroticism.

In *Henry James and Masculinity* (1994), Kelly Cannon, for example, argued that James's male characters are all marginal figures, as was James himself in what Cannon says was a "fiercely heterosexual world" (58). Cannon asserts that Strether "more than any other marginal figure sacrifices the voices of conventional masculinity to the interest of voices from within, including that of his sexuality" (49–50). Both Strether and Marcher create fictions of identity for themselves as self-protection against their vulnerability. While Strether resorts to surrender and accommodation of his emotional needs, Marcher creates a self-image as an aggressive hunter, an image of heightened "conventional maleness" (58).

One arguably marginal character who appears useful in deconstructing James's attitudes toward gender is Ralph Touchett in *The Portrait of a Lady*. According to Dana Luciano in "Invalid Relations: Queer Kinship in Henry James's *The Portrait of a Lady*" (2002), Touchett offers an alternative to the homosexual/heterosexual dichotomy that some scholars find too rigid. Homosexuality was not the only form of sexual deviance in James's time, Luciano argues; the term "third sex," put forth by Honoré de Balzac, "denoted a combination of male and female elements in one body which explained homosexual desire" (200). This combination appears evident in Touchett's character and perspective; he refuses to accept the gender opposition — strong/weak, active/passive — that formed, Luciano says, "the cherished cornerstone of Victorian ideology." The third-sex movement "diversified and disrupted the gender-sex configuration of normative heterosexuality . . . [and] conceived the third sex as a sort of vanguard, exempted from the characteristic incompleteness of the traditional sexes" (201). This idea of a continuum of sexual identities serves to support the argument that for James, sexuality that transcends binary circumscriptions offers an individual subtle and perhaps subversive power.

Womanhood

Studies of James's women often focus on *The Bostonians* and *The Portrait of a Lady*, both of which lend themselves to analysis of gender identity, sexuality, and power. In *The Bostonians*, James suggests the potential for same-sex relationships to liberate women from the constrictions of cultural expectations, even though the lesbian relationship is not fulfilled. In *The Portrait of a Lady*, James implies that heterosexual relationships can undermine a woman's independence, authority, and even sense of her own identity, while also suggesting that homoerotic bonds can be as manipulative as heterosexual involvements. Sexuality is a problem in both novels, scholars agree, and so is the possibility of achieving intimacy.

As Terry Castle noted in "Haunted by Olive Chancellor" (1993), *The Bostonians* was the first major novel to present a sympathetic portrait of a lesbian character, yet the relationship between Olive Chancellor and Verena Tarrant mirrors the rivalrous heterosexual triangles that James created in other fictions. This time, however, James invents same-sex desire, and explores the forces that ultimately defeat its realization. Although early critics tended to characterize Olive Chancellor as unappealing, strident, and hysterical, Castle sees her as the first lesbian tragic heroine (177, 179). James does not allow her to fulfill her desire for Verena, but still she survives and, as Castle notices, she receives from James a subtle benediction: that she is " 'distinguished and discriminating' " (177). As Sheldon Novick noted in his introduction to John Bradley's edition of essays, *Henry James and Homo-Erotic Desire* (1999), Olive's tragedy "is not that she is a lesbian, but that she is a lesbian who falls hopelessly in love with a woman who is not" (19). In this futile love, she enacts the plight of many other Jamesian characters.

In "Claiming Center Stage: Speaking Out for Homoerotic Empowerment in *The Bostonians*" (2000), Kathleen McColley suggested that besides the homoerotic relationship between Olive and Verena, James celebrates the "empowered alliance" that emerges from "their continued discourse together. Individual boundaries begin to dissipate as each takes on characteristics of the other the longer they share conversations and listen to the same maternal language regarding the suffering of women" (153–54). As partners, McColley says, they exert a power that they could not exert individually. Part of that power seems to be the ability to resist socially constructed models of womanhood, such as that represented by Adeline Luna, Olive's sister.

As Denis Flannery noted in "The Appalling Mrs. Luna: Sibling Love, Queer Attachment, and Henry James's *The Bostonians*" (2005), Mrs. Luna is portrayed as stereotypically feminine, with curls, a tight corset, tiny feet, and a manner of ebullient flirtatiousness. Mrs. Luna's love for Olive transforms into jealousy and rage when she perceives Olive's passion for Verena.

Sibling intimacy exists as a mirror of a homoerotic relationship, not only of its physical attraction but also the dynamics of power between lover and beloved. Mrs. Luna's attempt to wrest Olive from her obsession with Verena, Flannery argues, creates "layer upon layer of quite remarkably primal aggression and desire between the two sisters as constitutive of their interaction and as a shadowy model of queer desire and attachment" (16). At the same time that James apparently imagined a way for women to be free of prescribed roles, he undermined that freedom in their futile quest for love.

Isabel Archer, purportedly a New Woman, seemed more likely than Olive or Verena to break free of social prescriptions and reinvent a new role for herself. For some scholars, that reinvention involved sexuality. In her 1997 essay, "The Female World of Exorcism and Displacement (Or, Relations between Women in Henry James's Nineteenth Century *The Portrait of a Lady*)," Melissa Solomon examined Isabel's shifting gender identity once she meets Merle and characterizes theirs as a lesbian relationship, not, she cautions "as a medicalized identity . . . but as a site of same-sex female erotic complication" (462). Merle's manipulation of Isabel, Solomon says, is charged with sexuality: their desire for each other is implicit in the use they make of each other. Merle discovers in Isabel the "affluent wife" that crowned her achievements as a social climber. In arranging Isabel's marriage to Osmond, Merle, Solomon argues, is "displacing her own lesbian attachment to Isabel" while at the same time fulfilling Isabel's fantasy to reinvent herself in an unimagined future (460–61). Prominent in James's fiction, then, is a tension between desire for intimacy and for power, and the entanglement of sexual yearning, manipulation, and betrayal.

Like Solomon, Kristin Sanner also focused on Isabel's sexuality in " 'Wasn't All History Full of the Destruction of Precious Things?' Missing Mothers, Feminized Fathers, and the Purchase of Freedom in Henry James's *The Portrait of a Lady*" (2005). As "an orphaned heiress" without a maternal figure on which to model herself, Isabel nevertheless internalizes her culture's imperatives for women. As determined as she is to break free of them, her choice to marry Gilbert Osmond reflects her performance of gender expectations that she cannot evade. As Sanner argues, her relationship with Madame Merle, who desires to possess her as fiercely — if not sexually — as Olive desired Verena, undermines Isabel's hopes. According to Sanner, Merle's ability to manipulate Isabel forces her into a stereotypical passivity that she had strived to reject and into an unexpected and ill-suited maternal relationship with Merle's daughter, Pansy, and also with her ex-lover, Gilbert Osmond, for whom pity takes the form of a maternal tenderness (161).

Donatella Izzo called upon Foucault and narrative theory to examine gender and power in *Portraying the Lady: Technologies of Gender in the*

Short Stories of Henry James (2001). Besides considering such well-known stories as "The Last of the Valerii" and "The Beast in the Jungle," Izzo focuses on some stories not often afforded critical attention — such as "Rose-Agatha" and "Georgina's Reasons" — which helps to make her study fresh. Although her Foucauldian perspective might suggest that she sees all characters as culturally repressed, Izzo refuses to see James's women merely as victims. According to Izzo, James sometimes represented women as art objects, and in some stories allowed women to exert power through subversive strategies, such as silence.

Sex and Power

"The Beast in the Jungle" has been the focus of much critical analysis by scholars interested in the question of power. In "The Double Narrative of 'The Beast in the Jungle': Ethical Plot, Ironical Plot, and the Play of Power" (1997), for example, Michiel Heyns explored connections between the sexual and the ethical in that tale, arguing that May's characterization as Marcher's "kind wise keeper" puts her in a position of power. "May's complete absorption in Marcher's history is not so much an extinction of her own self as an appropriation of his . . ."; in effect, she has helped him to become helpless (113). In contrast to Sedgwick, who argues that May wants to free Marcher to acknowledge his homosexuality, Heyns says "that power seems to me to be derived exactly from a heterosexual imperative of which May is, in fact, the exponent in the tale" (121). As Heyns reads the plot, Marcher can be manipulated by May precisely because of his acute sensitivity, and Heyns argues against critics who fail "to discriminate the power plot, with its inherent ruthlessness, from the ethical plot, with its scruples and renunciations" (122). Characters such as May Bartram "are not mere victims" but participants in fluctuating power relationships.

Questions of power, as well as sexuality, have concerned scholars who look for evidence of James's homoeroticism and homosexuality in his life. In his 1992 biography of James, Fred Kaplan saw a change in James's fiction beginning in the 1890s, when he fell in love several times. These intimate relationships were qualitatively different from his many previous friendships, Kaplan asserts, more deeply emotional and more intense. Although the result of his feelings were intimate friendships rather than physical consummation, these relationships — all with younger men — urged James to examine his own desire for — and fear of — intimacy, yearning for power, and capacity for love. Kaplan, therefore, sees "The Beast in the Jungle" through the lens of James's own frustration: Marcher is haunted by his inability to love. "Deeply repressed feelings lie in wait to take revenge against him," Kaplan writes, "to spring out as a hallucinatory embodiment of his inner emptiness, his massive unfeeling egoism, and his lifelong repression of his own sexuality" (457). Although certainly Kaplan sees the beast as homoerotic, still he allows for the complication of James's resistance to intimacy as a possible compromise of his power.

This resistance appears most tellingly in Lyndall Gordon's *A Private Life of Henry James* (1998), which examines James's relationship with his cousin Minny Temple, an outspoken and independent young woman who died in 1870, when James was twenty-seven; and his friend Constance Fenimore Woolson, a writer, who apparently committed suicide in 1894, when James was fifty-one and at the height of his career. According to Gordon, James's ties with these women were "more intimate than sex, closer than those of family and friends" (8). In these relationships, we can see James's vulnerabilities, and most certainly his fear of intimacy, that are not as blatantly apparent when we examine his other friendships. Whether or not Minny figured as a model for Isabel Archer in *Portrait of a Lady* or Millie Theale in *The Wings of the Dove*, whether or not James stole Fenimore's notes for the plot of "The Beast in the Jungle," as well as other stories, Gordon makes the case that these women served as disturbing forces in James's life and art. Surely, in their independence and refusal to conform to prescribed gender roles, they urged James to consider alternative models for both men and women. Surely, James used them as material for his fiction. But in using them, he drew them perilously close to his heart. "It is consistent with the Lesson of the Master," Gordon writes, "that art, of necessity, preys on others. This is the questionable point where James the man meets James the writer. He drew women out as no other man, exposing needs . . . and then swerved from responsibility" (327). He did not respond to Minny's dream of traveling to Europe, although he himself might have escorted her, nor did he respond to Fenimore's dream of an intimate relationship with him; "he was strong, resolute, formidable," Gordon asserts, "when he drew women into his drama of unstated communion — and then withdrew at a telling moment to shut himself in the tower of art" (364).

When Gordon considers the evidence for James's homosexuality and homoeroticism, she is less inclined than such scholars as Novick or Kaplan to label him as a repressed homosexual. Certainly, she admits, James was "conspicuously demonstrative" with both men and women (302), but how to translate his protestations of affection in letters, or even his physical embraces, remains a question. "He was a complex person," Gordon writes, "who could be extravagantly open in his feelings for both sexes, and at the same time intensely, even enjoyably, secretive" (75). As Gordon sees his relationships, James was more interested in possessing another person's soul — or his potential for artistic inspiration — than his body.

Kristin Boudreau, in "Henry James's Inward Aches" (1999), similarly noted the failure of sympathy in James's life and in his fiction. "In a world governed by social conventions," she writes, "James found true contact between individuals often impossible, in spite of his lifelong efforts to cultivate sympathy, to share with his fellow mortals what he called the 'inward ache'" (69). As his brother William claimed in his essays and in *The Principles of Psychology*, there existed an unbridgeable gap between individual minds, a gap that left each person yearning for true understanding. Boudreau sees "The Beast in the Jungle" and "A Round of Visits" as exemplary of "the supreme failure of sympathy — our blindness to the feelings of others, our obsessions with our own narrow interests, our inability to connect with other people's claims except insofar as they intersect with our own" that both Henry and William James regretfully believed (70). The lonely John Marcher, for example, "cannot conceive of any human experience outside the realm of public behavior. Since he has no inkling of a secret in the lives of others, he identifies these lives as meaningless, just as his own life becomes empty once the beast has pounced, undetected . . ." (74). In "A Round of Visits," Mark Monteith returns to New York from expatriation in Europe, to discover that his savings have been embezzled by a person he thought was his friend. Hoping to share his dismay with someone, he encounters nothing but rebuffs and, finally, disillusionment when he finds a man he thinks understands him. As Boudreau sees it, James repeatedly demonstrated the failure of sympathy, the risks involved in trying to connect with another human being, and the unfathomed secrets that each of us harbors. For some scholars, one such secret, for James, was his homosexuality.

Like Gordon, however, Leland Person also cautioned against taking James's homosexuality for granted. In *Henry James and the Suspense of Masculinity* (2003), Person offered an overview of scholarship investigating gender and sexuality, urging others to pay careful attention "to the terms in which James himself understood and represented gender and sexuality and to avoid . . . 'retrolabeling'" (11). As Wendy Graham put it in *Henry James's Thwarted Love* (1999), Eve Sedgwick's analysis of James, although liberating for many scholars, needs to be read with this caution in mind: "Sedgwick's reinvention of James as a self-deceiving or sexually dormant homosexual, though a step forward, is not entirely satisfying, for in spite of herself, she seems to equate genital activity (endpleasure) with sexual identity" (11). For Graham and others, James found communication with his beloved friends pleasurable in itself, and this alternative to physical intimacy, Graham argues, can help critics understand James's particular expression of sexuality and intimacy.

In search of biographical evidence for James's sexuality, scholars have turned to James's letters to male friends, letters so effusive and melodramatic that they become problematic rather than definitive. Although Person sees that James "clearly felt desire for other men," he believes "it would be counterproductive from a literary standpoint to reduce James's sexuality to simple terms when it is the terms themselves that are so provocative" (14). Furthermore, as Person and others have noted, the letters that have been available to scholars are so few and often compromised that they do not afford reliable evidence.

Available letters, nevertheless, have proved fruitful for Susan E. Gunter, editor of two volumes of correspondence: *Dear Munificent Friends: James's Letters to Four Women* (1999), and, with Stephen H. Jobe, *Dear Beloved Friends: Henry James's Letters to Younger Men* (2002). In an article on James's relationship with Jocelyn Persse published in 2001, Gunter focused on thirteen letters that give evidence both of the effusive affection of James's rhetoric and the "unequal power" of James's male friendships. In many of these friendships, James positioned himself as an experienced and urbane adviser to a younger man at the beginnings of an artistic career. Although Gunter says that James "works hard in his letters to deconstruct the hierarchical positions that Edwardian society assigned them" (336), she points to an important connection between sexuality and power that other scholars have explored in James's fiction.

Michael Cooper investigates some of these tales in "Discipl(in)ing the Master, Mastering the Discipl(in)e: Eronotomies of Discipleship in James' Tales of Literary Life" (1990). Cooper invents the term *erotonomy* to refer to "a mutual desire of the participants for personal interaction with each other and a mutually accepted system for exchanging satisfactions" (66). This special interaction recurs in James's stories between a master and his younger disciple: Cooper cites "The Real Right Thing," "The Author of Beltraffio," and "The Aspern Papers" as examples. The master offers his knowledge and experience; the disciple offers affirmation of the master's power. When the master is a writer, the disciple is an adoring reader — more adoring and protective than any of the female characters in the story. "The homosocial bond with this disciple," Cooper writes, "becomes the fertile relationship that allows the feminized male author the space in which to bear his aesthetic offspring" (70).

Not surprisingly, other scholars interested in the theme of discipleship have focused their analytic attention on "The Pupil," a tale that has yielded a rich mine of interpretation. Although Millicent Bell, in her contribution to *The Cambridge Companion to Henry James* (1998), argued that the "unmentionable subject" in the story is money, queer theorists have decided that it is the sexual attraction between the tutor Pemberton and his pupil, the young Morgan Moreen. As Fred Kaplan sees it, Pemberton and Morgan represent James at two stages of his life — the middle-aged author and the young boy he once was. Pemberton falls in love with Morgan, but at the end of the tale, given the chance to take Morgan away from his family, Pemberton, although filled with desire, experiences nothing less than homosexual panic, and Morgan dies of a broken heart (304).

In "Homotextual Duplicity in Henry James's 'The Pupil'" (1993), Helen Hoy saw the tale even more fraught with homosexual panic — that is, panic experienced by James himself in writing the story. According to Hoy, James's fear of writing a tale in which consummation was possible caused James to repeatedly assert Morgan's boyishness even as the boy obviously was growing into a man. Finally, when consummation seemed inevitable, James could do nothing else but kill Morgan in order, Hoy says, to protect himself from creating an overtly homoerotic tale. Michael Moon complicates the tale by arguing for Mrs. Moreen's incestuous desire for her son, evidence of which he sees in her erotically charged handling of a pair of dirty kid (read "child") gloves.

Refuting such readings, Philip Horne, in "Henry James: The Master and the 'Queer Affair' of 'The Pupil'" (1995), acknowledged a theme of homoerotic tension, but argued that the story is more complicated than simply a tale of unfulfilled desire. Pemberton struggles not only with his attraction to Morgan, but also with his feelings of responsibility to the child as tutor and caretaker, his own poverty and response to Mrs. Moreen's manipulation of him, and his recognition of the way the Moreen family strives to protect its honor and social standing. All of these themes, which recur in many of James's fictions, thicken the plot of attraction between two men of disparate ages.

Still, these homoerotic tales have urged many scholars to look for biographical evidence of such attraction, and they have identified several relationships between James and younger men, such as Persse, Howard Sturgis, Morton Fullerton, Percy Lubbock, and Hugh Walpole; one relationship that has attracted scholarly attention is James's infatuation with the sculptor Hendrik C. Andersen, which lasted, with diminishing intensity, from 1899 to 1915. In her introduction to Rosella Mamoli Zorzi's *Beloved Boy: Letters to Hendrik C. Andersen* (2004), a collection of James's letters, Millicent Bell acknowledged that James's effusive letters to Andersen suggest a sexual relationship, but she and other biographers doubt that the affair ever was consummated physically. James was fifty-six when they met; Andersen was twenty-six, at the start of his career as an artist, receptive to aesthetic advice and definitely to financial help. Although early in his infatuation James proposed that the two men live together at his home in Rye, eventually, James not only gave up this idea, but also cooled in his admiration of Andersen's work — and possibly of Andersen himself. It seemed, then, that James enjoyed the fantasy of a relationship, a fantasy that he could invent and control, rather than the complications of reality.

Pierre Walker and Greg Zacharias, editors of the multi-volume letters being published by the University of Nebraska Press, are contributing significantly to James studies through their scrupulous editing and annotating of the material that they are discovering. In "James's Hand and Gosse's

Tail: Henry James's Letters and the Status of Evidence" (1998), Walker and Zacharias detailed the publication of James's 1894 letter to Edmund Gosse mentioning James's desire "to put a little salt on your tail" in order to insure that Gosse remain at his home for a visit. In the manuscript, the authors reveal, James crossed out a word and added a phrase that may or may not be significant to understanding the relationship between the two men: "I hope this will be in time to put my hand [hand is crossed out] a little [added] salt on your tail" (72). How did James intend to end the sentence after the word "hand," the authors ask? Where did he hope to put his hand? "No one will ever know how James initially meant to conclude the sentence. But since the 'my' and the crossed-out 'hand' are still legible in the letter (though 'hand' is only barely so), it will never be possible not at least to suspect that James meant to write about putting his hand on Gosse's tail or to suspect that, by leaving 'hand' barely legible, James might have wanted Gosse to read his joke" (73). Since the letter was published without the orthography of the original, scholars have not been allowed to ask such questions; Walker and Zacharias, however, aim to correct the evidence in their edition of James's complete correspondence, a work that no doubt will change future scholarship.

The question that underlies such scholarship is whether James ever had a physical sexual relationship with a man. As John Bradley notes in *Henry James's Permanent Adolescence* (2000), assertions such as Sheldon Novick's, put forth in *Henry James: The Young Master* (1996), that James had a sexual relationship with Oliver Wendell Holmes when both were young men in Cambridge, Massachusetts, have generated considerable hostility among other scholars. Philip Horne, Lyndall Gordon, and David Van Leer believe that Novick read too much into James's effusive letters to his youthful friend, and Novick himself seems to have qualified his assertion after his biography of James was published.

In his introduction to John Bradley's *Henry James and Homo-Erotic Desire*, published three years after *Henry James: The Young Master*, Novick questioned the meaning of "homo-erotic," which Leon Edel applied to James's relationships with men. "In his and some other hands," Novick writes, "the word 'homo-erotic' implied a desire for sexual relations while awkwardly seeking to evade the stigma attached to homosexual acts themselves. It suggested sexual desire, a one-dimensional or single-minded thing, rather than the more common and more complex homosocial bond, and it evaded the question of realisation. The word conveyed a sort of impotence: what one truly desired was not achieved" (2). Edel, like other writers in the 1950s, '60s, and '70s, alluded to rumors about James's impotence, and perpetuated the portrait of James as celibate. Because James was "a Victorian gentleman with conservative views" (11), who adhered to the literary conventions of his time, Novick understands why some critics argue that "James's writing about sexuality was somehow unconscious, a helpless expression of neurotic fears" (14). But Novick takes a bolder stand: the evidence from his letters and fiction suggests "two conclusions: one concerns a presence of feeling in James's relations to men, and the other concerns an absence of feeling in his relations to women" (8). Novick argues, furthermore, "that he loved certain men, and that this love was a feature of his selfhood, of his conscious understanding of himself. . . . He formed friendships with slender, handsome, manly, passive young men who greatly resembled the male protagonists of his stories and novels" (8–9). These young men respond to their older and more powerful lover by paying homage, and literally falling to their knees. Whether this enactment of homage was James's wish or actual experience remains a mystery.

Besides evidence from James's letters, scholars have looked at James's autobiographical writings, especially *A Small Boy and Others*, for any evidence of when James first appeared conscious of homosexual or homoerotic feelings. Michael Moon, in *A Small Boy and Others: Imitation and Initiation in American Culture from Henry James to Andy Warhol* (1998), examined James's recollections of visits to the Louvre to argue that James's "boyhood initiation as an artist took place not in relation to a set of literary texts . . . but amidst the display of a celebrated collection of 'queer' (his recurrent term) images: the intensely male-homoerotic mythology and history paintings associated with the French Revolution and the First Empire. . . ." (12). These paintings evoke classical sculpture, which represents the cult of the beautiful male nude. Although James himself grew into a somewhat corpulent man, hardly the image of the male nudes he so admired, Moon notes that James's way of dress was theatrical and notably conspicuous (37). His contemporaries remarked that James seemed intent on having others notice his body, and some felt that in his foppish way of dressing, he appeared decidedly effeminate. Moon argues that in his later years, James displayed "an at least slightly grotesque exhibitionism, and a decreasing fear of being perceived as behaving in a ridiculous manner . . ." (38).

Besides these critical interpretations, since 1990, James's life and work have been appropriated by fiction writers who create James as a character in their own novels and stories, or who take up and reinvent his themes for our own time — a time of uncloseted homosexuals and AIDS. In Colm Tóibín's *The Master* (2004), James is the central character, and Tóibín weaves passages from James's writings, Alice James's diary, and the family's correspondence into his fictionalized retelling of James's life as a gay man and an artist who craved solitude. In addition to primary sources, Tóibín relies on Edel for biographical information and interpretation, including the conclusion that Henry and William enacted a tense rivalry. David Lodge takes a different view, rejecting the idea of a homosexual James in his 2004 novel *Author, Author* and instead portraying James as a celibate ascetic, devoted to his art.

David Leavitt in his collection of stories, *A Place I've Never Been* (1990), follows his gay characters, Jamesian but not James himself, abroad as they reinvent their lives. As Julie Rivkin notes, "Behind the stories in this collection hover Jamesian tales of lives not lived, vicarious doubles, regrets, returns, and specters of second chances. Yet if Leavitt's stories echo James's, it is James with a difference," she points out. "In Leavitt's version . . . the smudge of mortality is AIDS, the article manufactured at Woollett might be a condom" (283). Nicholas Guest, Alan Hollinghurst's central character in *The Line of Beauty* (2004), is a graduate student writing a dissertation on James; besides quoting from James throughout the novel, Guest seems modeled on Milly Theale, surrounded as she was by characters who betray her. These contemporary writers indebted to James, Rivkin asserts, echo the "particular tracings of desire, duplicity, and renunciation that characterize James's fiction" (283). One might ask, as Rivkin does, why, if characters in the fictional worlds of Leavitt or Hollinghurst have no need to dissimulate, if they have no need to hide their sexuality, do they recreate James's nineteenth-century vision of thwarted desires? As Rivkin sees it, although these reinvented characters are free to experience sex without proscriptions (beyond the need to protect themselves from HIV), they still struggle to find intimacy and love. Experience, for these contemporary writers as for James, still is fraught with risk, still centers on power relationships, still can be subverted by differences in class, by corruption, by greed.

As exciting as queer studies has been in energizing James criticism, some scholars have cautioned temperance. Like Zwinger, they do not believe that decoding James is as enriching as reading; they worry about reductionism. Sometimes this admonition of caution is interpreted by other scholars as homophobia: a resistance to admitting that James was gay because one finds it distasteful, if not shameful. Yet Philip Horne, in his essay about "The Pupil," responsibly reminds us of "the abuse of speculation. A crux is summarised and a hypothetical interpretation presented explicitly as hypothetical. Building on this hypothesis, the critic reaches a third and a fourth." Soon, the hypotheses become "scaffolding" that serves to generate an argument. When the scaffolding is removed in the course of an essay, the argument suddenly loses its basis in speculation and "becomes more like fact" (81). These kinds of conjectures, Horne reminds us — and he points to the work of Sedgwick and Moon as examples — appealing and stimulating as they are, need to be evaluated carefully.

In "The Queer Subject of 'The Jolly Corner'" (1999), for example, Eric Savoy asserted his resistance to what he calls the "tyranny of the 'biographical James'" and "the referential tendencies of biographical criticism toward coherent identity." Instead, he posits a complex argument that rests on "the unbinding of the coherent subject" in the tale. "If I am correct in suggesting that Spencer Brydon returns to America as a self-knowing 'gay' bachelor — closeted, to be sure, but with a sexual affliliation richly and connotatively established — whose provisional identity is contested and unravelled by his encounter with his hypothetical and rather differently closeted double, then 'The Jolly Corner' might be read as a supple and prescient allegory of the queer undoing of the gay subject" (2). Rather than ascribe a queer or straight identity to Spencer Brydon, Savoy sees the story as representing "the unbinding" or "undoing" of any fixed — albeit precarious — sexual identity (19).

Peggy McCormack, in her introduction to *Questioning the Master: Gender and Sexuality in Henry James's Writings* (2000), wrote that the essays she commissioned for the collection focus exclusively on textual analysis, without "an a priori premise about how James lived and how his life may be read into his works" (11), a goal that proves unattainable for some contributors. Nevertheless, the collection offers a generous range of perspectives from feminist and queer theorists — among them, John Carlos Rowe, Eric Haralson, and Leland Person — who respond to the political, cultural, and biographical questions raised by James's works. Sarah B. Daugherty's "James and the Representation of Women: Some Lessons of the Master (')s" asks a reasonable question about the extent to which we may call James a feminist author, even though he seems more sympathetic to women's oppression than do some of his contemporaries. She concludes that James reinscribed some recurring themes about women's position in society, themes he saw in works by Balzac, Hawthorne, and Trollope, for example, rescuing them from sentimentality and complicating the portrayal of female protagonists. Despite James's occasional chauvinism, Daugherty argues, "for reasons both humane and aesthetic, James sided with female characters against male writers who belatedly defended the status quo" and without emerging as a political critic (179). Priscilla Walton, who established her reputation as a feminist scholar with *The Disruption of the Feminine in Henry James* (1992), reflects on transformations of James's fiction to the cinema and television by male, female, homosexual, and heterosexual directors in her contribution, "The Janus Face of James: Gender, Transnationality, and James's Cinematic Adaptations." Recent cinematic translations, Walton writes, heighten the realization that James transcended national boundaries and belonged exclusively to none; and direct our attention to James's use of the female body "as an object of control in national ventures" (52). In general, the essays in McCormack's collection represent the least polemical writings emerging from feminist and queer theory, writings that sometimes seem shrill in their insistence on James's enactment of his homosexual identity through his fiction.

"Without disputing either James's perspective on pleasure or the homoeroticism of his fiction and later letters," Christopher Lane wrote in "Jamesian Inscrutability" (1990), "I . . . am questioning the rash suggestion that his complex aesthetic formulations are reducible to buried sexual secrets" (247). James's style, his literary choices, his characters' striving for authority and connection, the thwarted loves and desperate dreams — all these, Lane writes, cannot be accounted for by James's apparent homosexuality: homoeroticism, he says, cannot be "the fundamental cause of nebulosity in James's writing . . ." (249). If there are truths to be discovered about James, secrets to be unearthed, they will not be exclusively, or even merely, sexual.

"Discussion, suggestion, formulation, these things are fertilizing when they are frank and sincere," James wrote in "The Art of Fiction" (*Literary Criticism* 45). A look at recent issues of the *Henry James Review*, particularly the 2006 spring and winter editions, reveals the range and fertility of James studies at the beginning of the twenty-first century. Queer theory is represented by one article, arguing that the erotic is best understood in linguistic, rather than representational, terms. Several scholars take up the ongoing question of James's identity, examining various characterizations of him: as old maid, fussbudget, and as an aesthete fearful of the vulgar tastes of the masses. A few articles place James's fiction in historical context: one traces the publication of "The Real Thing"; another considers *The Portrait of a Lady* in the context of divorce debates of the 1860s and '70s. One scholar is interested in the theme of intrusion and disclosure, a variation, it seems, of the often-examined themes of privacy and betrayal; another scholar focuses on the theme of patience. Still another examines metaphor and metonyms in "In the Cage" from a new formalist perspective.

Investigating James seems inexhaustible, questions set forth by his contemporaries remain unsettled, and new conjectures are ingeniously crafted as James's critical reception continues to be shaped. If James himself never could have foreseen the direction criticism of his work would take, still, as he wrote in "The Art of Fiction," "Art lives upon discussion, upon experiment, upon curiosity, upon variety of attempt, upon the exchange of views and the comparison of standpoints; and there is a presumption that those times when no one has anything particular to say about it, and has no reason to give for practice or preference, though they may be times of honor, are not times of development — are times, possibly even, a little of dulness" (*Literary* 44–45). However abashed James might be about scholarly inquiry into his sexual experiences, his intimate friendships, his coveting of popularity, and his literary choices, he would have to admit that ours are not times of dullness, but rather of energy and even exuberance about the works and world of Henry James.

Works Cited

Bell, Millicent. Introduction to *Beloved Boy: Letters to Hendrik C. Andersen, 1899–1915*. Edited by Rosella Mamoli Zorzi, ix–xxxv. Charlottesville: U of Virginia P, 2004.

Bell, Millicent. "The Unmentionable Subject in 'The Pupil.'" In Freedman, 139–50.

Boudreau, Kristin. "Henry James's Inward Aches." *Henry James Review* 20, no. 1 (1999): 69–80.

Bradley, John R., ed. *Henry James and Homo-Erotic Desire*. New York: St. Martin's, 1999.

———. *Henry James's Permanent Adolescence*. New York: Palgrave, 2000.

Buelens, Gert, ed. *Enacting History in Henry James: Narrative, Power, and Ethics*. Cambridge: Cambridge UP, 1997.

Cannon, Kelly. *Henry James and Masculinity: The Man at the Margins*. New York: St. Martin's, 1994.

Castle, Terry. "Haunted by Olive Chancellor." *The Apparitional Lesbian: Female Homosexuality and Modern Culture*, 150–85. New York: Columbia UP, 1993.

Cooper, Michael A. "Discipl(in)ing the Master, Mastering the Discipl(in)e: Erotonomies of Discipleship in James' Tales of Literary Life." In *Engendering Men*, edited by Joseph Boone and Michael Cadden, 66–86. New York: Routledge, 1990.

Daugherty, Sarah B. "James and the Representation of Women: Some Lessons of the Master(')s." In McCormack, 176–95.

Eakin, Paul John. "Henry James's 'Obscure Hurt': Can Autobiography Serve Biography?" *New Literary History* 19, no. 3 (Spring 1988): 675–92.

Flannery, Denis. "The Appalling Mrs. Luna: Sibling Love, Queer Attachment, and Henry James's *The Bostonians*." *Henry James Review* 26, no. 1 (2005): 1–19.

Freedman, Jonathan. *The Cambridge Companion to Henry James*. Cambridge: Cambridge UP, 1998.

Gordon, Lyndall. *A Private Life of Henry James: Two Women and His Art*. New York: Norton, 1998.

Graham, Wendy. *Henry James's Thwarted Love*. Stanford, CA: Stanford UP, 1999.

Griffin, Susan. "Scar Texts: Tracing the Marks of Jamesian Masculinity." *Arizona Quarterly* 53, no. 4 (1997): 61–82.

Gunter, Susan E, ed. *Dear Munificent Friends: Henry James's Letters to Four Women*. Ann Arbor: U of Michigan P, 1999.

———. "'You Will Fit the Tighter into My Embrace!' Henry James's Letters to Jocelyn Persse." *GLQ: A Journal of Lesbian and Gay Studies* 7, no. 2 (2001): 335–54.

Gunter, Susan E., and Steven H. Jobe, eds. *Dear Beloved Friends: Henry James's Letters to Younger Men*. Ann Arbor: U of Michigan P, 2002.

Habegger, Alfred. "'What Maisie Knew': Henry James's *Bildungsroman* of the Artist as Queer Moralist." In Buelens, 93–108.

Haralson, Eric. *Henry James and Queer Modernity*. New York: Cambridge UP, 2003.

Henke, Richard. "The Man of Action: Henry James and the Performance of Gender." *Henry James Review* 16, no. 2 (1995): 227–41.

Heyns, Michiel W. "The Double Narrative of 'The Beast in the Jungle': Ethical Plot, Ironical Plot, and the Play of Power." In Buelens, 109–25.

Hollinghurst, Alan. *The Line of Beauty.* London: Macmillan, 2004.

Horne, Philip. "Henry James: The Master and the 'Queer Affair' of 'The Pupil.'" *Critical Quarterly* 37, no. 3 (Autumn 1995): 75–92.

Hoy, Helen. "Homotextual Duplicity in Henry James's 'The Pupil.'" *Henry James Review* 14, no. 1 (Winter 1993): 34–42.

Izzo, Donatella. *Portraying the Lady: Technologies of Gender in the Short Stories of Henry James.* Lincoln: U of Nebraska P, 2001.

James, Henry. *Autobiography.* Edited by F. W. Dupee. Princeton, NJ: Princeton UP, 1983 [1913, 1914, 1917].

———. *Literary Criticism: Essays on Literature, American Writers, English Writers.* New York: The Library of America, 1984.

Kaplan, Fred. *Henry James: The Imagination of Genius.* New York: Morrow, 1992.

Lane, Christopher. "Jamesian Inscrutability." *Henry James Review* 20, no. 3 (1999): 244–54.

Leavitt, David. *A Place I've Never Been.* New York: Penguin, 1990.

Lodge, David. *Author, Author.* New York: Viking Penguin, 2004.

Luciano, Dana. "Invalid Relations: Queer Kinship in Henry James's *The Portrait of a Lady.*" *Henry James Review* 23, no. 2 (2002): 196–217.

Matthiessen. F. O. *Henry James: The Major Phase.* New York: Oxford UP, 1944.

McColley, Kathleen. "Claiming Center Stage: Speaking Out for Homoerotic Empowerment in *The Bostonians.*" *Henry James Review* 21, no. 2 (2000): 151–69.

McCormack, Peggy, ed. *Questioning the Master: Gender and Sexuality in Henry James's Writings.* Baltimore: U of Delaware P, 2000.

Monteiro, George, ed. *The Correspondence of Henry James and Henry Adams, 1877–1914.* Baton Rouge: Louisiana State UP, 1992.

Moon, Michael. *A Small Boy and Others: Imitation and Initiation in American Culture from Henry James to Andy Warhol.* Durham, NC: Duke UP, 1998.

Novick, Sheldon. *Henry James: The Young Master.* New York: Random, 1996.

———. Introduction to *Henry James and Homo-Erotic Desire.* Edited by John R. Bradley, 1–23.

Person, Leland S. *Henry James and the Suspense of Masculinity.* Philadelphia: U of Pennsylvania P, 2003.

Rivkin, Julie. "Writing the Gay '80s with Henry James: David Leavitt's *A Place I've Never Been* and Alan Hollinghurst's *The Line of Beauty.*" *Henry James Review* 26, no. 3 (2005): 282–92.

Rosenzweig, Saul. "The Ghost of Henry James." *Partisan Review* 11 (Fall 1944): 436–55.

Rowe, John Carlos. *The Other Henry James*. Durham, NC: Duke UP, 1998.

Sanner, Kristin. "'Wasn't All History Full of the Destruction of Precious Things?' Missing Mothers, Feminized Fathers, and the Purchase of Freedom in Henry James's *The Portrait of a Lady*." *Henry James Review* 26, no. 2 (2005): 147–67.

Savoy, Eric. "The Queer Subject of the 'Jolly Corner.'" *Henry James Review* 20, no. 1 (Winter 1999): 1–21.

Sedgwick, Eve. "The Beast in the Closet: James and the Writing of Homosexual Panic." In *Sex, Politics, and Science in the Nineteenth-Century Novel*, edited by Ruth Bernard Yeazell, 148–86. Selected Papers from the English Institute, 1983–1984, n.s., no. 10. Baltimore: Johns Hopkins UP, 1986.

———. *Epistemology of the Closet*. Berkeley: U of California P, 1990.

———, ed. *Novel Gazing: Queer Readings in Fiction*. Durham, NC: Duke UP, 1997.

Solomon, Melissa. "The Female World of Exorcisim and Displacement (Or, Relations between Women in Henry James's Nineteenth-Century *The Portrait of a Lady*). In Sedgwick, *Novel Gazing*, 444–64.

Stevens, Hugh. *Henry James and Sexuality*. Cambridge: Cambridge UP, 1998.

———. "Homoeroticism, Identity, and Agency in James's Late Tales." In Buelens, 126–47.

———. "Queer Henry *In the Cage*." In Freedman, 120–38.

———. "The Resistance to Queory: John Addington Symonds and 'The Real Right Thing.'" *Henry James Review* 20, no. 3 (1999): 255–64.

Thurschwell, Pamela. *Literature, Technology and Magical Thinking, 1880–1920*. Cambridge: Cambridge UP, 2001.

Tóibín, Colm. *The Master*. New York: Scribner's, 2004.

Van Leer, David. "The Beast of the Closet: Homosociality and the Pathology of Manhood." *Critical Inquiry* 15, no. 3 (Spring 1989): 587–605.

Walker, Pierre A., and Greg W. Zacharias. "James's Hand and Gosse's Tail: Henry James Letters and the Status of Evidence." *Henry James Review* 19, no. 1 (1998): 72–79.

Walton, Priscilla. *The Disruption of the Feminine in Henry James*. Toronto: U of Toronto P, 1992.

———. "The Janus Faces of James: Gender, Transnationality, and James's Cinematic Adaptations." In McCormack, 37–53.

Zwinger, Lynda. "Bodies that Don't Matter: The Queering of 'Henry James.'" *Modern Fiction Studies* 41, nos. 3–4 (Fall–Winter 1995): 657–80.

Selected Henry James Bibliography

First Editions

A Passionate Pilgrim and other Tales. Boston: James R. Osgood, 1875.
Transatlantic Sketches. Boston: James R. Osgood, 1875.
Roderick Hudson. Boston: James R. Osgood, 1875. London: Macmillan, 1879 (revised).
The American. Boston: James R. Osgood, 1877. London: Macmillan, 1879.
French Poets and Novelists. London: Macmillan, 1878. Leipzig: Bernhard Tauchnitz, 1883.
Watch and Ward. Boston: Houghton Mifflin, James R. Osgood, 1878.
The Europeans. London: Macmillan, 1878. Boston: Houghton Mifflin, James R. Osgood, 1879.
Daisy Miller. New York: Harper & Brothers, 1879. London: Macmillan, 1879.
An International Episode. New York: Harper & Brothers, 1879.
The Madonna of the Future. London: Macmillan, 1879.
Hawthorne. London: Macmillan, 1879. New York: Harper & Brothers, 1880.
Confidence. London: Chatto & Windus, 1880. Boston: Houghton Mifflin, James R. Osgood, 1880.
The Diary of a Man of Fifty and A Bundle of Letters. New York: Harper & Brothers, 1880.
Washington Square. New York: Harper & Brothers, 1880. London: Macmillan, 1881.
The Portrait of a Lady. London: Macmillan, 1881. Boston: Houghton Mifflin, 1882.
Daisy Miller: A Comedy. Boston: James R. Osgood, 1883.
The Siege of London. Boston: James R. Osgood, 1883. Leipzig: Bernhard Tauchnitz, 1884.
Portraits of Places. London: Macmillan, 1883. Boston: James R. Osgood, 1884.
A Little Tour in France. Boston: James R. Osgood, 1884. London: Heinemann, 1900.
Tales of Three Cities. Boston: James R. Osgood, 1884. London: Macmillan, 1884.
The Author of Beltraffio. Boston: James R. Osgood, 1884.

The Bostonians. London and New York: Macmillan, 1886.

The Princess Casamassima. London and New York: Macmillan, 1886.

Partial Portraits. London and New York: Macmillan, 1886.

The Reverberator. London and New York: Macmillan, 1888.

The Aspern Papers. London and New York: Macmillan, 1888.

A London Life. London and New York: Macmillan, 1889.

The Tragic Muse. Boston and New York: Houghton Mifflin, 1890. London and New York: Macmillan, 1890.

The Lesson of the Master. London and New York: Macmillan, 1892.

The Real Thing. London and New York: Macmillan, 1893.

Picture and Text. New York: Harper & Brothers, 1893.

The Private Life. London: James R. Osgood, McIlvaine & Co., 1893. New York: Harper & Brothers, 1893.

Essays in London and Elsewhere. London: James R. Osgood, McInvaine & Co., 1893. New York: Harper & Brothers, 1893.

The Wheel of Time. New York: Harper & Brothers, 1893.

Theatricals. London: James R. Osgood, McIlvaine & Co., 1894.

Theatricals: Second Series. London: James R. Osgood, McIlvaine & Co., 1894.

Terminations. London: Heinemann, 1895. New York: Harper & Brothers, 1895.

Embarrassments. London: Heinemann, 1896. New York: Macmillan, 1896.

The Other House. London: Heinemann, 1896. New York: Macmillan, 1986.

The Spoils of Poynton. London: Heinemann, 1897. Boston: Houghton Mifflin, 1897.

What Maisie Knew. London: Heinemann. Chicago: Herbert S. Stone, 1897.

In the Cage. London: Duckworth and Co., 1898. Chicago: Herbert S. Stone, 1898.

The Two Magics, The Turn of the Screw, Covering End. London: Heinemann, 1898. New York: Macmillan, 1898.

The Awkward Age. London: Heinemann, 1899. New York: Harper & Brothers, 1899.

The Soft Side. London: Methuen & Co., 1900. New York: Macmillan, 1900.

The Sacred Fount. New York: Scribner's, 1901. London: Methuen, 1901.

The Wings of the Dove. New York: Scribner's, 1902. Westminster: Archibald Constable and Co., 1902.

The Better Sort. London: Methuen, 1903. New York: Scribner's, 1903.

The Ambassadors. London: Methuen, 1903. New York: Harper & Brothers, 1903.

William Wetmore Story and His Friends. Edinburgh and London: William Blackwood and Sons, 1903. Boston: Houghton Mifflin, 1903.

The Golden Bowl. New York: Scribner's, 1904. London: Methuen, 1904.

The Question of Our Speech. Boston: Houghton Mifflin, 1905.

English Hours. London: Heinemann, 1905. Boston: Houghton Mifflin, 1905.

The American Scene. London: Chapman and Hall, 1907. New York: Harper & Brothers, 1907.

The Novels and Tales of Henry James "New York Edition." 24 vols. Published two volumes at a time between 14 December 1907 and 31 July 1909. New York: Scribner's. London: Macmillan, 1908–9.

Views and Reviews. Boston: The Ball Publishing Co., 1908.

Julia Bride. New York: Harper & Brothers, 1909.

Italian Hours. London: Heinemann, 1909. Boston: Houghton Mifflin, 1909.

The Finer Grain. New York: Scribner's, 1910. London: Methuen, 1910.

The Henry James Year Book. Boston: Richard G. Badger, 1911. London: J. M. Dent, 1912.

The Outcry. London: Methuen, 1911. New York: Scribner's, 1911.

A Small Boy and Others. New York: Scribner's, 1913. London: Macmillan, 1913.

Notes of a Son and Brother. New York: Scribner's, 1914. London: Macmillan, 1914.

Notes on Novelists. London: J. M. Dent, 1914. New York: Scribner's, 1914.

The Question of the Mind. London: Central Committee for National Patriotic Organisations, 1915.

Pictures and Other Passages from Henry James. Selected by Ruth Head. London: Chatto & Windus, 1916.

The Ivory Tower. London: W. Collins Sons, 1917. New York: Scribner's, 1917.

The Sense of the Past. London: W. Collins Sons, 1917. New York: Scribner's, 1917.

The Middle Years. London: W. Collins Sons, 1917. New York: Scribner's, 1917.

Gabrielle de Bergerac. New York: Boni & Liveright, 1918.

Within the Rim. London: W. Collins Sons, 1919.

Travelling Companions. New York: Boni & Liveright, 1919.

A Landscape Painter. New York: Scott & Seltzer, 1919.

Refugees in Chelsea. Chelsea: Ashendene Press, 1920.

Master Eustace. New York: Thomas Seltzer, 1920.

Works Consulted

Adams, Timothy Dow. "Material James and James's Material: Coburn's Frontispieces to the New York Edition." *Henry James Review* 21, no. 3 (2000): 253–60.

Agnew, Jean-Christophe. "The Consuming Vision of Henry James." In *The Culture of Consumption: Critical Essays in American History, 1880–1980*, edited by Richard Wightman Fox and T. J. Jackson Lears, 65–100. New York: Pantheon, 1983.

Allen, Elizabeth. *A Woman's Place in the Novels of Henry James*. New York: St. Martin's, 1984.

Anderson, James William. "An Interview with Leon Edel on the James Family." *Psychohistory Review* 8, no. 1–2 (1979): 15–22.

Anderson, Quentin. *The American Henry James*. New Brunswick, NJ: Rutgers UP, 1957.

Andreas, Osborn. *Henry James and the Expanding Horizon*. Seattle: U of Washington P, 1948.

Anesko, Michael. "The Eclectic Architecture of Henry James's New York Edition." *"Friction with the Market": Henry James and the Profession of Authorship*, 141–62. New York: Oxford UP, 1986.

———. "'God Knows they are Impossible': James's Letters and Their Editors." *Henry James Review* 18, no. 2 (1997): 140–48.

Armstrong, Paul B. *The Challenge of Bewilderment: Understanding and Representation in James, Conrad, and Ford*. Ithaca, NY: Cornell UP, 1987.

———. "History and Epistemology: The Example of *The Turn of the Screw*." In Esch and Warren, 245–54.

———. *The Phenomenology of Henry James*. Chapel Hill: U of North Carolina P, 1983.

———. "Reading James's Prefaces and Reading James." In McWhirter, 125–37.

Ash, Beth Sharon. "Narcissism and the Gilded Image: A Psychoanalytic Reading of *The Golden Bowl*." *Henry James Review* 15, no. 1 (1994): 55–90.

Auerbach, Nina. "*The Bostonians*: Feminists and the New World." In *American Novelists Revisited: Essays in Feminist Criticism*, edited by Fritz Fleishmann, 189–208. Boston: G. K. Hall, 1982.

Banta, Martha. "The Excluded Seven: Practice of Omission, Aesthetics of Refusal." In McWhirter, 240–60.

———. *Henry James and the Occult*. Bloomington: Indiana UP, 1972.

———. Review of *Henry James: A Life*. *American Literature* 58, no. 4 (December 1986): 639–43.

Beach, Joseph Warren. *The Method of Henry James*. Philadelphia: Albert Saifer, 1954 [1918].

Beidler, Peter G., ed. *The Turn of the Screw by Henry James*. 2nd ed. Boston: Bedford/St. Martin's, 2004.

Bell, Millicent. "Henry James: The Man Who Lived." *Massachusetts Review* 14 (Spring 1973): 391–414.

———. Introduction to *Beloved Boy: Letters to Hendrik C. Andersen, 1899–1915*. Edited by Rosella Mamoli Zorzi, ix–xxxv. Charlottesville: U of Virginia P, 2004.

———. "Jamesian Being." *Virginia Quarterly Review* 52, no. 1 (Winter 1976): 115–32.

———. *Meaning in Henry James*. Cambridge, MA: Harvard UP, 1991.

———. "The Unmentionable Subject in 'The Pupil.'" In Freedman, *Cambridge*, 139–50.

Bennett, Arnold. "Henry James." *Books and Persons*, 263–66. New York: Doran, 1917.

Bersani, Leo. *A Future for Astyanax: Character and Desire in Literature*. Ithaca, NY: Cornell UP, 1984.

Blackmur, Richard, ed. *The Art of the Novel: Critical Prefaces by Henry James*. New York: Scribner's, 1934.

———. "Henry James." In *Literary History of the United States*. Vol. 2, edited by Robert Spiller, et al., 1039–64. New York: Macmillan, 1948.

———. *The Lion and the Honeycomb: Essays in Solicitude and Critique*. New York: Harcourt, Brace and World, 1955.

———. *Studies in Henry James*. Edited by Veronica A. Makowsky. New York: New Directions, 1983.

Blair, Sara. "Documenting America: Racial Theater in *The American Scene*." *Henry James Review* 16, no. 3 (1995): 264–72.

———. *Henry James and the Writing of Race and Nation*. New York: Cambridge UP, 1996.

———. "In the House of Fiction: Henry James and the Engendering of Literary Mastery." In McWhirter, 58–73.

Bogardus, Ralph F. *Pictures and Texts: Henry James, A. L. Coburn, and New Ways of Seeing in Literary Culture*. Ann Arbor, MI: UMI Research Press, 1984.

Booth, Wayne C. *The Rhetoric of Fiction*. Chicago: U of Chicago P, 1983 [1961].

Boudreau, Kristin. "Henry James's Inward Aches." *Henry James Review* 20, no. 1 (1999): 69–80.

Bradley, John R., ed. *Henry James and Homo-Erotic Desire*. New York: St. Martin's, 1999.

———. *Henry James's Permanent Adolescence*. New York: Palgrave, 2000.

Brooks, Peter. *The Melodramatic Imagination: Balzac, Henry James, Melodrama and the Mode of Excess*. New Haven, CT: Yale UP, 1976.

Brooks, Van Wyck. *The Pilgrimage of Henry James*. New York: Dutton, 1925.
Buelens, Gert, ed. *Enacting History in Henry James: Narrative, Power, and Ethics*. Cambridge: Cambridge UP, 1997.
———. "Possessing the American Scene: Race and Vulgarity, Seduction and Judgment." In Buelens, 166–92.
Burr, Anna Robeson. *Alice James: Her Brothers—Her Journal*. New York: Dodd, Mead, 1934.
Bynner, Witter. "On Henry James' Centennial: Lasting Impressions of a Great American Writer." *Saturday Review of Literature* 2 (22 May 1943): 23, 26, 28.
Calisher, Hortense. "A Short Note on a Long Subject: Henry James." *Texas Quarterly* (Summer 1967): 57–59.
Cameron, Sharon. "The Prefaces, Revision, and Ideas of Consciousness." *Thinking in Henry James*, 32–82. Chicago: U of Chicago P, 1989.
Cannon, Kelly. *Henry James and Masculinity: The Man at the Margins*. New York: St. Martin's, 1994.
Cargill, Oscar. *The Novels of Henry James*. New York: Macmillan, 1961.
———. Review of *Henry James*, 5 vols. *American Literature* 44, no. 2 (May 1972): 330–32.
Carroll, David. *The Subject in Question: The Languages of Theory and the Strategies of Fiction*. Chicago: U of Chicago P, 1982.
Castle, Terry. "Haunted by Olive Chancellor." *The Apparitional Lesbian: Female Homosexuality and Modern Culture*, 150–85. New York: Columbia UP, 1993.
Chesterton, G. K. *The Autobiography of G. K. Chesterton*. New York: Sheed and Ward, 1936.
Clemens, Cyril. "Bret Harte and Henry James as Seen by Marie Belloc Lowndes." *Mark Twain Quarterly* 2 (Fall 1937): 21–23.
———. "A Visit to Henry James' Old Home." *Mark Twain Quarterly* 5 (Spring 1943): 9.
Cohen, Philip. "The Lesson of the Master: The New York Edition, James Studies, and Contemporary Textual Scholarship." Review of McWhirter. *Studies in the Novel* 31, no. 1 (Spring 1999): 98–116.
Conrad, Joseph. "An Appreciation." In Edel, *Collection*, 11–17.
Cooper, Michael A. "Discipl(in)ing the Master, Mastering the Discipl(in)e: Erotonomies of Discipleship in James' Tales of Literary Life." In *Engendering Men*, edited by Joseph Boone and Michael Cadden, 66–86. New York: Routledge, 1990.
Cormier, Harvey. "Jamesian Pragmatism and Jamesian Realism." *Henry James Review* 18, no. 3 (1997): 288–96.
Crews, Frederick C. *The Tragedy of Manners: Moral Drama in the Later Novels of Henry James*. Hamden, CT: Archon Books, 1971 [1957].
Daugherty, Sarah B. "James and the Ethics of Control: Aspiring Architects and Their Floating Creatures." In Buelens, 61–74.

Daugherty, Sarah B. "James and the Representation of Women: Some Lessons of the Master(')s." In McCormack, 176–95.

Davidson, Rob. *The Master and the Dean: The Literary Criticism of Henry James and William Dean Howells.* Columbia: U of Missouri P, 2005.

Dupee, Frederick W. *Henry James.* New York: Sloane, 1951.

———, ed. *The Question of Henry James: A Collection of Critical Essays.* New York: Holt, 1945.

Dwight, H. G. "H. G. Dwight on American Hostility to James, and Its Probable Causes." In Gard, 432–49.

Eakin, Paul John. "Henry James's 'Obscure Hurt': Can Autobiography Serve Biography?" *New Literary History* 19, no. 3 (Spring 1988): 675–92.

Edel, Leon. "Confessions of a Biographer." In *Psychoanalytic Studies of Biography*, ed. Moraitis and Pollock, 3–27.

———. *Henry James.* Pamphlets on American Writers, no. 4. Minneapolis: U of Minnesota P, 1960.

———. *Henry James.* Vol. 1, *The Untried Years, 1843–1870.* Philadelphia: Lippincott, 1953.

———. *Henry James.* Vol. 2, *The Conquest of London, 1870–1883.* Philadelphia: Lippincott, 1962.

———. *Henry James.* Vol. 3, *The Middle Years, 1882–1895.* Philadelphia: Lippincott, 1962.

———. *Henry James.* Vol. 4, *The Treacherous Years, 1895–1901.* Philadelphia: Lippincott, 1969.

———. *Henry James.* Vol. 5, *The Master, 1901–1916.* Philadelphia: Lippincott, 1972.

———, ed. *Henry James: A Collection of Critical Essays.* Englewood Cliffs, NJ: Prentice Hall, 1963.

———, ed. *Henry James: Selected Letters.* Cambridge, MA: Belknap Press of Harvard UP, 1987.

———, ed. *Henry James Letters.* Vol. 4. Cambridge, MA: Belknap Press of Harvard UP, 1984.

———. *Literary Biography.* London: Rupert Hart-Davis, 1957.

———. Review of *The Legend of the Master: Henry James. New England Quarterly* 21, no. 4 (December 1948): 544–47.

———. *Stuff of Sleep and Dreams.* New York: Harper & Row, 1982.

———. *Writing Lives: Principia Biographica.* New York: Norton, 1984.

Edel, Leon, and Dan Laurence. *A Bibliography of Henry James.* 3rd ed. Oxford: Clarendon Press, 1982.

Edel, Leon, and Lyall H. Powers, eds. *The Complete Notebooks of Henry James.* New York: Oxford UP, 1987.

Edel, Leon, and Gordon N. Ray, eds. *Henry James and H. G. Wells, A Record of Their Friendship, Their Debate on the Art of Fiction, and Their Quarrel.* Urbana: U of Illinois P, 1958.

Edgar, Pelham. *Henry James: Man and Author*. Boston: Houghton Mifflin, 1927.

Eliot, T. S. "Henry James." In *The Shock of Recognition*, edited by Edmund Wilson, 854–65. New York: Modern Library, 1943.

Esch, Deborah, and Jonathan Warren, eds. *The Turn of the Screw by Henry James: A Norton Critical Edition*. 2nd ed. New York: Norton, 1999.

Felman, Shoshana. "Henry James: Madness and the Risks of Practice (Turning the Screw of Interpretation)." In Esch and Warren, 196–228.

———. *Writing and Madness (Literature/Philosophy/Psychoanalysis)*. Translated by Martha Noel Evans, Shoshana Felman, and Brian Massumi. Ithaca, NY: Cornell UP, 1985.

Fetterly, Judith. "*The Bostonians*: Henry James's Eternal Triangle." *The Resisting Reader: A Feminist Approach to American Fiction*, 101–53. Bloomington: Indiana UP, 1978.

Flannery, Denis. "The Appalling Mrs. Luna: Sibling Love, Queer Attachment, and Henry James's *The Bostonians*." *Henry James Review* 26, no. 1 (2005): 1–19.

Fleet, Simon. "The Nice American Gentleman." *Vogue* (1 October 1949): 136, 183–85.

Fluck, Winfried. "Power Relations in the Novels of James: The 'Liberal' and the 'Radical' Version." In Buelens, 16–39.

Fogel, Daniel Mark. *Henry James and the Structure of the Romantic Imagination*. Baton Rouge: Louisiana State UP, 1981.

———. "In Memoriam: Adeline R. Tintner (1912–2003)." *Henry James Review* 25, no. 1 (2004): 1–3.

———. "Leon Edel's Henry James." In Powers, *Leon Edel and Literary Art*, 73–82.

———. "A New Reading of Henry James's 'The Jolly Corner.'" In Gargano, *The Late Novels*, 190–203.

Ford, Ford Madox. *Henry James: A Critical Study*. New York: Octagon Books, 1964 [1913].

———. "Henry James: The Master." *Portraits from Life*. Boston: Houghton Mifflin, 1937.

Fowler, Virginia C. *Henry James's American Girl: The Embroidery on the Canvas*. Madison: Uy of Wisconsin P, 1984.

Freedman, Jonathan, ed. *The Cambridge Companion to Henry James*. Cambridge: Cambridge UP, 1998.

———. *Professions of Taste: Henry James, British Aestheticism, and Commodity Culture*. Stanford, CA: Stanford UP, 1990.

———. Review of *Imagination and Desire in the Novels of Henry James; Henry James and the Art of Power*. *New England Quarterly* 58, no. 2 (June 1985): 323–30.

Fromm, Gloria, ed. *Essaying Biography: A Celebration for Leon Edel*. Honolulu: The Biographical Research Center, 1986.

Fryer, Judith. *The Faces of Eve: Women in the Nineteenth Century American Novel.* Oxford: Oxford UP, 1976.

Funston, Judith E. *Henry James, 1975–1987: A Reference Guide.* Boston: G. K. Hall, 1991.

Gale, Robert. *Plots and Characters in the Fiction of Henry James.* Hamden, CT: Archon Books, 1965.

Gard, Roger, ed. *Henry James: The Critical Heritage.* London: Routledge, 1968.

Gargano, James W., ed. *Critical Essays on Henry James: The Early Novels.* Boston: G. K. Hall, 1987.

———. *Critical Essays on Henry James: The Late Novels.* Boston: G. K. Hall, 1987.

Garland, Hamlin. "I Have Lost Touch with My Own People." In *Henry James, Interviews and Recollections,* edited by Norman Page, 91–95. London: Macmillan, 1984.

Gass, William. "The High Brutality of Good Intentions." In Gargano, *The Early Novels,* 136–44.

Geismer, Maxwell. *Henry James and the Jacobites.* Boston: Houghton Mifflin, 1963.

Gide, André. "Henry James." *Yale Review* 19, no. 3 (March 1930): 641–43.

Goetz, William R. "Criticism and Autobiography in James's Prefaces." *American Literature* 51 (1979): 333–48.

Goode, John, ed. *The Air of Reality: New Essays on Henry James.* London: Methuen, 1972.

Gordon, Lyndall. *A Private Life of Henry James: Two Women and His Art.* New York: Norton, 1998.

Gosse, Edmund. *Aspects and Impressions.* New York: Scribner's, 1922.

Graham, Kenneth. *Henry James, The Drama of Fulfillment.* Oxford: Clarendon Press, 1975.

———. Review of *Henry James: The Treacherous Years, 1895–1901. Review of English Studies,* New Series 22, no. 86 (May 1971): 235–37.

Graham, Wendy. *Henry James's Thwarted Love.* Stanford, CA: Stanford UP, 1999.

Grattan, Clinton Hartley. "The Calm within the Cyclone." *Nation* 134 (17 February 1932) 201–3.

———. *The Three Jameses: A Family of Minds; Henry James, Sr., William James, Henry James.* New York: New York UP, 1932.

Greene, Graham. *The Lost Childhood and other Essays.* New York: Viking, 1952.

Griffin, Susan. *The Historical Eye: The Texture of the Visual in Late James.* Boston: Northeastern UP, 1991.

———. "Scar Texts: Tracing the Marks of Jamesian Masculinity." *Arizona Quarterly* 53, no. 4 (1997): 61–82.

Griffin, Susan. "Seeing Doubles: Reflections of the Self in James's *Sense of the Past*." *Modern Language Quarterly* 45, no. 1 (March 1984): 48–60.

———. "The Selfish Eye: Strether's Principles of Psychology." *American Literature* 56, no. 3 (October 1984): 396–409.

Grover, Philip. *Henry James and the French Novel*. New York: Barnes & Noble, 1973.

Gunter, Susan E., ed. *Dear Munificent Friends: Henry James's Letters to Four Women*. Ann Arbor: U of Michigan P, 1999.

———. "'You Will Fit the Tighter into My Embrace!' Henry James's Letters to Jocelyn Persse." *GLQ: A Journal of Lesbian and Gay Studies* 7, no. 2 (2001): 335–54.

Gunter, Susan E., and Steven H. Jobe, eds. *Dear Beloved Friends: Henry James's Letters to Younger Men*. Ann Arbor: U of Michigan P, 2002.

Habegger, Alfred. *Gender, Fantasy, and Realism in the American Novel*. New York: Columbia UP, 1982.

———. *Henry James and the 'Woman Business.'* Cambridge: Cambridge UP, 1989.

———. "'What Maisie Knew': Henry James's *Bildungsroman* of the Artist as Queer Moralist." In Buelens, 93–108.

Hale, Dorothy J. "Henry James and the Invention of Novel Theory." In Freedman, 79–101.

Hanson, Ellis. "Screwing with Children in Henry James." *GLQ: A Journal of Lesbian and Gay Studies* 9, no. 3 (2003): 367–91.

Haralson, Eric. *Henry James and Queer Modernity*. New York: Cambridge UP, 2003.

———. "Lambert Strether's Excellent Adventure." In Freedman, *Cambridge*, 169–86.

Haviland, Beverly. "The Return of the Alien: Henry James in New York, 1904." *Henry James Review* 16, no. 3 (1995): 257–63.

Hayes, Kevin J., ed. *Henry James: The Contemporary Reviews*. Cambridge: Cambridge UP, 1996.

Hellman, Geoffrey T. "Chairman of the Board." *New Yorker*, 13 March 1971: 46+.

Henke, Richard. "The Man of Action: Henry James and the Performance of Gender." *Henry James Review* 16, no. 2 (1995): 227–41.

Heyns, Michiel W. "The Double Narrative of 'The Beast in the Jungle': Ethical Plot, Ironical Plot, and the Play of Power." In Buelens, 109–25.

Hicks, Priscilla Gibson. "A Turn in the Formation of James's New York Edition: Criticism, the Historical Record, and the Siting of *The Awkward Age*." *Henry James Review* 16, no. 2 (1995): 195–221.

Hochman, Barbara. "Disappearing Authors and Resentful Readers in Late-Nineteenth Century American Fiction: The Case of Henry James." *ELH* 63, no. 1 (1996): 177–201.

Hocks, Richard A. *Henry James and Pragmatistic Thought: A Study of the Relationship between the Philosophy of William James and the Literary Art of Henry James.* Chapel Hill: U of North Carolina P, 1974.

———. "Multiple Germs, Metaphorical Systems, and Moral Fluctuation in *The Ambassadors.*" In Buelens, 40–60.

———. "Recollecting and Reexamining William and Henry." *Henry James Review.* 18, no. 3 (1997): 280–87.

———. Review of *Desire and Love in Henry James: Study of the Late Novels; Thinking in Henry James. Nineteenth Century Literature* 45. 3 (Dec. 1990): 338–91.

Holland, Laurence B. *The Expense of Vision: Essays on the Craft of Henry James.* Princeton, NJ: Princeton UP, 1964.

Hollinghurst, Alan. *The Line of Beauty.* London: Macmillan, 2004.

Horne, Philip. "The Editing of James's Letters." *Cambridge Quarterly* 15 (1986): 126–41.

———. *Henry James: A Life in Letters.* New York: Viking, 1998.

———. "Henry James: The Master and the 'Queer Affair' of 'The Pupil.'" *Critical Quarterly* 37, no. 3 (Autumn 1995): 75–92.

———. *Henry James and Revision: The New York Edition.* Oxford: Clarendon Press, 1990.

———. "The Question of Our Texts." In Freedman, 63–78.

Hound and Horn. 7 (April–May 1934). Special issue on Henry James.

Howe, Irving. "The Political Vocation." In Edel, *Critical Essays,* 156–71.

Howells, William Dean. "Henry James, Jr." *Century* 25, no. 1 (1882): 25–29.

———. Review of *The Passionate Pilgrim.* In Vann, 10–16.

Hoy, Helen. "Homotextual Duplicity in Henry James's 'The Pupil.'" *Henry James Review* 14, no. 1 (Winter 1993) 34–42.

Izzo, Donatella. *Portraying the Lady: Technologies of Gender in the Short Stories of Henry James.* Lincoln: U of Nebraska P, 2001.

Jacobson, Marcia. *Henry James and the Mass Market.* University: U of Alabama P, 1983.

James, Henry. *Autobiography.* Edited by F. W. Dupee. Princeton, NJ: Princeton UP, 1983 [1913, 1914, 1917].

———. *Literary Criticism: Essays on Literature, American Writers, English Writers.* New York: The Library of America, 1984.

Johanningsmeier, Charles. "How Real American Readers Originally Experienced James's 'The Real Thing.'" *Henry James Review* 27, no. 1 (2006): 75–99.

Jordan, Elizabeth. "Mr. James and the London Season." *Three Rousing Cheers,* 195–221. New York: Appleton-Century, 1938.

Kaplan, Fred. *Henry James: The Imagination of Genius.* New York: Morrow, 1992.

Kaplan, Fred. "James Without Beret." In *Biography and Source Studies*, edited by Frederick R. Karl, 1–8. New York: AMS Press, 1996.

Kaston, Carren. *Imagination and Desire in the Novels of Henry James*. New Brunswick, NJ: Rutgers UP, 1984.

Kazin, Alfred. Review of *Henry James: The Untried Years*. *New York Herald Tribune Book Review*, 3 May 1953: 1.

Kimbrough, Robert, ed. *The Turn of the Screw by Henry James*. New York: Norton, 1966.

Kress, Jill. *The Figure of Consciousness: William James, Henry James, and Edith Wharton*. New York: Routledge, 2002.

Krook, Dorothea. *The Ordeal of Consciousness in Henry James*. New York: Cambridge UP, 1962.

LaFarge, John. "Henry James's Letters to the LaFarges." *New England Quarterly* 22 (June 1949): 173–92.

Lane, Christopher. "Jamesian Inscrutability." *Henry James Review* 20, no. 3 (1999): 244–54.

Leavis. F. R. "The Appreciation of Henry James." *Scrutiny* 14 (Spring 1947): 229–37.

———. *The Great Tradition: George Eliot, Henry James, Joseph Conrad*. Garden City, NY: Doubleday, 1954.

———. "Henry James." *Scrutiny* 5 (March 1939): 398–417.

———. "Henry James's First Novel." *Scrutiny* 14 (Spring 1947): 295–301.

Leavitt, David. *A Place I've Never Been*. New York: Penguin, 1990.

Leslie, Shane. "A Note on Henry James." *Horizon* 7 (June 1943): 405–13.

Leuschner, Eric. "'Utterly, Insurmountably, Unsaleable': Collected Editions, Prefaces, and the 'Failure' of Henry James's New York Edition." *Henry James Review* 22, no. 1 (2001): 24–40.

Levenson, J. C. Review of *Henry James: The Untried Years, 1843–70*. *New England Quarterly* 26, no. 4 (December 1953): 533–37.

Levin, Jonathan, and Sheldon M. Novick. "Realism and Imagination in the Thought of Henry and William James: A Conversation." *Henry James Review* 18, no. 3 (1997): 297–307.

Lichtenberg, Joseph D. "Henry James and Leon Edel." In Moraitis and Pollock, 49–58.

Lodge, David. *Author, Author*. New York: Viking Penguin, 2004.

Lubbock, Percy. *The Craft of Fiction*. New York: Scribner's, 1921.

———, ed. *The Letters of Henry James*. 2 vols. New York: Scribner's, 1920.

Luciano, Dana. "Invalid Relations: Queer Kinship in Henry James's *The Portrait of a Lady*." *Henry James Review* 23, no. 2 (2002): 196–217.

Ludwig, Sami. *Pragmatist Realism: the Cognitive Paradigm in American Realist Texts*. Madison: U of Wisconsin P, 2002.

Lynn, Kenneth S. Review of *Henry James, The Conquest of London: 1870–1881; Henry James, The Middle Years: 1882–1895*. *New England Quarterly* 36, no. 2 (June 1963): 260–63.

MacKenzie, Compton. "Henry James." *Life and Letters* 39 (December 1943): 147–55.

Marshall, Adré. *The Turn of the Mind: Constituting Consciousness in Henry James*. London: Associated Universities Press, 1998.

Matthiessen. F. O. *Henry James: The Major Phase*. New York: Oxford UP, 1944.

———. *The James Family: Including Selections from the Writings of Henry James, Senior, William, Henry, and Alice James*. New York: Knopf, 1947.

McColley, Kathleen. "Claiming Center Stage: Speaking Out for Homoerotic Empowerment in *The Bostonians*." *Henry James Review* 21, no. 2 (2000): 151–69.

McCormack, Peggy, ed. *Questioning the Master: Gender and Sexuality in Henry James's Writings*. Baltimore: U of Delaware P, 2000.

McCulloch, Jeanne. "The Art of Biography I: Leon Edel." *Paris Review* 98 (Winter 1985): 157–207.

McWhirter, David. "Henry James, (Post)Modernist?" *Henry James Review* 25. no. 2 (2004): 168–94.

———, ed. *Henry James's New York Edition: The Construction of Authorship*. Stanford, CA: Stanford UP, 1995.

———. "'A Provision Full of Responsibilities': Senses of the Past in Henry James's Fourth Phase." In Buelens, 148–65.

Meissner, Colin. *Henry James and the Language of Experience*. New York: Cambridge UP, 1999.

Mencken, H. L. *A Mencken Chrestomathy*. New York: Knopf, 1920.

Michaels, Walter Benn. "Jim Crow Henry James?" *Henry James Review* 16, no. 3 (1995): 286–91.

Miller, J. Hillis. "The 'Grafted' Image: James on Illustration." In McWhirter, 138–41.

Miller, James E. "Henry James in Reality." *Critical Inquiry* 2, no. 3 (Spring 1976): 585–604.

Monteiro, George, ed. *The Correspondence of Henry James and Henry Adams, 1877–1914*. Baton Rouge: Louisiana State UP, 1992.

Moon, Michael. *A Small Boy and Others: Imitation and Initiation in American Culture from Henry James to Andy Warhol*. Durham, NC: Duke UP, 1998.

Moore, Rayburn S. "'The Full Light of a Higher Criticism': Edel's Biography and Other other Recent Studies of Henry James." *South Atlantic Quarterly* 63 (1964): 104–14.

———. "Henry James Ltd., and the Chairman of the Board: Leon Edel's Biography." Review of *The Life of Henry James*. *South Atlantic Quarterly* 73 (1974): 261–69.

Moraitis, George, and George H. Pollock, eds. *Psychoanalytic Studies of Biography*. Madison, CT: International Universities Press, 1987.

Murray, Donald M. "Henry James and The English Reviewers, 1882–1890." *American Literature* 24, no. 1 (March 1952): 1–20.

Nadel, Ira. "Visual Culture: The Photo Frontispieces to the New York Edition." In McWhirter, 90–108.

Nevius, Blake. Review of *Henry James, The Treacherous Years: 1895–1901*. *Nineteenth Century Fiction* 25, no. 1 (June 1970): 118–21.

Novick, Sheldon. *Henry James: The Young Master*. New York: Random House, 1996.

———. Introduction to *Henry James and Homo-Erotic Desire*. Edited by John R. Bradley, 1–23.

Parker, Herschel. "The Authority of the Revised Text and the Disappearance of the Author: What Critics of Henry James Did with Textual Evidence in the Heyday of the New Criticism." *Flawed Texts and Verbal Icons: Literary Authority in American Fiction*, 85–114. Evanston, IL: Northwestern UP, 1984.

———. "Deconstructing the Art of the Novel and Liberating James's Prefaces." *Henry James Review* 14, no. 3 (1993): 284–307.

Parrington, Vernon. "Henry James and the Nostalgia of Culture." *Main Currents in American Thought*. Vol. 3, 239–41. New York: Harcourt, Brace and World.

Pearson, John. *The Prefaces of Henry James: Framing the Early Modern Reader*. University Park: Pennsylvania State UP, 1997.

Person, Leland S. *Henry James and the Suspense of Masculinity*. Philadelphia: U of Pennsylvania P, 2003.

———. "In the Closet with Frederick Douglass: Reconstructing Masculinity in *The Bostonians*." *Henry James Review* 16, no. 3 (1995): 292–98.

Petrie, Dennis W. "Vision of the Artist: Leon Edel's *Henry James*." In Powers, *Leon Edel and Literary Art*, 63–71.

Poirier, Richard. *The Comic Sense of Henry James: A Study of the Early Novels*. New York: Oxford UP, 1960.

———. *The Performing Self: Compositions and Decompositions in the Languages of Contemporary Life*, 86–111. New York: Oxford UP, 1971.

Porter, Carolyn. *Seeing and Being: The Plight of the Participant Observer in Emerson, James, Adams, and Faulkner*. Middleton, CT: Wesleyan UP, 1981.

Posnock, Ross. "Affirming the Alien: The Pragmatist Pluralism of *The American Scene*. In Freedman, *Cambridge*, 224–46.

———. "Breaking the Aura of Henry James." In McWhirter, 23–28.

———. *The Trial of Curiosity: Henry James, William James, and the Challenge of Modernity*. New York: Oxford UP, 1991.

Pound, Ezra. "Henry James." In *Literary Essays of Ezra Pound*, edited by T. S. Eliot, 295–338. New York: New Directions, 1968 [1918].

Powers, Lyall, *Henry James and the Naturalist Movement.* East Lansing: Michigan State UP, 1971.

———. *Henry James's Major Novels; Essays in Criticism.* East Lansing: Michigan State UP, 1973.

———, ed. *Leon Edel and Literary Art.* Ann Arbor, MI: UMI Press, 1988.

———. "Leon Edel, The Life of a Biographer." *American Scholar* 66 (Autumn 1997): 598–607.

Przybylowicz, Donna. "The 'Lost Stuff of Consciousness': The Priority of Futurity and the Deferral of Desire in 'The Beast in the Jungle.'" In *Henry James's Daisy Miller, The Turn of the Screw, and Other Tales,* edited by Harold Bloom, 93–116. New York: Chelsea House, 1987.

Rahv, Philip. "Attitudes to Henry James." *New Republic* 108, no. 7 (15 February 1943): 220–24.

———. "The Cult of Experience in American Writing" (1940). In *Essays on Literature and Politics, 1932–1972,* edited by Arabel J. Porter and Andrew J. Dvosin, 8–22. Boston: Houghton Mifflin, 1978.

———. "Henry James and His Cult." In *Essays on Literature and Politics, 1932–1972,* edited by Arabel J. Porter and Andrew J. Dvosin, 93–104. Boston: Houghton Mifflin, 1978.

Review of *The Novels and Tales of Henry James. Literary Digest,* 21 March 1908: 418.

Rhoads, Linda Smith. Review of *Henry James: Letters, Volume 4, 1895–1916. New England Quarterly* 58, no. 1 (March 1985): 135–39.

Richardson, Lyon N. Review of *Henry James: The Conquest of London, 1870–1881; Henry James: The Middle Years. American Literature* 35, no. 3 (November 1963): 377–79.

Rivkin, Julie. "The Logic of Delegation in *The Ambassadors.*" *PMLA* 101, no. 5 (October 1986): 819–31.

———. "Writing the Gay '80s with Henry James: David Leavitt's *A Place I've Never Been* and Alan Hollinghurst's *The Line of Beauty.*" *Henry James Review* 26, no. 3 (2005): 282–92.

Rosenzweig, Saul. "The Ghost of Henry James." *Partisan Review* 11 (Fall 1944): 436–55.

Ross, Melanie H. "'The Mirror with a Memory': Tracking Consciousness in the Preface to *The Golden Bowl.*" *Henry James Review* 26, no. 3 (Fall 2005): 246–55.

Rowe, John Carlos. *The Other Henry James.* Durham, NC: Duke UP, 1998.

———. *The Theoretical Dimensions of Henry James.* Madison: U of Wisconsin P, 1984.

Rundle, Vivienne. "Defining Frames: The Prefaces of Henry James and Joseph Conrad." *Henry James Review* 16, no. 1 (1995): 66–92.

Ryan, Judith. "Henry James." *The Vanishing Subject: Early Psychology and Literary Modernism,* 75–88. Chicago: U of Chicago P, 1991.

Salmon, Richard. *Henry James and the Culture of Publicity.* Cambridge: Cambridge UP, 1997.

Sanner, Kristin. "'Wasn't All History Full of the Destruction of Precious Things?' Missing Mothers, Feminized Fathers, and the Purchase of Freedom in Henry James's *The Portrait of a Lady.*" *Henry James Review* 26, no. 2 (2005): 147–67.

Savoy, Eric. "Embarrassments: Figure in the Closet." *Henry James Review* 20, no. 3 (1999): 227–36.

———. "The Queer Subject of the 'Jolly Corner.'" *Henry James Review* 20, no. 1 (Winter 1999): 1–21.

Scudder, H. E. Review of *The Tragic Muse.* In Vann, 19–22.

Scura, Dorothy McInnis. *Henry James, 1960–1974: A Reference Guide.* Boston: G. K. Hall, 1979.

Sears, Sallie. *The Negative Imagination: Form and Perspective in the Novels of Henry James.* Ithaca, NY: Cornell UP, 1968.

Sedgwick, Eve. "The Beast in the Closet: James and the Writing of Homosexual Panic." In *Sex, Politics, and Science in the Nineteenth-Century Novel,* edited by Ruth Bernard Yeazell, 148–86. Selected Papers from the English Institute, 1983–1984, n.s., no. 10. Baltimore: Johns Hopkins UP, 1986.

———. *Epistemology of the Closet.* Berkeley: U of California P, 1990.

———. "Is the Rectum Straight? Identification and Identity in *The Wings of the Dove. Tendencies,* 73–103. Durham, NC: Duke UP, 1993.

———, ed. *Novel Gazing: Queer Readings in Fiction.* Durham, NC: Duke UP, 1997.

———. "Shame and Performativity: Henry James's New York Edition Prefaces." In McWhirter, 206–39.

Segal, Ora. *The Lucid Reflector: The Observer in Henry James' Fiction.* New Haven, CT: Yale UP, 1969.

Seltzer, Mark. *Henry James and the Art of Power.* Ithaca, NY: Cornell UP, 1984.

Shaw, Bernard. *Dramatic Opinions and Essays with an Apology.* Vol. 1. New York: Brentano's, 1922 [1907].

Sherman, Stuart P. "The Aesthetic Idealism of Henry James." *On Contemporary Literature,* 226–55. New York: Holt, 1923.

Simson, George. "Interview with Leon Edel." *Literature and Belief* 4 (1984): 17–31.

Skrupskelis, Ignas, and Elizabeth Berkeley, eds. *The Correspondence of William James.* Vol. 1, *William and Henry, 1861–1884.* Charlottesville: U of Virginia P, 1992.

———. *The Correspondence of William James.* Vol. 2, *William and Henry, 1885–1896.* Charlottesville: U of Virginia P, 1993.

———. *The Correspondence of William James.* Vol. 3, *William and Henry, 1897–1910.* Charlottesville: U of Virginia P, 1994.

Smith, Logan Pearsall. "Notes on Henry James." *Atlantic Monthly* 172 (August 1943): 75–77.

———. "Slices of Cake." *New Statesman and Nation* 25 (1 June 1943): 367–68.

Sofer, Naomi Z. "'Why Different Vibrations . . . Walk Hand in Hand': Homosocial Bonds in *Roderick Hudson*." *Henry James Review* 20, no. 3 (1999): 185–205.

Solomon, Eric. "The Return of the Screw." In Kimbrough, 237–45.

Solomon, Melissa. "The Female World of Exorcism and Displacement (Or, Relations between Women in Henry James's Nineteenth-Century *The Portrait of a Lady*)." In Sedgwick, *Novel Gazing*, 444–64.

Spender, Stephen. *The Destructive Element*. Philadelphia: Albert Saifer, 1953 [1935].

Spilka, Mark. "Turning the Freudian Screw: How Not to Do It." In Kimbrough, 245–53.

Stafford, William T. "Literary Allusions in James's Prefaces." *American Literature* 35, no. 1 (March 1963): 60–70.

Stevens, Hugh. *Henry James and Sexuality*. Cambridge: Cambridge UP, 1998.

———. "Homoeroticism, Identity, and Agency in James's Late Tales. In Buelens, 126–47.

———. "Queer Henry *In the Cage*." In Freedman, *Cambridge*, 120–38.

———. "The Resistance to Queory: John Addington Symonds and 'The Real Right Thing.'" *Henry James Review* 20, no. 3 (1999): 255–64.

Stevenson, Elizabeth. *The Crooked Corridor: A Study of Henry James*. New York: Macmillan, 1949.

Tate, Allen. "The Beast in the Jungle." In Vann, 75–78.

Taylor, Andrew. *Henry James and the Father Question*. Cambridge: Cambridge UP, 2002.

Thurschwell, Pamela. *Literature, Technology and Magical Thinking, 1880–1920*. Cambridge: Cambridge UP, 2001.

Tintner, Adeline R. "Biography and the Scholar: *The Life of Henry James*." In Fromm, 21–35.

———. *The Book World of Henry James*. Ann Arbor, MI: UMI Research Press, 1987.

———. *The Museum World of Henry James*. Ann Arbor, MI: UMI Research Press, 1985.

———. *The Pop World of Henry James*. Ann Arbor, MI: UMI Research Press, 1989.

Todorov, Tzvetan. "The Fantastic." In Esch and Warren, 193–96.

Tóibín, Colm. *The Master*. New York: Scribner's, 2004.

Trilling, Lionel. *The Liberal Imagination*. New York: Doubleday, 1950.

Troy, William. "The Altar of Henry James." *New Republic* 108, no. 7 (15 February 1943): 228–30.

Tuttleton, James, ed. *The American by Henry James: A Norton Critical Edition.* New York: Norton, 1978.

Van Leer, David. "The Beast of the Closet: Homosociality and the Pathology of Manhood." *Critical Inquiry* 15, no. 3 (Spring 1989): 587–605.

Vann, J. Don, ed. *Critics on Henry James.* Coral Gables, FL: U of Miami P, 1972.

Veeder, William. *Henry James — The Lessons of the Master: Popular Fiction and Personal Style in the Nineteenth Century.* Chicago: U of Chicago P, 1975.

Vincec, Sister Stephanie. "'Poor Flopping Wings': The Making of Henry James's *The Wings of the Dove*." *Harvard Library Bulletin* 24 (January 1976): 60–93.

Wagenknecht, Edward. *Eve and Henry James: Portraits of Women and Girls in His Fiction.* Norman: U of Oklahoma P, 1978.

———. *The Novels of Henry James.* New York: Ungar, 1983.

———. "Our Contemporary Henry James." *College English* 10, no. 3 (December 1948): 123–32.

———. Review of *Henry James: The Untried Years. Chicago Sunday Tribune,* 3 May 1953: 2.

———. *The Tales of Henry James.* New York: Ungar, 1984.

Walker, Pierre A., ed. *Henry James on Culture: Collected Essays on Politics and the American Social Scene.* Lincoln: U of Nebraska P, 1999.

———. "Leon Edel and the 'Policing' of the Henry James Letters." *Henry James Review* 21, no. 3 (2000): 279–89.

———. *Reading Henry James in French Cultural Contexts.* DeKalb: Northern Illinois UP, 1995.

———. Review of *The Other Henry James. Modern Philology* 98, no. 1 (August 2000): 121–24.

———. "Seeing A Life through Biography, Letters, and Fiction." *Chronicle for Higher Education (The Chronicle Review)*, 12 November 2004: 11.

Walker, Pierre A., and Greg W. Zacharias. "James's Hand and Gosse's Tail: Henry James Letters and the Status of Evidence." *Henry James Review* 19, no. 1 (1998): 72–79.

Walton, Priscilla. *The Disruption of the Feminine in Henry James.* Toronto: U of Toronto P, 1992.

———. "The Janus Faces of James: Gender, Transnationality, and James's Cinematic Adaptations." In McCormack, 37–53.

Warren, Austin. "Henry James: Symbolic Imagery in the Later Novels." *Rage for Order: Essays in Criticism,* 142–61. Chicago: U of Chicago P, 1948.

Warren, Kenneth W. *Black and White Strangers: Race and American Literary Realism.* Chicago: U of Chicago P, 1993.

Wegelin, Christof, ed. *Tales of Henry James*. New York: Norton, 1984.

Wegelin, Christof, and Henry B. Wonham, eds. *Tales of Henry James*. 2nd ed. New York: Norton, 2003.

Wellek, René. "Henry James's Literary Theory and Criticism." *American Literature* 30, no. 3 (November 1958): 293–321.

Wells, H. G. "Of Art, Of Literature, Of Mr. Henry James." In *Henry James and H. G. Wells: A Record of their Friendship, Their Debate on the Art of Fiction, and Their Quarrel*, edited by Leon Edel and Gordon N. Ray, 234–60. Urbana: U of Illinois P, 1958.

West, Rebecca. *Henry James*. London: Nisbet, 1916.

"Why Mr. James 'Revised.'" Literary *Digest*, 21 August 1909: 275–76.

Wilson, Edmund. "The Ambiguity of Henry James." *The Triple Thinkers*, 88–132. New York: Harcourt, 1938.

———. "The Pilgrimage of Henry James." *Shores of Light*, 217–28. New York: Farrar, Straus, and Young, 1952.

Winner, Viola Hopkins. *Henry James and the Visual Arts*. Charlottesville: U of Virginia P, 1970.

Winters, Yvor. "Maule's Well, or Henry James and the Relation of Morals to Manners." *In Defense of Reason*, 300–43. Denver: Alan Swallow, 1943 [1938].

Woolf, Virginia. "Henry James." *The Death of the Moth and other Essays*, 129–55. New York: Harcourt, Brace, 1942.

———. "Henry James's Ghost Stories." In *The Essays of Virginia Woolf*. Vol. 3, *1919–1924*, edited by Andrew McNeillie, 319–26. New York: Harcourt, Brace, 1988.

Yeazell, Ruth, ed. *Henry James: A Collection of Critical Essays*. Englewood Cliffs, NJ: Prentice Hall, 1994.

———. *Language and Knowledge in the Late Novels of Henry James*. Chicago: U of Chicago P, 1976.

———. Review of *Thinking in Henry James*. *Modern Philology* 89, no. 2 (November 1991): 302–6.

Zorzi, Rosella Mamoli, ed. *Beloved Boy: Letters to Henrik C. Andersen, 1899–1915*. Charlottesville: U of Virginia P, 2004.

Zwinger, Lynda. "Bodies that Don't Matter: The Queering of 'Henry James.'" *Modern Fiction Studies* 41, nos. 3–4 (Fall–Winter 1995): 657–80.

Index

Adams, Henry, 97, 116–17
Adler, Alfred, 62, 63
Agar, Herbert, 48
Agnew, Jean-Christophe, 77, 88–89
Alcott, Louisa May, 85
Allen, Elizabeth, 84–85
Andersen, Hendrik C., 66, 127, 132
Anderson, James William, 62
Anderson, Quentin, 54–55, 57, 108
Anderson, Sherwood, 45
Andreas, Osborn, 51–52, 95
Anesko, Michael, 29
Armstrong, Paul, 3, 34–35, 36, 100, 101, 105–7
Ash, Beth Sharon, 100
Auerbach, Nina, 85, 114

Balzac, Honoré de, 4, 29, 57, 87, 90, 120, 131
Banta, Martha, 29, 69–70, 77, 86
Barzun, Jacques, 43, 47
Beach, Joseph Warren, 47, 50, 56
Beckett, Samuel, 95
Beebe, Maurice, 57, 76
Bedford/St. Martin's Case Studies in Contemporary Criticism, 3, 75
Beilder, Peter G., 3,
Bell, Millicent, 70, 77, 100–101, 126, 127
Berkeley, Elizabeth M., 11, 12, 18, 19, 20, 64, 82
Bersani, Leo, 96–97, 99, 100
Blackmur, Richard P., 1, 30, 33–34, 37, 42, 43, 56, 67, 80
Blair, Sara, 38, 109–10
Blake, William, 91
Booth, Wayne C., 78–79, 82
Bosanquet, Theodora, 6
Boudreau, Kristin, 124–25
Bradley, John R., 121, 128
Bragdon, Claude, 22
Brooks, Peter, 86–87
Brooks, Van Wyck, 1, 5, 45–46, 80, 89
Brownell, W. C., 16
Buelens, Gert, 109

Burlinghame, Edward L., 14
Burr, Anna Robeson, 52
Bynner, Witter, 43, 44

Cabell, James Branch, 45
Calisher, Hortense, 42
Cameron, Sharon, 35–36, 102–3
Cannon, Kelly, 120
Cargill, Oscar, 76
Castle, Terry, 121
Charles Scribner's Sons. *See* Scribner's Publishers
Chesterton, G. K., 44
Clemens, Cyril, 44
Clemens, Samuel. *See* Mark Twain
Coburn, Alvin Langdon, 28
Cohen, Philip, 36
Cohn, Dorrit, 98
Coleridge, Samuel Taylor, 91
Conrad, Joseph, 22–23, 36
consciousness, 6, 8, 35–36, 81, 95–111
Cooper, Frederic Taber, 23
Cooper, Michael A., 126
Cormier, Harvey, 104
Crews, Frederick C., 78
critical perspectives:
  cultural studies, 2, 6, 7, 75, 86
  deconstruction, 7
  feminism, 2, 6, 75, 84–86, 91, 109, 121–23
  formalism, 31–32, 50, 56, 77, 81
  Freudian, 2, 6, 52–53, 68, 69, 75, 77, 81, 87, 100, 108
  gender studies, 3, 86, 114–32
  Marxism, 2, 3, 75, 91, 97, 109
  New Criticism, 31, 32, 56, 57, 88
  new historicism, 2, 6
  phenomenological, 7, 91
  psychoanalytic, 2, 3, 6, 53, 75, 85, 87, 91, 100
  queer studies, 2, 6, 86, 114–32
  reader-response, 3, 7, 75, 91
  semiotics, 75
  structuralism, 2, 7, 84

Darwin, Charles, 108
Daudet, Alphonse, 90
Daugherty, Sarah B., 75, 131
Davidoff, Robert, 64
Davidson, Rob, 37–38
Derrida, Jacques, 39
Dickens, Charles, 4, 17, 57, 88
Dickinson, Emily, 72
Dreiser, Theodore, 45, 49, 51, 75
DuBois, W. E. B., 110
Dupee, Frederick W., 1, 54, 56, 80
Dwight, H. G., 23–24, 95

Eakin, Paul John, 118–19
Edel, Leon, 1, 6, 11, 23, 27, 28, 29, 30, 36, 39, 44, 57, 61–72, 76, 77, 82, 90, 91, 108, 118, 128, 129
Edgar, Pelham, 52, 56
Edman, Irwin, 47
Eliot, George, 4, 22, 27, 57
Eliot, T. S., 5, 42, 83
Emerson, Ralph Waldo, 54, 70, 75, 97, 99
Esch, Deborah, 3, 21
evil, 2, 3, 21, 55, 76, 86, 87, 108

Faulkner, William, 57, 95, 97
Felman, Shoshana, 3, 87, 100
Ferguson, Francis, 42
Fetterly, Judith, 84, 85, 92
Fielding, Henry, 16
Fields, Annie, 39
Flannery, Denis, 121–22
Flaubert, Gustave, 4, 57, 90
Fleet, Simon, 44
Fluck, Winfried, 100, 109
Fogel, Daniel Mark, 75, 76, 89–90, 91
Ford, Ford Madox, 23
Foucault, Michel, 75, 95, 99, 122–23
Fowler, Virginia, 85
Frankenstein, 38
Freedman, Jonathan, 30, 39, 77, 88, 89, 96
Freud, Sigmund, 62
Fryer, Judith, 84, 114
Fuller, Henry B., 22
Fullerton, Morton, 127
Funston, Judith, 75

Gadamer, Hans-Georg, 107
Gale, Robert, 76
Gard, Roger, 10, 13, 14, 16, 17, 18, 21, 22, 24, 44
Gargano, James, 13, 14, 16, 19, 22, 77, 90
Gaskell, Elizabeth, 85
Gass, William, 55
Geismer, Maxwell, 80–81, 89
gender, 1, 2, 3, 7, 8, 38, 51, 84–86, 91, 110, 111, 114–32
Gide, André, 42
Goethe, Johann Wolfgang von, 91
Goncourt, Edmond de, 90
Goode, John, 77
Gordon, Lyndall, 124, 128
Gosse, Edmund, 30, 44, 127–28
Graham, Kenneth, 69, 77
Graham, Wendy, 115, 117, 125
Grattan, Clinton Hartley, 46
Greene, Graham, 30, 55
Griffin, Susan, 101–2, 118–19
Grover, Philip, 90–91
Gunter, Susan E., 66, 126

Habegger, Alfred, 51, 85–86, 108, 114, 117
Hale, Dorothy J., 30, 31
Haralson, Eric, 117, 118–20, 131
Haviland, Beverly, 110–11
Hawthorne, Nathaniel, 4, 57, 75, 91, 131
Hayes, Kevin, 5, 13, 14, 15, 16, 18, 22, 23
Head, Ruth, 139
Hellman, Geoffrey T., 64
Henke, Richard, 115
Henry James Society, 8, 75, 76
Herrick, Robert, 29
Heyns, Michiel W., 123
Hitler, Adolf, 47
Hocks, Richard A., 82–83, 101–3
Holland, Laurence, 81
Hollinghurst, Alan, 130
Holmes, Oliver Wendell, 128
homoeroticism, 2, 38, 72, 116, 117, 120, 121, 122, 123, 124, 127, 129, 131, 132
homosexuality, 2, 38–39, 72, 114, 118, 120–25, 132
Horne, Philip, 2, 39, 65–66, 77, 127, 128, 130
Hound and Horn, 33, 42

Howells, William Dean, 10, 13, 16–17, 37, 42, 75
Hoy, Helen, 117, 127

intimacy, 8, 63, 81, 96, 114–32
Izzo, Donatella, 7, 122–23

Jacobson, Marcia, 88
James, Alice (sister), 52, 129
James, Edward Holton (nephew), 11
James, Garth Wilkinson (brother), 52
James, Henry, works by:
　"The Altar of the Dead," 48
　The Ambassadors, 10, 20, 21, 22, 23, 42, 75, 76, 78, 81, 91, 98, 101, 103, 104, 105, 120, 138
　The American, 5, 10, 13, 14, 19, 29, 37, 76, 137
　The American Scene, 23, 24, 27, 88, 99, 102, 103, 104, 109, 110, 139
　"The Art of Fiction," 4, 17, 42, 110, 132
　"The Aspern Papers," 12, 77, 88, 91, 126, 138
　"The Author of Beltraffio," 44, 126, 137
　The Awkward Age, 20, 21, 42, 91, 138
　"The Beast in the Jungle," 2, 75, 100, 114, 120, 123, 124, 125
　The Better Sort, 138
　The Bostonians, 10, 12, 14, 17, 18, 29, 49, 51, 85, 88, 90, 91, 109, 111, 121, 138
　Confidence, 14, 29, 137
　Daisy Miller, 2, 10, 11, 14, 75, 116, 137
　Diary of a Man of Fifty and a Bundle of Letters, 137
　Embarrassments, 138
　English Hours, 139
　Essays in London and Elsewhere, 138
　The Europeans, 5, 13, 29, 137
　"The Figure in the Carpet," 104
　The Finer Grain, 139
　French Poets and Novelists, 137
　"The Future of the Novel," 11–12
　Gabrielle de Bergerac, 139
　"George Eliot," 75
　"Georgina's Reasons," 123
　The Golden Bowl, 11, 12, 20, 21–22, 24, 28, 39, 44, 78, 81, 84, 88, 91, 99, 100, 138, 141
　Guy Domville, 10, 19–20
　Hawthorne, 137
　The Henry James Year Book, 139
　"In the Cage," 114, 116, 118, 132, 138
　An International Episode, 137
　Italian Hours, 139
　The Ivory Tower, 139
　"The Jolly Corner," 75, 89–90, 130–31
　Julia Bride, 139
　"The Landscape Painter," 10, 139
　"The Last of the Valerii," 123
　"The Lesson of the Master," 5, 12, 138
　A Little Tour of France, 137
　A London Life, 138
　The Madonna of the Future, 137
　Master Eustace, 139
　The Middle Years, 37, 53, 139
　"Middlemarch," 61
　Notebooks, 32
　Notes of a Son and Brother, 37, 118, 139
　Notes on Novelists, 139
　The Novels and Tales of Henry James "New York Edition." See New York Edition
　"The Novels of George Eliot," 22, 27
　The Other House, 29, 138
　The Outcry, 139
　Partial Portraits, 138
　A Passionate Pilgrim and Other Tales, 10, 13, 137
　Picture and Text, 138
　Pictures and Other Passages from Henry James, 139
　The Portrait of a Lady, 10, 15, 16, 29, 51, 75, 76, 81, 84, 88, 96, 98, 102, 108, 109, 116, 120, 121, 122, 124, 132, 137
　Portraits of Places, 137
　The Princess Casamassima, 10, 12, 17, 18, 49, 55, 90, 91, 96, 99, 110, 138
　The Private Life, 138
　"The Pupil," 2, 19, 53, 126, 127, 130
　The Question of Our Speech, 139
　The Question of the Mind, 139

"The Real Right Thing," 126
"The Real Thing," 12, 19, 108, 132, 138
Refugees in Chelsea, 139
The Reverberator, 138
Roderick Hudson, 13, 14, 29, 51, 116, 137
"Rose-Agatha," 123
"A Round of Visits," 125
The Sacred Fount, 10, 20, 22, 24, 29, 65, 88, 98, 138
The Sense of the Past, 139
The Siege of London, 137
A Small Boy and Others, 37, 110, 129, 139
The Soft Side, 138
The Spoils of Poynton, 20, 77, 81, 88, 99, 138
Tales of Three Cities, 137
Terminations, 138
Theatricals, 138
Theatricals: Second Series, 138
"A Tragedy of Error," 10
The Tragic Muse, 10, 18, 19, 28, 88, 90, 91, 110, 138
Transatlantic Sketches, 137
Travelling Companions, 139
"Trollope," 110
The Turn of the Screw, 2, 3, 20, 21, 52–53, 68, 75, 76, 81, 87, 91, 100, 104, 108, 114, 138
The Two Magics, The Turn of the Screw, Covering End, 138
Views and Reviews, 139
Washington Square, 5, 10, 14, 15, 29, 76, 91, 137
Watch and Ward, 29, 88, 137
What Maisie Knew, 1, 20, 21, 22, 23, 24, 68, 104, 111, 117, 138
The Wheel of Time, 138
William Wetmore Story and His Friends, 138
The Wings of the Dove, 10, 20, 21, 22, 32, 42, 61, 77, 78, 81, 91, 124, 138
Within the Rim, 139
James, Henry Sr. (father), 13, 16, 46, 53, 54–55, 70, 108, 118
James, Henry III (nephew), 63
James, Mary (mother), 68
James, Robertson (brother), 52

James, William (brother), 11, 12, 18, 19–20, 24, 37, 46, 47, 53, 54, 63, 64, 68, 82, 101–2, 103–5, 107–8, 110, 118, 119, 125, 129
Jobe, Steven H., 66, 126
Johanningsmeier, Charles, 19
Jordan, Elizabeth, 44
Joyce, James, 24, 57, 61, 95

Kant, Immanuel, 105
Kaplan, Fred, 71–72, 120, 123–24, 126
Kaston, Carren, 98–99
Kazin, Alfred, 43, 47, 67
Keats, John, 91
Kimbrough, Robert, 2,
Kipling, Rudyard, 29
knowledge, 76, 77, 78, 83, 89, 95, 98, 105–7, 109, 126
Kress, Jill, 107–8
Krook, Dorothea, 81, 83, 87, 89

Lacan, Jacques, 75, 85, 87
LaFarge, John, 44
LaFarge, Margaret, 44
Lane, Christopher, 131–32
Lawrence, D. H., 57
Leavis, F. R., 43, 48, 51, 67, 81
Leavitt, David, 130
LeClair, Robert C., 57
Leslie, Shane, 44
Leuschner, Eric, 29
Levenson, J. C., 68
Levin, Jonathan, 104
Lewes, George, Henry, 108
Lewis, Sinclair, 45
Lodge, David, 129
Logan, Annie, 18
Lowndes, Marie Belloc, 44
Lubbock, Percy, 5, 30, 42, 52, 56, 64, 65, 71, 127
Luciano, Dana, 120
Ludwig, Sami, 108–9
Lukacs, Georg, 97
Lynn, Kenneth S., 69

MacKenzie, Compton, 44
Marshall, Adré, 98
Marx, Karl, 47
Matthiessen, F. O., 1, 6, 43, 48, 50–51, 54, 56, 57, 64, 66–67, 80, 82, 115

Maupassant, Guy de, 90
McClure, Samuel S., 19
McColley, Kathleen, 121
McCormack, Peggy, 131
McCulloch, Jeanne, 62, 63, 64, 67–68, 72
McWhirter, David, 8, 28, 32, 33, 36–37, 38
Meissner, Colin, 100, 107
Melville, Henry, 75
Mencken, H. L., 46
Meredith, George, 29
Michaels, Walter Benn, 111
Miller, J. Hillis, 28
Miller, James E., 83
modernism, 6, 7, 22, 89, 104, 114
Monteiro, George, 117
Moon, Michael, 129, 130
Moore, Marianne, 42
Moore, Rayburn S., 71
morality, 3, 7, 8, 12, 33, 46, 47–55, 56, 78, 79, 81–83, 87, 95–111, 123
Morse, J. H., 16
Moss, Mary, 22
Murray, Donald, 17, 57

Nadel, Ira, 28
naturalism, 75
New York Author's Club, 24
New York Edition, 5, 27–39, 96, 102, 139
Norton Critical Editions, 2–4, 75
Novick, Sheldon, 104, 120, 121, 124, 128–29
Nowell-Smith, Simon, 6, 65

Oechsner, Frederick, 48

Parker, Herschel, 31, 32, 34, 71
Parrington, Vernon, 5, 45–46, 89
Perry, Ralph Barton, 82
Persse, Jocelyn, 126, 127
Person, Leland S., 111, 125–26, 131
pluralism, 82, 103–5, 110
Poe, Edgar Allan, 57, 75
Poirier, Richard, 79–80
Porter, Carolyn, 77, 79, 97
Porter, Katherine Anne, 43
Posnock, Ross, 33–34, 103–4, 110
postmodernism, 6, 7, 8
Pound, Ezra, 5, 46

power, 7, 35, 38, 52, 62, 76, 77, 81, 84, 85, 86, 90, 96–100, 109, 115, 120, 121–16, 130
Powers, Lyall, 57, 63, 76, 77, 90
pragmatism, 78, 82–83, 91, 96, 101–5, 108–9, 110, 111
Przybylowicz, Donna, 100

race, 109–10, 111
Rahv, Philip, 6, 43, 47, 48–49, 51, 57, 75
Ray, Gordon, 44
realism, 6, 10, 15, 33, 49, 51, 55, 75, 105, 111
religion, 48, 54, 55, 108
Richardson, Lyon N., 68–69
Richardson, Samuel, 16
Rivkin, Julie, 39, 130
romance, 10, 17, 33, 105
Rosenzweig, Saul, 53, 118
Ross, Melanie H., 39
Rowe, John Carlos, 2, 6, 7, 34, 91, 114, 116–17, 131
Rundle, Vivienne, 36
Ryan, Judith, 104

Saintsbury, George, 18
Sanner, Kristin, 122
Savoy, Eric, 117, 130–31
Scribner's Publishers, 27, 28, 29, 36, 139
Scudder, Horace E., 19
Scura, Dorothy McInnis, 75–76
Sears, Sallie, 82, 83
Sedgwick, Eve, 2, 38–39, 77, 100, 114, 115, 117, 125, 130
Segal, Ora, 79
Seltzer, Mark, 96, 99–100
sexuality, 7, 8, 53, 55, 72, 100, 114–32
Skrupskelis, Ignas, 11, 12, 18, 19, 20, 64, 82
Smith, Logan Pearsall, 44
Solomon, Eric, 2
Solomon, Melissa, 122
Spencer, Herbert, 108
Spender, Stephen, 42, 47, 50, 57
Spilka, Mark, 2
spiritualism, 12, 21, 86–87
Stafford, William T., 34–35, 36, 76
Stevens, Hugh, 77, 114, 116–17
Stevenson, Elizabeth, 56
Stevenson, Robert Louis, 17, 29

Sturgis, Howard, 127
style, 5, 7, 10, 12, 13, 14, 18, 19, 20, 22, 24, 43, 53, 70, 83, 88, 104, 131
Swedenborg, Emanuel, 70

Tate, Allen, 57
Taylor, Andrew, 108
Temple, Minny, 124
Thackeray, William Makepeace, 17
Thoreau, Henry David, 81
Thurschwell, Pamela, 119
Tintner, Adeline R., 76, 91
Todorov, Tzvetan, 3,
Tóibín, Colm, 129
Trilling, Lionel, 1, 6, 45–46, 48–50, 51, 57, 67, 80
Trollope, Anthony, 88, 91, 131
Troy, William, 43, 47, 48
truth, 8, 82, 95, 96, 106
Turgenev, Ivan, 90
Twain, Mark, 45

Van Leer, David, 128
Vann, J. Don, 10, 14, 18, 44
Veeder, William, 88
Vincec, Sister Stephanie, 32

Wagenknecht, Edward, 53, 67, 76
Walker, Pierre, 63–64, 71, 72, 91, 109, 127–28

Wallace, Henry, 51
Walpole, Hugh, 6, 127
Walton, Priscilla, 131
Ward, Joseph, 57
Warhol, Andy, 129
Warren, Austin, 57
Warren, Jonathan, 3, 21
Warren, Kenneth, 109
Wegelin, Christof, 2,
Wellek, René, 31
Wells, H. G., 23, 43, 44, 67
Wharton, Edith, 43–44, 71, 107–8
Whitman, Walt, 72
Wilde, Oscar, 19, 89
Wilson, Edmund, 1, 2, 6, 42, 43, 50, 52–53, 81, 87, 100
Winters, Yvor, 43, 47, 50
Wonham, Henry B., 2,
Woolf, Virginia, 5, 24, 57, 61, 72, 82, 95
Woolson, Constance Fenimore, 124

Yeats, William Butler, 57
Yeazell, Ruth Bernard, 77, 83, 103

Zabel, Morton, 43, 67
Zacharias, Greg, 64, 127–28
Zola, Emile, 4, 57, 90
Zorzi, Rosella Mamori, 66, 127
Zwinger, Linda, 115–16, 130

Although some of Henry James's contemporary critics deemed him just short of a great writer, history has elevated him to indisputable preeminence in the American canon. Linda Simon provides an overview of James criticism, beginning with newspaper and magazine reviews by James's contemporaries and ending with current academic criticism. The story begins in the 1870s, when critics focused on James's works as mirrors of American identity and sought to establish his place in the nation's newly evolving indigenous literary culture. James himself tried to secure that place by publishing a 24-volume standard edition of his works, with prefaces designed to shape readers' responses; Simon considers both contemporary and current criticism about those prefaces.

James's reputation became contested after his death in 1916: praised by some critics for his psychological insights and stylistic innovations, he was dismissed by others as socially and politically irrelevant. Beginning in the 1940s, as Simon shows, such critics as Lionel Trilling, Philip Rahv, and F. R. Leavis championed James, placing him in the forefront of the American literary canon. None of his champions, however, was as influential as Leon Edel, whose Freudian reading of James and editing of James's letters and notebooks deepened critical interest and opened new perspectives; Simon devotes a chapter to Edel's role.

In the past several decades, James scholarship has focused provocatively on sexuality and gender, race and morality, and the nature of consciousness; the final two chapters consider these current critical trends. Simon's book, clearly written and comprehensive, is the only overview of the main arguments in James criticism over the past 140 years. It helps readers understand the paths the criticism has taken and how scholars and critics have built upon past work.

LINDA SIMON is Professor of English at Skidmore College and Editor-in-Chief of *William James Studies*. Her books include *Dark Light: Electricity and Anxiety from the Telegraph to the X-Ray* and *Genuine Reality: A Life of William James*, which was a *New York Times* Notable Book of 1998. She has received fellowships from the American Philosophical Society and from the Bakken Library on Electricity and Life.

This lucid, absorbing study offers thorough coverage of criticism of James's works. . . . [N]ot only covers all James criticism but also outlines a pattern of changing perspectives in the field of literary criticism itself.
— CHOICE

One of the achievements of Simon's book is her ability to identify points of continuity among generations of James's readers. . . . Seeing the key critical trends [in the "major scholarly industry" of James studies] is no small feat, and Simon has done well to chart a current road map to this critical archive.
— NEW ENGLAND QUARTERLY

The only work that gives an overview of all of James criticism. . . . It is also completely up to date. It enables readers to "get a handle" on the huge corpus that is James criticism. . . . Thanks to Simon's book, James scholars and students will be able to see clearly where the uncharted territory lies, and as a result, it represents a significant and lasting contribution.
— Pierre A. Walker, Salem State College

www.ingramcontent.com/pod-product-compliance
Lightning Source LLC
Chambersburg PA
CBHW060955230426
43665CB00015B/2212